Morton Smith and Gershom Scholem, Correspondence 1945–1982

Jerusalem Studies in Religion and Culture

Editors

Guy G. Stroumsa
David Shulman
Hebrew University of Jerusalem
Department of Comparative Religion

VOLUME 9

Morton Smith and Gershom Scholem, Correspondence 1945–1982

Edited with an introduction by

Guy G. Stroumsa

BRILL

LEIDEN • BOSTON
2008

This book is printed on acid-free paper.

Library of Congress Cataloging-in-Publication Data

Morton Smith and Gershom Scholem, correspondence, 1945–1982 / edited with an introduction by Guy Stroumsa.
p. cm. — (Jerusalem studies in religion and culture, 1570-078X ; v. 9)
Includes index.
ISBN 978-90-04-16839-8 (hardback : alk. paper)
1. Scholem, Gershom Gerhard, 1897–1982—Correspondence. 2. Smith, Morton, 1915—Correspondence. I. Stroumsa, Guy G. II. Title. III. Series.

BM755.S295A4 2008
296.092—dc22
[B]

2008009748

ISSN 1570-078x
ISBN 978 90 04 16839 8

PRINTED IN THE NETHERLANDS

CONTENTS

INTRODUCTION

Gershom Scholem (1897–1982) stands among the towering historians of religions in the twentieth century. Although less prominent, Morton Smith (1915–1991) was a leading student of ancient Mediterranean religions. They came from very different religious, cultural and linguistic milieus: Scholem from the assimilated Jewish bourgeoisie of Berlin, Smith from an affluent Episcopalian family from Philadelphia. They met in 1940 in Jerusalem, while Smith was a research student at the Hebrew University, where Scholem taught. Their correspondence, which starts with Smith's return to the USA in 1945, ending only with Scholem's death in 1982, provides a rare perspective on the growing friendship of these two remarkable scholars. It reflects their shifting scholarly pursuits and their lasting intellectual interests. Both men show some similar traits of character, in particular an abiding interest in religious phenomena, grounded in youthful experiences, but always kept under the rigorous control of stringent rational criticism. These 121 letters (72 written by Smith, and 49 by Scholem) are kept in the Scholem archive at the Jewish National and University Library in Jerusalem.[1] They offer a rare glimpse into the odd and complex ways of *translatio studii* through continents and across fields, following the vagaries of displaced scholars in turbulent times – the *République des Lettres* in a dark century.

Smith came to Jerusalem in 1940 and stayed there during the war years. He would return to the United States only in 1945. During those years, he registered as a graduate student at the Hebrew University and submitted a PhD thesis, in Hebrew, entitled "Tannaitic Parallels to the

---

[1] Only three of these letters have been published in Gershom Scholem's correspondence: two, dated August 6 and August 29, 1948, in G. Scholem, *Briefe, II, 1948–1970*, ed. Thomas Sparr (Munich: Beck, 1995), 9–11, and one from June 9, 1974 (quoted below), in G. Scholem, *Briefe, III, 1971–1982*, ed. Itta Shedletzky (Munich: Beck, 1999), 104–106. The first three long letters from 1945, two from Smith to Scholem, and one from Scholem to Smith are in Hebrew; all the others are in English. Smith's Hebrew is a bit stilted.

I should like to thank Albert I. Baumgarten, Hans Dieter Betz, Scott Brown, Jan Bremmer, Allan Pantuck, Mark Silk, Alan Thomas and William V. Harris for their useful comments on a draft of this Introduction.

Gospels" (Scholem refers to "the first Christian PhD of the Hebrew University"). This thesis was supervised by Professor Moshe Schwabe, who was the founder of the Department of Classics at the Hebrew University and had been a student of Wilamowitz-Moellendorff. During that period, Gershom Scholem was Smith's mentor. Smith took his courses on the history of Jewish mysticism, and translated from Hebrew to English the text of Scholem's lectures on the origins of Kabbalah.[2] When he went back to the United States, Smith began a correspondence with his Jerusalem mentor.

The correspondence as a whole highlights a peculiar chapter in the history of scholarship (and in particular of Jewish scholarship) during almost the first four decades after the Second World War, both in the USA and in Israel. Among the American scholars mentioned in the letters, often time and again, are (in alphabetical order) Alexander Altmann, Zvi Ankori, Salo W. Baron, Elias Bickermann, William Braude, Millar Burrows, Gerson Cohen, Erwin Ramsdell Goodenough, Werner Jaeger, Helmut Koester, Saul Lieberman, Jacob Neusner, Arthur Darby Nock, Shalom Spiegel, Harry Austryn Wolfson. Among the scholars from the Hebrew University, some of them former teachers or friends of Smith during his Jerusalem years, one finds Martin Buber, David Flusser, Amos Funkenstein, Hans Lewy, Hans Jonas, Hans Jacob Polotsky, Shmuel Sambursky, Moshe Schwabe, Yeshayahu Tishby, Zvi Werblowsky and Haim Wirszubski.

The scholarly topics that recur time and again in these letters are all related to the study of religion, in particular to Kabbalah, messianism, magic, Gnosticism, monasticism, Patristics and *Hekhalot* literature (i.e., late antique Hebrew mystical texts dealing with Ezekiel's Chariot). For years after his return to the USA, Smith worked on translating *Hekhalot* texts. The letters also offer some sharp observations about the study of religion, for instance when Smith rhetorically asks Scholem: "Why is it that the study of religion attracts so many nitwits?" (Letter 84). Moreover, they reflect on academic politics, in particular over the difficulties in Smith's career before his appointment as Professor

[2] This translation was never published, and Smith mistakenly destroyed it, as the letters make clear. Scholem eventually published in German a much more thorough study on the same theme, *Ursprung und Anfänge der Kabala* (Berlin: de Gruyter, 1962). This work was published in French in 1966, and in English in 1987. In Jerusalem, Smith had also worked on the English version of Scholem's lectures, which would eventually become *Major Trends in Jewish Mysticism* (first published in New York, Schocken, 1941).

of Ancient History at Columbia, side by side with Elias Bickermann, whom he eventually replaced after Bickermann's retirement.[3] In 1956, Scholem writes: "How American Universities let a scholar like yourself sit around and wait for a good appointment is above my understanding" (Letter 53). The letters also illuminate Scholem's various teaching trips to the USA.

The letters also reflect, from time to time, on contemporary political conditions and events. Smith tells Scholem about anti-Semitism in post-war USA; Scholem refers to a distressing trip to Germany after the war, in order to save remaining books of Jewish interest. The political situation in Palestine in 1948 is referred to: there are some vignettes on the siege of Jerusalem. On 22 May 1967, Smith had these prophetic words: "Needless to say, I have no fears for Israel – save that you may punch so hard you give yourselves a black eye" (Letter 83).

Both show a clear and deep interest in the other's field of research: Scholem, whose long-standing interest in Gnosticism (which he saw as the source of Jewish mysticism)[4] is well known, sees the Carpocratians) as "the Frankists of antiquity" (Letter 66). Scholem indeed does not hide his deep interest in "religious nihilism" (Letter 27) and in "comparative mysticism." The differences in age and status, as well as in culture, do not prevent their friendship and the warmth in their relationship from growing. In 1956–1957 (Letters 54–55), since Scholem's stay in the USA, which Smith had a large part in organizing, they start calling one another "Dear Morton," "Dear Gershom."

These letters, then, shed new light on these two great philologists, on their highly complex personalities and ways of thinking, on their struggles with facts and ideas, on their reactions to contemporary events. Scholem, whose deep friendship with Walter Benjamin, exemplified by their correspondence and by Scholem's book on it, has been widely acknowledged, much beyond scholarly circles, as a leading intellectual figure of the twentieth century.[5] Almost single-handedly, Scholem

---

[3] Smith got a junior position in the college, while Bickermann was teaching only in the Graduate School. I owe this precision to Al Baumgarten.

[4] See for instance his *Jewish Gnosticism, Merkabah Mysticism and Talmudic Tradition* (New York: Jewish Theological Seminary, 1960).

[5] Gershom Scholem, ed., *Walter Benjamin, Gershom Scholem, Briefwechsel, 1933–1940* (Frankfurt: Suhrkamp, 1980); English translation: G. Scholem, ed., *The Correspondence of Walter Benjamin and Gershom Scholem, 1932–1940* (Cambridge, Mass.: Harvard University Press, 1992). See further G. Scholem, *Walter Benjamin: die Geschichte einer Freundschaft*

established, over a long life of relentless study of mostly Medieval texts, often available only in manuscripts, the field of Kabbala and Jewish mysticism studies.[6]

Scholem's fame is strongly established upon two pillars: the one, his leading role in the development of Jewish Studies in the contemporary scene, both in Israel and in the world; the other, his connections with a small group of Jewish intellectual exiles from Nazi Germany, which included, of course, Walter Benjamin, the close friend of his youth, but also Hannah Arendt, Theodor Adorno and Max Bloch. We know Scholem's complex personality rather well, thanks in particular to the three volumes of his published correspondence, together with the two volumes of his youth journals and his autobiographical work *Von Berlin nach Jerusalem*. But it is precisely the obvious nature of these two pillars, the success of Jewish studies as well as the curiosity and respect given to Adorno, Arendt, Benjamin and their likes, that might be misleading. One forgets too often that Scholem intended to "redeem" the study of Judaism by rooting it into the general history of religion (*allgemeine Religionswissenschaft*).[7] This field was rather distinguished in Weimar Germany, since the glorious days of the *Religionsgeschichtliche Schule* at the end of the nineteenth century, when Wilhelm Bousset and his Göttingen colleagues were preaching through example of the comparative study of ancient Near Eastern and Jewish material together with that of biblical material, both from the Old and the New Testaments. Just as Scholem's deep Zionist convictions were meant to bring the Jews back into history, so his scholarly approach searched for a way to re-integrate the religious history of the Jews into the history of religions. While the importance of Scholem's works for the phenomenological understanding of mystical phenomena is now widely recognized, his deep interest in the religious upheaval in the first Christian centuries seems to be hardly mentioned. Scholem, in particular, attached a very high importance to the birth of Christianity and of Gnosticism. Together with the work of

(Frankfurt: Suhrkamp, 1975); English translation: G. Scholem, *Walter Benjamin: The Story of a Friendship* (Philadelphia: Jewish Publication Society, 1981).

[6] We still need a thorough intellectual biography of Scholem. One may consult D. Biale, *Gershom Scholem: Kabbalah and Counter-History* (Cambridge, Mass.: Harvard University Press, 1979), and P. Mendes-Flohr, ed., *Gershom Scholem: The Man and His Work* (Albany, 1994), as well as Scholem's autobiographical work: *Von Berlin nach Jerusalem: Jugenderinnerungen* (Frankfurt: Suhrkamp, 1977).

[7] See E. Hamacher, *Gershom Scholem und die Allgemeine Religionsgeschichte* (Religionsgeschichtliche Versuche und Vorarbeiten, 45; Berlin, New York: Walter de Gruyter, 1999).

Bousset, that of Rudolph Bultmann and Max Lidzbarski meant much for Scholem: Gnosis, then perceived to have been a "world religion" of sorts, was a major phenomenon, and Scholem never doubted its significance for a proper understanding of the formation of Rabbinic Judaism and of the earliest stages of Jewish mysticism. The Gnostic upheaval of religious traditions and rejection of canonical texts had a strong appeal for Scholem's "religious anarchism." And his interest in the earliest stages of Christianity never abated. Scholem worked hard over a long period to promote at the Hebrew University the comparative study of religion and the study of Christianity.[8] While some of these efforts bore fruit, the comparative study of religious phenomena has retained a modest place in the mind of the Israeli public compared to that of Jewish Studies. Scholem's long correspondence with Smith, which deals frequently with issues of early Christianity, should help in restoring the proper balance. Another new emphasis of these letters is the place of the United States in Scholem's career. Scholem is usually and naturally understood through his German intellectual background and his major role in the development of Jewish Studies at the Hebrew University (which remained for some critical decades the only institution of higher learning and research in the Humanities in Jewish Palestine and early Israel), but this approach prevents a proper appreciation of his major impact upon Jewish and religious studies in the USA. Here too, the publication of the Scholem-Smith letters should permit a better understanding of his pioneering role.

While Scholem's striking intellectual and scholarly legacy is clearly delineated in today's study of Jewish mysticism, that of Morton Smith remains much less well known, and much harder to define. Smith's research had mainly to do with antiquity. In his necrology, W. M. Calder, III states: "*Religionsgeschichte* in the US has lost its most erudite and controversial figure, an exponent of Böckh's *totius antiquitatis cognitio*."[9] Smith's interests brought him to fields as different as ancient Israel, early Christianity, Judaism in late antiquity and magic in the

[8] For his role in the early years of the Hebrew University in seeking to establish an Institute for the Study of Religion, see for instance G. Stroumsa, "Buber as an Historian of Religion: Presence, not Gnosis," in *Archives de Sciences Sociales des Religions* 101 (1998), 1–17. [Also in P. Mendes-Flohr, ed., *Martin Buber: A Contemporary Perspective* (Syracuse, Jerusalem: Israel Academy of Sciences and Humanities, 2002), 25–47.]

[9] In *Gnomon* 64 (1992), 382–384.

Greco-Roman world.[10] His scholarly interests intersected with those of Scholem at the meeting point between Judaism and Christianity, between magic and mysticism, between the ancient and the medieval worlds. Arguing against the intellectually pernicious and heuristically dangerous segregation of knowledge into sealed compartments, Smith was quite effective as a radical critic of traditionally held views. Probably because he was working in areas more densely traveled and closer to the heart of Christian believers, his work generated much more animosity than Scholem's. Thus, he was usually considered to be much more convincing as a critic than when he offered his own interpretation. Smith consistently shunned disclosure of his personal life and, in striking contradistinction with Scholem, almost never showed an interest in publicly expressing views outside scholarly circles.[11] While Scholem, since his youth, kept systematic care of his diaries and letters,[12] Smith ordered his own personal correspondence to be destroyed after his death (his archival papers donated to the Jewish Theological Seminary in New York contain considerable professional correspondence; after Scholem's death, he must have returned all letters Scholem had sent him to his widow Fania). While he was an intellectual iconoclast, Smith maintained all his life very conservative political ideas. Scholem, on the other hand, who in his youth had been some kind of an anarchist, remained very much on the left of the political spectrum to his late years – although he very rarely expressed himself publicly on political matters.

The psychological differences between them, compounded by the difference in age and status when the correspondence starts, explain why the letters as a whole are more revealing about Smith than about Scholem. The letters shed light, in particular, on Smith's intellectual evolution, on the deep impact his studies at the Hebrew University had upon him, and on the genesis and development of some of his most important insights and discoveries. Professor Shaye Cohen, Smith's literary executor, wrote that Smith revived the old *religionsgeschichtlisch*

---

[10] The preface to the second edition of H. D. Betz, ed., *The Greek Magical Papyri in Translation, Including the Demotic Spells* (Chicago: Chicago University Press, 1992 [1st ed. 1986]) is dedicated to Smith's memory.

[11] *Hope and History: an Exploration* (New York: Harper and Row, 1980) is an exception.

[12] Scholem's youth *Tagebücher* have now been published in two volumes, by K. Gründer and F. Niehwöhner (Frankfurt am Main: Jüdischer Verlag, 1995 and 2000). See also Gershom Scholem, *A Life in Letters*, edited and translated by A. D. Skinner (Cambridge, Mass. and London: Harvard University Press, 2002). This volume includes two letters from Scholem to Smith, both from 1948 (pp. 357–359).

approach to the New Testament.[13] This is certainly true, but one should add that Smith put Judaism at the core of his approach, while too many contemporary scholars claiming to work within this methodological school tend to ignore or downplay the crucial role of Judaism in Christian origins. On the other hand, those scholars who approach early Christianity from the angle of its Jewish background too often ignore or downplay the broader context of the Hellenistic and Roman religious world. Smith, who was equally conversant in Greek and in Hebrew, and felt at home among pagans, Jews and Christians, never sought to avoid or circumvent difficult problems, always attacking them upfront – and always with panache. More than anyone else, perhaps, Smith sought to work on the meeting-points between traditionally defined religious identities. At the intersection between Judaism and Christianity, and in the background of mysticism, he saw magic. Scholem's fascination with religious antinomianism, from his youthful flirt with nihilism to the *opus maximum* of his maturity, his biography of Sabbatai Zvi,[14] left, as we shall see, a powerful imprint on the mind of his young Christian student, who would serve, for a short while, as an Episcopalian priest, before deciding, later in life, that Jesus had been a magician.

If Smith achieved notoriety in circles much broader than those of philological scholarship, this is due to his discovery, in the Palestinian monastery of Mar Saba, of a letter of Clement of Alexandria mentioning a previously unknown secret Gospel of Mark.[15] This discovery is of major significance for both New Testament studies and early Church history. The passage of the Secret Gospel quoted in Clement's letter has usually been interpreted, by Smith as by most of his detractors, as

[13] Shaye J. D. Cohen, "*In memoriam* Morton Smith: Morton Smith and his Scholarly Achievement," in F. Parente and J. Sievers, eds., *Josephus and the History of the Greco-Roman Period: Essays in Memory of Morton Smith* (Studia Post-Biblica 41; Leiden, 1994), 1–8. These pages are reprinted in Morton Smith, *Studies in the Cult of Yahweh* (Religions in the Greco-Roman World, 130–131; Leiden, New York, Köln: Brill, 1996), vol. II, pp. 279–285. See, in the same volume, pp. 251–278, a bibliography of Smith's works.

[14] Sholem's magisterial biography of Sabbatai Tvi appeared in Hebrew in 1957. See in English G. Scholem, *Sabbatai Sevi: The Mystical Messiah, 1626–1676* (Princeton: Princeton University Press, 1975); [transl. R. J. Z. Werblowsky].

[15] Smith presented his discovery in a popular book, *The Secret Gospel: The Discovery and Interpretation of the Secret Gospel according to Mark* (New York: Harper and Row, 1973), and in a scholarly book, *Clement of Alexandria and a Secret Gospel of Mark* (Cambridge, Mass.: Harvard University Press, 1973), which offers a thorough analysis of its contents, a study of its implications, and a demonstration of its authenticity.

alluding to strange rituals, with homoerotic intimations, practiced by Jesus and his disciples. The very fact that such a Secret Gospel was kept by the Church authorities in late-second-century Alexandria is noteworthy. The official "orthodox" Church thus appears to be dangerously close to some of the Gnostic (and libertine) sects it was fighting, and in particular of the Carpocratians, mentioned in Clement's letter.

Smith, obviously expecting strong resistance to accepting the new document, spent years of careful research to demonstrate the authenticity of Clement's letter. His lengthy argument, in *Clement of Alexandria and a Secret Gospel of Mark*, shows a philologist fully mastering his craft. But Smith was not satisfied with simply providing a philological demonstration of Clement's authorship. From the letter attributed to Clement, he also subsequently developed his own view on the nature of Jesus' rituals. For him, the very first Christian ritual, the Eucharist, needed to be understood as a case of erotic magic, a view he first expresses to Scholem in 1974 (see Letter 97).

Smith's discovery and his interpretation aroused a particularly violent polemic in the world of New Testament and early Christianity scholarship, especially in the United States.[16] The discovery itself seems to have deeply offended the religious sensibilities of many scholars, who could not conceive of such a picture of the Lord emerging from a credible ancient text. Various attempts were made to show the inauthentic character of the new text. Moreover, Smith himself was accused, in various quarters, directly or through *innunendo* (as a homosexual, he would have had a personal interest in representing Jesus' homosexual practice) of having forged the famous letter.[17]

This polemic, which started more than thirty years ago, has been recently rekindled, at least in America.[18] Suspicion has been much aug-

[16] See M. Smith, "Clement of Alexandria and Secret Mark: The Score at the End of the First Decade," *Harvard Theological Review* 75 (1982), 449–461.

[17] Smith's homosexuality was widely speculated upon in the American academic community.

[18] See for instance Stephen Carlson, *The Gospel Hoax: Morton Smith's Invention of Secret Mark* (Waco, Texas: Baylor University Press, 2005). The author's legal training and his lack of philological acumen clearly show throughout the book. For a refutation of Carlson's argument, see S. G. Brown, "Factualizing the Folklore: Stephen Carlson's Case against Morton Smith," *Harvard Theological Review* 99 (2006), 291–327; see also A. J. Pantuck and S. G. Brown, "Morton Smith as M. Madiotes: Stephen Carlson's Attribution of *Secret Mark* to a Bald Swindler," *Journal for the Study of the Historical Jesus* 6 (2008), 106–125. The most recent, and thorough attempt to show that Smith forged the document is that of Peter Jeffery, *The Secret Gospel of Mark Unveiled: Imagined Rituals of Sex, Death, and Madness in a Biblical Forgery* (New Haven, London: Yale University

mented by the strange disappearance of the manuscript of Clement's letter. The letter had been copied into the final blank pages of a seventeenth-century edition of Patristic writings. That book is now kept in the Library of the Greek Orthodox Patriarchate in Jerusalem, but the final pages, with Clement's letter, have been cut out and are not to be found anywhere.

While no definitive proof will ever satisfy Smith's debunkers, his correspondence with Scholem sheds some new light on Smith's Mar Saba discovery and on his state of mind afterwards, while he was working on the presentation of his discovery to the scholarly world. The correspondence should provide sufficient evidence of his intellectual honesty to anyone armed with common sense and lacking malice.[19]

Smith's letters show that already in 1950, Smith, then under the tutelage of Werner Jaeger at Harvard, was planning a research trip to Greek monasteries in order to photograph various patristic manuscripts – in particular those of Isidore of Pelusium (Letter 26, from December 4, 1950). In 1953, Smith had returned from his trip with 5,000 photos of manuscripts (Letter 31). On December 9, 1957, he writes of his plan "to spend the whole summer in the Near East, including a week in both Jerusalem and Istanbul, and a month in both Jordan and northern Greece, "hunting for collections of manuscripts in the monasteries of Chalcidice (excluding Athos)..." (Letter 55). On his Mar Saba discovery from that trip, in the summer of 1958, he writes to Scholem for the first time on August 7, 1959: "The material by Clement of Alexandria which I found at Mar Saba last year is turning out to be of great importance, and as soon as I get all minor nuisances off my hands, I must work hard at it" (Letter 63). On January 30, 1961, he writes: "There's so much to write about the Mar Saba MS – which I am sending by surface mail – that I just despair to do it justice" (Letter 68). A few months later, Smith's interpretation of the document has advanced: "I've been thinking a good deal...about the possibility

Press, 2006). See William V. Harris's review in the *Times Literary Supplement* of October 16, 2007.

[19] The following comments are based upon my "Comments on Charles Hedrick's Article: A Testimony", published in the *Journal of Early Christian Studies* 11 (2003), 147–153. For a convincing argument about the letter's authenticity, see A. Martin, "A propos de la lettre attribuée à Clément d'Alexandrie sur l'évangile secret de Marc," in L. Painchaud and P.-H. Poirier, eds., *Colloque international "L'Evangile de Thomas et les textes de Nag Hammadi", Québec 29–31 Mai 2003* (Louvain-Paris: Presses de l'Université Laval-Peeters, 2007), 277–300. See further Scott G. Brown, *Mark's Other Gospel: Rethinking Morton Smith's Controversial Discovery* (Waterloo, Ontario: Wilfrid Laurier University Press, 2005).

that Jesus may actually have taught a libertine Gospel – libertinism is so widespread in the New Testament, almost every book combats it; it cannot derive from Paul, there are a lot of libertine sayings in Jesus' mouth (the Law and the prophets were until John, since then!). Do you think the body and blood eaten and drunk can be a ritual expression of libertinism? (Eating a human sacrifice was a way of binding conspirators together, Apollonius of Tyana was charged with it). I talked about it with Bickerman[20] the other day and he was rather enthusiastic, saying this background would explain the reaction to the crucifixion, which I think it would. Any comments you may make on *mitzvah ha-ba'ah be-'averah* [in Hebrew characters; this is a reference to a theological justification of antinomian behavior in Sabbatianism] in or before the Tannaitic period will be most welcome" (Letter 72). A letter from October 6, 1962, reflects the further progress of his interpretation of the document: "...the edition of Clement on the Carpocratians creeps along by inches, but quite wonderful things keep turning up. I am really beginning to think that Carpocrates and the sort of things he represented (and especially the ascent through the heavens) were far closer to Jesus than has ever been supposed. What's more, I have the evidence. I wish you were here so that I could discuss it with you..." (Letter 76). The next letter referring to Clement's letter is from July 5, 1968: "The book on Mark goes forward, at glacial speed. But I shall finish revising the stylist's revision this summer (unless something quite unforeseen happens) so it should go off to the press by fall" (Letter 86).

Smith's letters also tell us something about Scholem's positive reaction to the discovery. On July 13, 1973, Smith writes: "I was delighted to get your letter with its kind remarks about my book..." (Letter 95), adding, on July 12, 1974: "That you are convinced of the Clementine authorship of the letter and find probable my account of the relation of the gospel fragment to canonical Mark, and above all that you agree with me as to the importance of magic and related libertinism in the Christian communities from which the Gospels and the Pauline epistles emerged – *dai li* [in Hebrew characters, meaning: 'this satisfies me completely']" (Letter 97). In the same letter, Smith writes at great length on Jesus as a libertine magician. These paragraphs reflect quite clearly the evolution of Smith's thought from Secret Mark to the very figure of Jesus. In the same letter, Smith writes: "My expectation is, however,

[20] Smith became in 1957 a colleague of Elias Bickerman, who was Professor of Ancient History at Columbia. See n. 3 above.

that with some exceptions the reviews [of the book on Clement and the secret Mark] will be only preliminary skirmishes; the real battle will be fought out in articles and book [sic] over the next ten or fifteen years. It will have to be, because the text is there and has to be explained, and the problems are there, and have to be answered." The last letter of Smith I want to quote is from September 27, 1976. Smith writes: "...I think I've learned more about Jesus from you and Shabbatai Zvi (I'm sometimes not sure which is which) than I have from any other source except the gospels and the magical papyri...Gospels and papyri have kept me busy all summer. I promised Harper's a book on "Jesus the Magician" which was going to be a mere collection of parallels to the Gospels from the magical papyri..." (Letter 104).

I hope these quotes from Smith's letters are enough to convince even the most skeptical reader about Smith's honesty. They reflect his long interest in searching for Patristic manuscripts in Greek monasteries, his astonishment and excitement about his find in 1958, and the long gestation of his interpretation of it in the following two decades, all the way up to the publication of *Jesus the Magician*.[21] These quotes reveal, moreover, perhaps for the first time, the deeper drive behind Smith's evolving perception of Jesus and of the very beginnings of Christianity. The continuing central importance of Scholem for Smith, decades after the formative Jerusalem years, is revealed in the last quotation: the decisive intellectual experience of Smith's life seems to have been

[21] M. Smith, *Jesus the Magician* (San Francisco: Harper and Row, 1978). In Letter 40, dated August 1, 1955, Smith mentions "a book on Mark," which he had finished writing the preceding summer (he refers again to this book in Letter 42 [October 27, 1955] and Letter 45 [February 28, 1956]), in which he argued that Jesus was conceived, in the "group that put together this collection," as "a healing god, by analogy with Asclepius and Sarapis." Smith adds that A. D. Nock had read his manuscript and commented on it. It would seem that after his discovery in Mar Saba, in 1958, Smith put his manuscript aside. It stands to reason that much of this material was reincorporated into *Jesus the Magician*. In private correspondence, Allan Pantuck adds the following: Although Smith says here the book had been completed, in fact he was continuing to work on it for several more years, and he still hadn't finished it when he moved to Drew in 1956–1957: in a letter to Goodenough from 1956, Smith states that the book deals with pagan elements in the first half of Mark, and seems to have been part of his greater interest in the Hellenization of Judaism. In his "On the Authenticity of the Mar Saba Letter of Clement," *Catholic Biblical Quarterly* 38 (1976), 196–199, Smith relates that this material that he had set aside in 1958 had finally been published as his "The Aretology used by Mark." In W. Wuellner, ed., *Protocol of the Sixth Colloquy of the Center for Hermeneutical Studies in Hellenistic and Modern Culture* (Berkeley, 1973), 1–25. Scott G. Brown, "The Question of Motive in the Case against Morton Smith," *Journal of Biblical Literature* 125 (2006), 351–83, seeks to trace the evolution of Smith's thought on Secret Mark.

his encounter with Scholem and with Jewish esoteric, magical and mystical literature. Ancient Jewish magic, mystical ascents to heaven, and the antinomian figure of the seventeenth-century false Messiah from Smyrna, Sabbatai Zvi, all profoundly marked Smith. With the loss of his faith, he gradually came to see Jesus as an antinomian figure, and it was the discovery of secret Mark which permitted him to build a sustained thesis in this direction. In a way, Smith pursued all his life the study he had begun in his Jerusalem PhD. thesis on the Tannaitic parallels to the Gospels. In his sustained search for the Jewish background of earliest Christianity, he went onto a path too little trodden: that of early Jewish esotericism. Of course, whether the emerging figure of Jesus and his followers, and of the earliest Christian rites, is convincing or not, is another issue, and one that certainly deserves to be debated seriously.

Scholem was immediately impressed by Smith's discovery: "I congratulate you most cordially on this discovery. Your arguments are very strong indeed, and I am curious to what valid objections Nock and Völker have to make.[22] I look forward to the book which must surely arouse great interest. What an unexpected testimony!!" (Jerusalem, not dated). "My cordial congratulations for your Mar Saba findings and discoveries. Please do not forget to send me all you publish about these matters." (Letter 69, from February 10, 1961). It should be noted, however, that Scholem, who obviously had very warm feelings for Smith, was not convinced by his interpretation of the text: "About libertinism in the New Testament I do not feel competent to comment although there may be something in what you say regarding libertine sayings put in Jesus' mouth. But I admit to an amount of scepticism regarding the hypothesis about the body and blood formula as a ritual expression of libertinism, Bickerman's enthusiasm notwithstanding" (Letter 73, from July 3, 1961. See also Letter 96, from June 9, 1974).

Upon receiving Smith's more popular book, accounting of his discovery, Scholem writes: "Your book is indeed very exciting and I am full of expectations regarding the proof forthcoming in your next volume announced by Harvard. Not so much because I have

---

[22] Allan Pantuck adds the following: After his announcement of the Letter at SBL, Smith sent out in early 1961 both the text of his talk as well as a summary to the scholars with whom he had consulted on the dating and style of Clement. This summarized their opinions, and in it Smith lists three scholars who disagreed with attribution of the letter to Clement: Munck, Nock, and Völker. This is what Scholem must be referring to here (Private correspondence).

any doubts about your point regarding the authenticity of the letter, but because of the consequences you draw. The Jesus of the Sermon on the Mountain and Jesus the Magician, suppressed by the church tradition – what perspectives! Was this the secret reason behind your projected study of Jewish magic in Hellenistic times I once supported vis-à-vis Bollingen?" (Letter 94, from July 3, 1973). On June 9, 1974 (Letter 96), Scholem writes a long letter on Smith's thesis: "...As to the magical part, I consider your evidence very good and convincing as far as it pertains to the tradition of the original church, whereas I am not sure whether the story can be truly taken as historical evidence about Jesus himself. That the magical element in these traditions of primitive Christianity was in conformity to generally accepted magical views and practices, I take as proven convincingly by you. As to the last part, the libertine character of Jesus' teaching for the initiates, I think it is a hypothesis which remains rather vague and I admit that I have not been convinced. That there were groups who drew libertinist consequences from the teachings about the kingdom of God, I take as firmly established by you and some of your predecessors. The further step to relate it to Jesus himself remains to me a hypothesis for which no hard evidence can be produced...My admiration for the scholarship and insight demonstrated in your book is enormous and I cannot imagine that it will not have its repercussions in future discussions...But there seems to me a great difference between the stringency of your deductions and the hypothetical character of your assumption of Jesus as a mystical libertinist."

Like his mentor Scholem, Smith was fascinated throughout his life with old manuscripts, finding new evidence on ancient religious history, in particular on magical, mystical, and heretical trends. His unexpected discovery of the Mar Saba document put him on the track of an interpretation of Jesus similar, *mutatis mutandis*, to Scholem's interpretation of Sabbatai Zvi. Moreover, like Scholem had done for Kabbalah in Judaism, Smith attempted to emphasize the centrality of esoteric traditions and rituals in early Christianity, traditions and rituals later suppressed or transformed by emerging orthodoxy. That in this attempt he was not as successful as he wished seems obvious. Probably, he overplayed his hand.[23] But no one should any longer seriously dispute

[23] For a recent and fair assessment of the reactions to Smith's publications, see C. W. Hedrick, "The Secret Gospel of Mark: Stalemate in the Academy," *Journal of Early Christian Studies* 11 (2003), 133–145. See further my article cited n. 19 above.

the authenticity of the Clementine letter he discovered, or deny that he did with it exactly what a scholar working in a library should do: photograph the text, publish a list of the documents analyzed, and put the book back on the shelf afterwards.[24] It is a well-known fact among scientists and epistemologists that it takes a long time, up to a generation, before scientific breakthroughs are widely acknowledged and their implications fully recognized. Smith published the account of his discovery in 1973. It is high time to accept it.

Habent sua fata litterae: the strange fate of Clement of Alexandria's letter to Theodore may be taken as the philological equivalent of Heisenberg's uncertainty principle – that the very attempt to observe a subatomic particle's trajectory changes its course. In the spring of 1976, a party of four, including the late David Flusser, Professor of New Testament, the late Shlomo Pines, Professor of medieval Arabic and Jewish philosophy, both at the Hebrew University of Jerusalem, Archimandrite Meliton, from the Greek Patriarchate in Jerusalem (at the time a research student at the Hebrew University) and myself (then a graduate student at Harvard University), drove (in my car) from Jerusalem to Mar Saba monastery, in the Judean wilderness, in the quest for Clement's letter. Together with Flusser and Pines, I had been intrigued by Morton Smith's sensational description of his find, and we wanted to see the text with our own eyes. When we reached the monastery, with the help of one of the monks, whose name I have forgotten, we began searching for Isaac Vossius' edition of the Letters of Ignatius on the very dusty shelves of the library in the monastery's tower. The young monk and Archimandrite Meliton explained to us that most books from the monastery's library had been moved to the Patriarchate library in Jerusalem after too many thefts had occurred. We did come with great expectations, and indeed the monk soon found the book, with "Smith 65" inscribed on its front page.[25] There, on the blank pages at the end of the book, were the three manuscript pages of Clement's letter, exactly as described by Smith. The book had clearly

---

[24] After Smith's death, Professor Robert Somerville, Smith's executor, found the photographs of Clement's letter in Smith's safe-deposit box (oral communication of Professor Joseph Sievers, 15 November 2006).

[25] I.e., number 65 in the list of books compiled by Smith during his examination of the monastery's library in 1958. This catalogued list was later published in 1960 in the periodical of the Greek Patriarchate: "Hellenika Cheirographa en tei Monei tou Hagiou Sabba," *Nea Sion* 52 (1960), 110–125, 245–356.

remained where Smith had found it, and where he had replaced it after having made his photographs. It was obvious to all of us that the precious book should not be left in place, but rather should be deposited in the library of the Patriarchate. So we took the book with us back to Jerusalem, and Father Meliton brought it to the library. We planned to analyze the manuscript seriously and contemplated an ink analysis. At the National and University Library, however, we were told that only at the Police Headquarters were people equipped with the necessary knowledge and tools for such an analysis. Father Meliton made it clear that he had no intention of putting the Vossius book in the hands of the Israeli police. We gave up, I went back to Harvard, and when I returned to Jerusalem to teach, more than two years later, I had other commitments. It was only recently, more than a quarter of a century later, in talking to American colleagues, that I realized that I am, as one of these colleagues put it, the "last living Western scholar" to have seen the Clement manuscript, and that I had a duty to testify in front of a still puzzled or skeptical scholarly world. What seems clear is that it was our journey of discovery that led to someone's excision, and possibly destruction, of the Clementine manuscript.[26]

Since I have been interested in early Christian esoteric traditions for many years, the idea of a secret Gospel in the Alexandrian Church never really surprised me.[27] Smith's analysis of the Secret Gospel, though brilliant, may be ultimately unconvincing, but the continuous skepticism about the very existence of Clement's letter, and accusations of forgery – a forgery perhaps made by Smith himself have always seemed to me to stem from quite unscholarly grounds, usually implicit rather than explicitly stated. To my mind, the new evidence strongly points to the total trustworthiness of Smith's account of his important discovery (though not necessarily of his interpretation of the document).

I met Smith a few times in the United States, but only once in Jerusalem. That was in the spring of 1982, a few months after Scholem's death. He was in town for a few days, and wanted, above all, to present his condolences to Mrs. Scholem. The same week, Professor Helmut

[26] See Bart D. Ehrman, *Lost Christianities: The Battles for Scripture and the Faiths we Never Knew* (New York: Oxford University Press, 2003), chapter four: "The Forgery of an Ancient Discovery? Morton Smith and the Secret Gospel of Mark," pp. 67–89, esp. 83–84.

[27] See my *Hidden Wisdom: Esoteric Traditions and the Roots of Christian Mysticism* (second edition, Leiden, 2005), 40–41, 112.

Koester, from Harvard University, was giving a lecture on the Secret Gospel of Mark at the Hebrew University. Professor Flusser invited Smith to lunch, together with Koester, before the latter's lecture. Quentin Quesnell was also in town, and Flusser had also invited him to lunch. Smith, naturally, refused to have lunch with a man who had accused him of forgery.[28] If Smith wanted nothing more than to pay his respects to Mrs. Scholem, this was because he had had, for more than forty years, a very close relationship with her late husband.

The main interest of the whole correspondence, to my mind, lies in the fact that while it ended less than twenty-five years ago, it captures for us, in a way that can hardly be followed today, a particularly vivid and sharp image of scholarship in the making. Meetings, exchange of ideas, manuscripts, books, bibliographical references, gossip, travels, translations, misunderstandings, letters of recommendation: all this, among scholars not yet quite familiar with the telephone. Since the death of these two scholars, the internet and email revolution has had a dramatic effect upon the daily lives of scholars. But this effect can barely be captured, as it remains in the electronic, virtual world.

While it may be true, as Steven Aschheim has written, that Scholem (Scholem the intellectual) still awaits his biographer, the daily life of a scholar is hardly exciting stuff for a biographer.[29] Throughout his life, Scholem, like Smith, was mainly a scholar: day after day, and often night after night, reading, interpreting, translating, annotating, emending, thinking about texts and their significance, all this while struggling through the thousand battles of life, in harsh times, when a life dedicated to scholarship is less than evident for society at large. Scholem and Smith were both, in different ways, free spirits, or rather spirits in search of freedom – a freedom probably harder to achieve in the study of religion than in any other field.[30]

For the editorial work, I have been blessed with a "dream team." This edition was made possible only through the intelligent assiduity of

[28] Q. Quesnell, "The Mar Saba Clementine: A Question of Evidence," *Catholic Biblical Quarterly* 37 (1975), 48–67.

[29] Steven E. Aschheim, "The Metaphysical Psychologist: On the Life and Letters of Gershom Scholem," *The Journal of Modern History* 76 (2004), 903–933, esp. 932.

[30] One may note that in their letters, both scholars do not deal with their own religious attitudes. In particular, Smith does not provide here any insight on the loss of his faith.

my students Sharon Weisser and Yonatan Moss. Both showed great diligence and perseverance in the long process of deciphering scripts and identifying figures. Sharon worked mainly on Smith's letters, and Yonatan mainly on Scholem's. Yonatan also translated the first letters from Hebrew to English. Both worked with me on the notes. I remember fondly our many working sessions, which were never tedious. In a previous stage of preparation, much help was provided by Yf'at Monikendam. The excellent conditions from which I benefited for three years at the Scholion Center of the Hebrew University made working on these letters possible.

The letters are published here in chronological order, and have been numbered accordingly. Two additional letters (Letters 122 and 123), from Smith to Fania after her husband's death, are also published. The first one refers to the request made by Professor Jacob Katz for Scholem's letters, with a view to their publication. It can be assumed that Smith obliged and sent all of Scholem's letters in his possession to Jerusalem. Some of the letters are typed (and in some cases, the carbon copy of Scholem's letters has been kept), many are handwritten. Some are written on postcards, some on aerograms.

Three appendices have been added. Appendix A is Smith's application for a research Fellowship, on magic in the ancient Mediterranean (cf. Letter 76). This undated proposal was submitted in the Fall of 1962, both to the Guggenheim Foundation and to the Bollingen Foundation. Smith's application was successful, and he spent a sabbatical year from June, 1963 through September, 1964 completing a survey of magic material from Hellenistic and Roman periods in American, European and Near East museums supported by the Guggenheim Foundation (cf. Letter 82, from Luxor, dated January 14, 1964). Appendix B is a letter of recommendation for the Guggenheim Foundation, by Scholem, dated October 29, 1962. Appendix C is a letter of recommendation by Scholem, dated January 4, 1966. It probably refers to a request for a renewal of the Fellowship.[31]

We have not corrected syntactical oddities, and have tried to keep the original orthography, except in obvious cases of *lapsus calami*. For instance, Smith usually spells the name of Scholem's wife "Fanya,"

---

[31] Allan Pantuck adds the following: In 1966, Smith eventually decided to spend time in Syria searching for Hebrew manuscripts supported by a grant from the American Council of Learned Societies. During this trip, Smith was arrested by the Syrian secret service, detained, and accused of being a spy for Israel. (Private correspondence).

while Scholem spells it "Fania." The spelling of some names, such as Sambursky or Hekhalot, has been unified, as have forms of dating and page-setting. Book titles are in italics, as are foreign words and expressions. Abbreviated titles (for instance of scholarly journals) have been given in full.

I should like to thank the staff of the Manuscripts Department at the Jewish National and University Library in Jerusalem, and in particular Margot Cohn, for their ever-readiness to help. Finally, I express my gratitude to Suhrkamp Verlag, which owns the rights for Scholem's works, and to Professor Shaye Cohen, from Harvard University, Smith's literary executor, for their permission to publish these letters.

1

Morton Smith
8 Laurina Hall
99 Brattle Street
Cambridge, Massachusetts
February 23, 1945

Dear Professor Scholem,[1]

I have waited to write to you until I could report that I delivered your cards to their addressees, and could relay their regards back to you. I was in New York on two occasions: once before the beginning of school and once before Christmas. On the first occasion I met with Lieberman[2] and we had a very interesting conversation (interesting to me, at least) about the relations between the Palestinian Midrashists[3] and the Church Fathers. On the second occasion I met with Spiegel[4] and we spoke mostly about Jerusalem and about you. We had a very nice time. They both inquired after Rehavia[5] and especially after the Scholems.[6] Unfortunately, Schocken[7] was not in New York on either occasion. I will therefore have to wait until Passover[8] before I will be able to meet up with him. I thank you profusely for these greeting-cards, for I very much enjoyed speaking with both Lieberman and Spiegel.

---

[1] Letter translated from the Hebrew by Yonatan Moss.

[2] Saul Lieberman (Motol, Belorussia, 1898–New York, 1983). Influential academic Talmud scholar. Professor of Talmud at the Jewish Theological Seminary. Author of *Greek in Jewish Palestine* (New York, 1942) and *Hellenism in Jewish Palestine* (New York, 1950).

[3] Midrashists are authors of *midrashim* (Hebrew for 'interpretation' or 'exegesis'). The term midrash refers either to an exegetical method, an exegetical compilation or an exegetical verse from the Rabbinical Literature.

[4] Shalom Spiegel (Stanesti de Jos, Rumania, 1899–New York, 1984). Professor of medieval letters at the Jewish Theological Seminary of America. Author of *The Last Trial* (New York, 1967).

[5] Western Jerusalem residential neighborhood, established in 1924. It was home to the Scholems and many other German-speaking Jewish academics and professionals.

[6] The original Hebrew here contains an untranslatable pun: *Shlom Ha'Shalomim*.

[7] Salman Schocken (Margonin, Poland, 1877–Tel Aviv, 1959). Businessman, publisher, collector, and Zionist philanthropist.

[8] It is also possible that Smith is referring here to Easter and not to Passover.

I must thank you as well for the article you sent me as a token for the days of the world's creation.[9] Your article[10] reminds me how many things there are in Jewish history that we just do not know. Yet, I think a bit can be deduced from parallels in Christian history. Even that death impulse that you wrote about is not unique to the Jews. Gibbon[11] reflected on his writing style just as Zunz[12] did on his footnotes: his entire great book is like a giant mausoleum of cold marble. Zunz's aim was not only not to be Jewish, but also simply not to be at all.[13] This was the case with many at the end of the 19th century (Beckford,[14] for example. Are you familiar with his book "*Vathek*"?). It was against this rule of Satan that the Romanticists rebelled; several of them even succeeded in reliving the past (Coleridge, for example, in his poem *The Ancient Mariner*), but most of them (and almost all of their disciples) succumbed to the snares of sentimentalism, and from that time until our own day people have been devoured either by this bear or by that lion. Perhaps the Kabbalist will encounter the serpent?[15]

---

[9] Smith's Hebrew is elliptical here. He is probably referring to an article sent to him by Scholem as a gift for the Jewish New Year. This holiday is traditionally considered the date of the creation of the world, and in mediaeval Hebrew poetry is referred to as *yom harat 'olam* – 'the day of the world's conception', a rereading of Jeremiah 20:17.

[10] The article in question '*Mitoch Hirhurim 'al Chokhmat Yisrael*' ('Some Reflections on the Scientific Study of Judaism') was written by Scholem for the *Haaretz* newspaper in honor of the Jewish New Year in September, 1944. It was later reprinted in E. Spicehandler and J. Petuchowski (eds.) *Perakim BeYehadut: Antologia* (Jerusalem, 1963).

[11] Edward Gibbon (1737–1794). English historian. Author of *The Decline and Fall of the Roman Empire*, 6 vols. (1776–1788).

[12] Leopold Zunz (Detmold, 1794–Berlin, 1886). Founder of what has been termed 'the scientifc study of Judaism', the critical investigation of Jewish literature, hymnology and ritual. Author of *Die gottesdienstlichen Vorträge der Juden, historisch entwickelt* (Berlin, 1832).

[13] Smith's precise intention in this strange paragraph is unclear. He seems, however, to be expanding Scholem's criticism of the 19th century conception of the scientific study of Judaism. To characterize this conception Scholem quotes a story in which a young, enthusiastic Zionist, upon seeing the vast library of the renowned scholar Moritz Steinschneider, began to expound ardently on the role to be played by the scientific study of Jewish literature in the cultural renaissance. To which the aged Steinschneider curtly replied: "We have no other role than providing all this with a proper burial". Smith reads this attitude as profoundly nihilistic. It seeks not only to extinguish Jewish cultural life, but life in general.

[14] William Beckford of Fonthill (1760–1844). Eccentric wealthy English novelist and collector. Author of *The History of the Caliph Vathek* (1786–7).

[15] Smith is paraphrasing a parable found in the *Babylonian Talmud, Berachot* 13a: 'A traveling man was attacked by a wolf. Having been saved from the wolf, the man continues on his way telling the tale of the wolf, only to be attacked again, by a lion. When saved once again, the man continues on his way telling the tale of the lion, only to be attacked again, by a serpent. When saved from the serpent the man forgets the

I am seriously engaged in this question since I must provide consultation on the question of the place of theology in the university curriculum: how should religion be taught and what should be taught as religion? I have not yet found a solution to this question, for there are all different kinds of students, each with his particular academic inclinations.[16]

A new book on the Kabbalah has recently come out here: J. L. Blau, *The Christian Interpretation of the Cabala in the Renaissance*, Columbia University Press, N.Y. Blau[17] holds your work in high esteem, I would therefore think that he has already sent you an exemplar. I would be very happy to know (confidentially)[18] your opinion of the book. I found it somewhat dry – useful as a list of names, and because of the bibliography it includes (but the bibliography it does *not* include is greater). But I do not wholly agree with his opinion that: "this type of speculation rapidly proved a blind alley... Like astrology, alchemy, and other pseudo-sciences, Kabbalah fell a legitimate victim to the development of scientific thinking."[19] I take this as evidence that he does not understand the essence of the matter. Further evidence can be found in his characterization of authors who did not know about Jewish occult as non-kabbalists. Instead, I would argue, if the Kabbalah is a way of thinking (a 'way' and not, as Blau thinks, a precise standard) it is possible to proceed along the way without knowing who foraged it out before you. It was thus possible, as you have said, for Boehme[20] and Waite[21] to be Kabbalists without knowing the "Kabbalistic standard".

---

tales of the wolf and the lion, and tells only the tale of the serpent. So is the case with the people of Israel: later sorrows cause the earlier ones to be forgotten.'

[16] Smith's Hebrew is unclear here.

[17] Leon Joseph Blau (1909–1986). Professor of Religion at Columbia University (1926–77). Author of *The Christian Interpretation of the Cabbala in the Renaissance* (New York, 1944); *The Story of Jewish Philosophy* (New York, 1962). Christian Kabbalah is a movement of the Renaissance's humanists, started with Giovanni Pico della Mirandola (1463–1494) that effected a Christian appropriation of the Jewish Kabbalah.

[18] Added in English.

[19] J. L. Blau, *The Christian Interpretation of the Cabbala*, 1.

[20] Jackob Boehme (1575–1624). German Christian Mystic. Author of *Aurora* (1610). Scholem, in his *Major Trends in Jewish Mysticism* (Jerusalem, 1941), 237, compares Boehme's mysticism with that of the Kabbalah.

[21] Arthur Edward Waite (New York 1857–1942). Co-creator of the Rider-Waite Tarrot deck and prolific author of occult texts on magic, alchemy, Kabbalah, etc. Author of the *Holy Kabbalah* (1930). Waite was qualified by Scholem (*Major Trends in Jewish Mysticism*, 2) as a Christian scholar of a mystical bent.

I wrote to Lewy[22] two days ago regarding the publication of his book and mistakenly told him that the American Philological Association may print it as a "Transaction". I should have said as a *Monograph.*[23] Please inform him of the correction as quickly as possible, lest he write something incorrect to them.

Has Wirszubski[24] yet managed to copy the *Hekhalot* translation we completed?[25] I promised I would show it to Cadbury[26] the moment I receive it, but I have not yet received it.

Regards to you and to Mrs. Scholem. I still remember fondly the lunch I had at your house right before I left.

With respect,

Morton Smith

[22] Hans Lewy (Berlin, 1901–Jerusalem, 1945). Classical scholar and lecturer at the Hebrew University.

[23] Eventually published as: H. Lewy, *Chaldean Oracles and Theurgy: Mysticism, Magic and Platonism in the Later Roman Empire* (Cairo, 1956). New, much enlarged edition by Michel Tardieu (Paris, 1978).

[24] Chaim Wirszubski (Vilna, 1916–Jerusalem, 1977). Classical scholar at the Hebrew University who also published on Jewish mysticism. Author of *Picco della Mirandola's encounter with Jewish Mysticism* (Cambridge, Mass., 1989).

[25] *Hekhalot Rabbati* (*The Greater Heavenly Halls*) is a core text of late antique Jewish mysticism. Smith had translated this text during his stay in Jerusalem. Scholem's plans to publish it never materialized, but he does quotes from it in his *Jewish Gnosticism, Merkabah Mysticism and Talmudic Tradition* (New York, 1960), 11, n. 4.

[26] Henry Joel Cadbury (1883–1974). Influential New Testament scholar at Bryn Mawr and then at Harvard. Chairman of the American Friends Service Committee (AFSC), a religious association devoted to humanitarian causes. In 1947, he received the Nobel Prize on its behalf. Author of *National Ideals in the Old Testament* (New York, 1920).

2

G. Scholem
28 Abarbanel Rd.
Jerusalem (Palestine)
April 9, 1945

Dear Mr. Smith,[27]

Your letter from the end of February was received here with great joy, for we had not heard anything from you over the course of the last year and we did not know what has been happening in your life. But even now we are disappointed on this account: you write not the least about your doings and your plans so we have no knowledge of where you are headed!

I informed Dr. Lewy of your correction to your letter to him. In the meantime he received the good news that the French Institute[28] in Cairo would be willing to publish his book (and thus he will be able to read over the proofs himself).[29] I assume that the Gnostic sect in Jerusalem will appear marvelous to you, and "rightly sinister".[30] At the university and around it people are very preoccupied with Gnosticism proper (Jonas),[31] Manichaeism (Polotzky),[32] post-Gnostic Greek Mysticism (Lewy), Kabbalah as well as all sorts of other occult sciences of

[27] Letter translated from the Hebrew by Yonatan Moss.

[28] The Institut Français d'Archéologie Orientale, established in 1898 in Cairo.

[29] Hans Lewy died of a sudden heart attack in the summer of 1945, just several months after Scholem wrote this letter. The institute did, however, proceed to publish eleven years later an English translation of Lewy's work.

[30] Scholem adds these words in English. In referring to this so-called 'Gnostic sect' Scholem is probably thinking mainly of the 'Pilegesh Club'. This was a group of friends that gathered around Scholem in the thirties and forties and used to meet on weekends for private discussions and exchanges of ideas. The name of the club (which means 'concubine' in Hebrew) is derived from the initials of the participants: J. Polotsky, H. Jonas, H. Lewy, G. Lichtheim, G. Scholem, Sh. Sambursky. See: H. Jonas, *Erinnerungen* (Frankfort, Leipzig, 2003), 144–8.

[31] Hans Jonas (Mönchengladbach, 1903–New York, 1993). Philosopher and interpreter of Gnosticism. Author of *Gnosis und spätantiker Geist*, 2 vols. (Göttingen, 1934, 1954); *The Imperative of Responsibility* (Chicago, 1984).

[32] Hans Jacob Polotsky (Zurich, 1905–Jerusalem, 1991). Versatile orientalist and philologist. Founder of the Department of Linguistics at the Hebrew University. Author of *Egyptian Tenses* (Jerusalem, 1965).

Israel – both in Buber's[33] school and my own.[34] Anyway, let's pray that there will also spring up a new Center for the Worship of Reason in Jerusalem – that could counter the attack of these scholars of the occult!

I heard last week that Mr. Singer has finally completed his work and is about to *now* give in your dissertation to the university authorities. Too much time has passed and we had no idea what got to him.

Wirszubski finished copying your translation and I can send you a copy. But there are still many places which, in my opinion, require still further corrections and polish. In some cases doubts arise from a careful reading of the text (reading, after all, tends to be more meticulous than hearing). In addition, there are some doubtful manuscript variants that you did not take into account. There are other cases where you assigned *different* equivalents to the *same* words in *different* places. I am not, however, technically able at the moment to go over it all and write out a long list and notes. I will, therefore, perhaps send you the translation as it is. Wirszubski is no longer in Palestine. To our great delight, he was granted a scholarship by the British Council to study at Cambridge, England.[35] He will stay there for about two years to continue his studies in classical philology and to finish his doctorate. I can think of few people as worthy as him for this. He has been writing letters from there displaying his satisfaction and delight; he has no concerns other than reading books and working on his subject.

The work on the Kabbalists remains, therefore, stuck where it was when Wiszubski departed – at least as far as the *Hekhalot* are concerned. Nevertheless, I will try to mark in pencil certain places in the English manuscript for you; hopefully, you will understand what I am referring to. You would also be interested to know that I recently obtained a photograph from the Vatican library of an elegant manuscript of the *Sefer Hekhalot* – a first dove from Europe! The manuscript is marvelous in its writing but horrendous in its readings.

---

[33] Martin Buber (Vienna, 1878–Jerusalem, 1965). A leading Jewish philosopher and Zionist. One of the founders of the Hebrew University.

[34] Scholem was strongly opposed to Buber' spiritualizing interpretation of Jewish mysticism.

[35] 'scholarship' and 'British Council': in English. Wirszubski spent the years 1945–1948 at Cambridge. It was there that he wrote his doctorate, later published as: *Libertas as a Political Idea at Rome during the Late Republic and Early Principate* (Cambridge, Mass., 1950).

I am very pleased that you saw Spiegel and Lieberman. And what is our friend Wolfson[36] up to? Please send him my regards if you chance to see him, which I presume you will. Schocken is not living in New York at the moment but in Stamford – and that is precisely what is so difficult. He will, no doubt, remain in the United States until the end of the year and I would be delighted if you met with him. He has recently telegraphed us that he is willing to publish the second edition of my English book[37] on a much broader scale. I am very interested in such an enlargement, but he has set a condition which cannot be met, namely that the entire book must be done printing by the end of the summer! I shall hope he will agree to postpone this deadline – for what difference does it make if such a book appears in October of this year, or in April of the next. For in any case, it is impossible to prepare everything that has to be prepared in just two months time. If you were here I would try to entice you to take upon yourself the translation of the new chapters. Now it will be very difficult to find a suitable translator. Lichtheim[38] is busy. If Schocken rejects the proposal to wait another half a year the book will be issued without changes in volume and content; in which case I should hope to finish my book on the Sabbatian movement over the summer.[39] Otherwise, I will dedicate the entire summer to updating the English book.

I have not yet received Joseph Blau's book on the Christian Kabbalah, but just in the past few days a letter from him arrived announcing the book's delivery. I saw only an article by him in the *Review of Religion* and it really is "a little thin".[40] I am wondering whether I should perhaps

---

[36] Harry Austryn Wolfson (Austryn, Lithuania, 1887–Cambridge, Mass., 1974). Very influential historian of philosophy and medieval religious thought at Harvard University. Was the first incumbent of a chair of Jewish studies in a non-Jewish American University. Author of many works on Philo, Patristic thought, medieval philosophy in Arabic and Hebrew, Islamic theology, and Spinoza.

[37] Scholem's *Major Trends in Jewish Mysticism*. The first edition of the book was published in Jerusalem in 1941; the second edition appeared in 1946. Scholem ended up making scattered revisions and additions for the second edition, but no new chapters were included.

[38] George Lichtheim (Berlin, 1912–1973). Sociologist and historian. Translator of Scholem's *Major Trends in Jewish Mysticism.*

[39] Sabbatianism is a 17th century Jewish messianic movement centered on the figure of the Turkish Jew Sabbatai Zevi, claimed to be the messiah. Scholem, ultimately published: *Shabbetai Ẓevi ve-haTenu'ah haShabbetait biYemey Chayav*, 2 vols. (Tel Aviv, 1957). (*Sabbatai Sevi: The Mystical Messiah*, 1626–1676 [trans. R. J. Z. Werblowsky, Princeton, 1973]).

[40] In English.

incorporate in the expanded version of my book also a chapter of my own on the Christian Kabbalah. This would, however, hardly qualify as a major trend in *Jewish* mysticism! But the matter is surely stimulating, and I have a thing or two to say about it.

Perhaps some time you could write us candidly about the state of anti-Semitism where you are. Does it appear to you to have changed over the course of the four years you were away from your country? It should be worthwhile to hear the opinion of an intelligent person who is not in involved party in the matter as we are. Have you also encountered a major intensification of Jew-hatred, as we have been hearing from various quarters?

My wife sends you her regards, and hopes that the meal at our house was not the last!

With full blessings and peace,

Yours,

Gerschom Scholem

3

Morton Smith
248 S. 8th St.
Philadelphia
Pennsylvania, U.S.A.
November 26, 1945

Dear Professor Scholem,[41]

I must beg your forgiveness again for not having responded earlier to your Hebrew letter. The truth of the matter is that there was never a time in my life in which I was as busy as I have been in the past half

[41] Letter translated from the Hebrew by Yonatan Moss.

a year. Your letter arrived in May; in June I had my university finals; in July I received my deacon's ordination; and immediately in August I was placed in charge of a church of 300 members.[42] During that same month we – that is my father and I – moved downtown (before that we lived in the suburbs).[43] Until now I have neither had time to install the curtains nor to unroll the rugs in our new apartment due to the very bad shape the church was in. The man who was there before me did nothing, and when I took over even the membership roster was incomplete. About thirty days ago I finished arranging the church and began working at home, writing letters and even reading some. Then all of a sudden war broke out[44] between the church officer[45] and the Young Peoples' Fellowship[46] and on that very same day the diocese secretariat requested that I take my examinations for becoming a minister. A week ago yesterday the 'war' in my church ended with a compromise and last week I completed my examinations. (Of the eleven examinations I had I was only able to prepare for three; I had to take all the others without prior preparation, and I do not know yet whether I passed them or not. In any case I will not be able to receive my minister's ordination before I have completed six months as deacon, that is, not before the beginning of January by which time there shall be another round of examinations).

That is, in short, the story of my life over the past six months. As you can imagine, as every day goes by, my memory is progressively dimming.[47] At least I will be able to speak from experience of the 'forgotten Torah'.[48] It's true; with the exception of the *book of Psalms* which I read daily I have been reading very little: a few pages of *Midrashei*

[42] Smith served as Vicar, St. Ambrose's Mission in Philadelphia in 1945–1946 (A.P.).

[43] Smith's father was H. J. Smith, whose business H. J. Smith & Sons (founded in 1871) designed and executed stained glass and memorial windows. The business was active in Pennsylvania, for example it designed the sanctuary window in St. Hugh's Church in Philadelphia (A.P.).

[44] Smith's Hebrew here is obscure.

[45] *Chazan haKenessiyah*, Smith's coinage presumably refers to some practical ecclesiastical office, such as the beadle.

[46] Smith writes his Hebrew equivalent and adds these English words in parentheses.

[47] Smith's Hebrew is obscure.

[48] Smith is referring here to the early Rabbinic awareness of the dangers of forgetting the Torah which was initially preserved only orally. See *Tosefta Berachot*, 6, 23–4; *Sifrei Deuteronomy* 48; *Babylonian Talmud, Shabbat* 138b.

Halakha[49] and a bit from the *Sefer Hasidim*.[50] I had begun reading the latter in bed every night, but stopped after two weeks when I realized that I was unable to keep track when it was I who was nodding off to sleep – and when it was the author. Of course, I always have time to read nonsense; over this past period I have read (among other things) a life of Mr. A. Crowley[51] along with a selection of his poetry and one of his plays. The play (a comedy by the name *Mortadello*)[52] turned out, to my pleasant surprise, to be quite good. The first three acts were especially good – they were full of power and life and demonstrated an unusual command of language. I found several of his poems very good as well, albeit in that inflated *fin-de-siècle* style. The book about his life was written by a certain P. R. Stephenson (*The Legend of Aleister Crowley*, London, The Mandrake Press, 1930), and its purpose was to whitewash him. Apparently either Crowley or one of his disciples had Stephenson write it when Crowley was growing old and wanted to return to England and quit his youthful ways. According to the account related therein, Crowley was born to a middle class, though wealthy, family. His mother was very devout, belonging to some Protestant sect, probably the 'Plymouth Brethren'.[53] Reacting to his upbringing he developed hatred towards Christianity and already at the age of twenty he published his first book: *White Stains*,[54] based on Krafft-Ebing's *Psychopathia Sexualis*.[55] *White Stains* was published in 1896, and from then until 1906

---

[49] A group of Tannaitic expositions of the latter four books of the Pentateuch, probably redacted around the turn of the fifth century.

[50] Classic Jewish ethical work produced by the '*Hasidei Ashkenaz*' movement in Germany of the 12th and 13th centuries. It is attributed to R. Judah the Pious of Regensburg.

[51] Aleister Crowley (Leamington, 1875–Hastings, 1947). Occultist, mystic, hedonist and sexual revolutionary. Dubbed by the media of his day: 'The Wickedest Man in the World' and 'The Great Beast'. Author of *Liber Al vel Legis* (*The Book of the Law*) (1904) which sets out the principles of what he calls 'Magick' or 'Thelema'.

[52] Aleister Crowley, *Mortadello, or The Angel of Venice* (London, 1912).

[53] The Plymouth Brethren is a Christian religious movement that began in Ireland in the late 1820s and was first established in England by John Nelson Darby at Plymouth in 1830.The movement is characterized by its anti-denominational, anti-clerical and anti-creedal ideology.

[54] *White Stains* was actually published in 1898, in Amsterdam. It is a collection of pornographic verse, posing as the literary remains of 'George Archibald Bishop, a neuropath of the Second Empire'. The volume is prefaced by the following notice: 'The Editor hopes that Mental Pathologists, for whose eyes alone this treatise is destined, will spare no precaution to prevent it falling into other hands'.

[55] Richard Freiherr von Krafft-Ebing, *Psychopathia Sexualis: eine klinisch-forensische Studie* (Stuttgart, 1886). A groundbreaking study of sexual pathology in which the terms 'sadism' and 'masochism' are first coined. The book places a special emphasis on

Crowley lived as a litterateur, off his parents' money. Then he became interested in magic. In 1910 he was sued by MacGregor Mathers[56] for having published the rite of the 'Neo-Hermetic Order of the Golden Dawn' in his periodical *Equinox*.[57] He spent the years 1914–1918 in the United States and wrote extensively for G. S. Viereck's[58] periodical the *International*. He was in Cefalu, Sicily from 1918 to 1923, but was expelled from Italy, probably after 1923, by Mussolini's government as a result of the scandal following the death of Raoul Loveday.[59] The book stops there; but based on various indications in the book I gather that Crowley traveled from Sicily to Tunisia and from there to France.[60] *Magick in Theory and Practice* was published in France (Paris) in around 1927.[61] Crowley was in England in the thirties when Stephenson's book was published. When was the article you have about the Mittel-Danj[62] "zwischen Schopenhauer und Busch" written?

Why am I interested in a fool like him? I cannot say. I just am. He has a certain "Keckheit, Kühnheit und Grandiosität"[63] (as Goethe said about Byron) which I find lacking in your usual research student and your average Anglican minister.

Regarding the *Hekhalot*, if you send me the corrected Hebrew text, as well as the text of the translation we made including your annotations

---

homosexuality and was arguably the most influential book on human sexuality prior to Freud.

[56] Samuel Liddell MacGregor Mathers (London, 1854–1918). Magician and key figure in modern Occultism. In 1887 Mathers co-founded the 'Hermetic Order of the Golden Dawn', a magical fraternity dedicated to theurgy and spiritual development, which went on to become a major influence in the development of Western Occultism.

[57] *The Equinox: The Review of Scientific Illuminism*, bi-annually published by Crowley in London in the years 1909–1909.

[58] George Sylvester Viereck (Munich, 1884–Hadley, Mass., 1962). German-American poet, writer and propagandist. Ardent supporter of the German cause in World War I and of Nazi ideology before and during World War II. Viereck was founder and editor of the *International*, a literary avant garde monthly publication.

[59] Crowley founded the 'Abbey of Thelema' in Cefalu in 1921. Rumors circulated purporting sexual orgies, child sacrifice and bestiality that were practiced there. Crowley never confirmed or denied the rumors, so that when the 23-year old Oxford undergraduate Raoul Loveday mysteriously died there in 1923, Crowley was forced to leave Italy and the Abbey was closed.

[60] Crowley was in Tunis in 1923, in Paris in 1924, and then he traveled between France, Germany and North Africa in 1925–1929. In 1929 he was expelled from France.

[61] *Magick in Theory and Practice* (Paris, 1929).

[62] Unclear.

[63] Cheekiness, boldness and grandiosity.

on the parts you do not like, I will do my best to improve the translation according to your wishes. Needless to say, I will not print something you find unsatisfactory. I can draft a list here of the English and Hebrew words and make sure that any given Hebrew word is always translated by the same English word, *provided that the Hebrew word has the same meaning.* Naturally, sometimes one Hebrew word has several different meanings, each to be translated by a different English equivalent. When in doubt I think it is best to render the general feeling conveyed by the original by capturing its style in the translation; he who desires literal accuracy, should go and learn Hebrew.

I find that there is less anti-Semitism here now than there was in the forties when I left for Palestine. At that time Father Coughlin[64] was well-known; now he is all but forgotten. Moreover, anti-Semitism is now considered Nazism, so many of those who in the past were very involved in it, at present are scared to express their anti-Semitism. Naturally, for various reasons (upon which the Nazis had based their propaganda) the same opinions about Jews can still be heard; whenever the name of a Jew comes up in conversation someone will always say: "they are very rich", or "no doubt, they have a very great influence", or "they are all repulsive"; but the same people who say these things will go buy in stores owned by Jews, and will give their votes to Jewish candidates in municipal elections. Regarding Zionism and the Palestine problem, most people here do not really have opinions on the matter and those that do usually think that we should not meddle in such affairs. For this reason some people are angry at Truman and say that he spoke both without understanding and without reason.[65] Does this sentiment have a substantial enough influence to oppose the Zionists' influence and organization? I do not know. I think that they could accomplish more with Truman on the personal level; but before we will be able to create an alliance with England regarding Palestine, this will have to pass through the Senate; and popular sentiment will have more power

[64] Charles Coughlin (Hamilton, Ontario, 1891–Birmingham, Michigan, 1979). Roman Catholic priest who spearheaded radio evangelical broadcasting. Extremely popular during the Great Depression, he later became increasingly anti-Semitic and pro-fascist. The Church forbade him to continue broadcasting in 1942.

[65] Smith is presumably referring to President Truman's criticism, in the summer of 1945, of the British policy of restricting the immigration of Jewish refugees to Palestine. On November 13, 1945, the British government announces the formation of an Anglo-American Committee of Inquiry to investigate Britain's handing of the Palestine situation.

in the Senate. I therefore think that the Zionists will never succeed in getting us into the government of Palestine. The newspapers here print very little on the matter, and the little that is printed is usually bad: "Jews Riot in Tel Aviv", "Jews Again on Strike in Palestine", etc. I do not know who the Zionist public relations manager in the United States is; but whoever he may be, he is not doing a good job.

I did not manage to meet with Schocken, nor have I seen Wolfson for five months now. He is working on Philo[66] and his book on him should come out, I think, at the beginning of next year.[67] Everything was written already a year ago, but whenever they want to begin publishing he decides to further revise it.

As for my own plans – I do not know. I could be a teacher of New Testament in a seminary but I naturally do not feel like reading all the learned nonsense written on that very interesting book. Day by day, I am beginning to sense more and more the difference between books, on the hand, that display a special way of thinking that is worth reflecting on, and all other books, on the other hand. I am sensing even more to what degree the books that I do read influence my mode of thought.[68] For this reason I am becoming more and more opposed to the reading of the nonsense that needs to be read to become an expert in any given research method. Since this is the case, what shall I do? I do not know. But, in any case, I must remain a deacon for two more months. After that, God willing, I will be made a minister. And after that – who knows?[69]

Regards to Mrs. Scholem, and to Mrs. Lewy[70] too. I received her dear letter, and will try to return an answer to her soon. Have the Samburskys[71] returned from the Antipodes? And, more specially, how

---

[66] Philo of Alexandria (Philo Judaeus) (*circ.* 20 B.C.E.–*post.* 40 C.E.). Jewish Alexandrian exegete and philosopher, that included in his writings both biblical religion and Greek wisdom. He had a major formative influence on Christian thought.

[67] Harry A. Wolfson, *Philo: Foundations of Religious Philosophy in Judaism, Christianity and Islam* (Cambridge, Mass., 1947).

[68] The Hebrew here is somewhat unclear. Smith may be intending the reverse: "…to what degree the books that I do read *echo* my mode of thought".

[69] Smith writes these words in colloquial Arabic: *man ba'arif.*

[70] Hans Lewy's widow. Lewi had died on July 22, 1945. Scholem spoke at a memorial meeting held in Jerusalem on November 18, 1945.

[71] Samuel Sambursky (Königsberg, 1900–Jerusalem, 1990). Physicist and historian of science, who was among the founders of the Physics Department at the Hebrew University. He was instrumental in bringing the Italian nuclear physicist Giulio Racah over to the Hebrew University in 1939. Author of *The Physical World of the Greeks* (New York, 1956).

is the book (or the books), and what is new in the world of the divine, i.e., in the Kabbalah in the city of the Kabbalists? Please do not requite my sluggish deeds, but rather write back please, speedily and soon[72] so that I may rejoice in the *parousia*[73] of your wisdom.

With utmost respect,

Morton Smith

4

Jerusalem
March 24, 1946

Dear Mr. Smith,

I am very much in your debt but I thought I would write you a long, long letter about many things between heaven and earth, about things in Palestine and in America, but now – *hélas* – there is a new factor which compels me to write immediately and to be very short. I will have to leave Palestine during the next few days quite suddenly on a special mission on behalf of the University which will take me to France, Germany (or what was Germany) and some other countries, and I have no time to arrange everything adequately. This mission will keep me away from here for several months. But what is more, I can tell you that it is most likely that I shall come to the U.S.A. after achieving what I have to do in Europe and shall stay there about half a year. Wise[74] has invited me for a second Strook lecture course[75] to be

[72] Smith uses the Aramaic expression *ba'agala u'vizman kariv* widely familiar from the *Kaddish* prayer.

[73] 'Presence' in Classical Greek. In the New Testament and later Church writings it came to refer to the Advent of Christ.

[74] Stephen Wise (Budapest, 1874–New York, 1949). Influential American Reform rabbi and Zionist leader.

[75] Scholem had delivered one set of Hilda Strook memorial lectures at the Jewish Institute of Religion in New York in 1938. His *Major Trends in Jewish Mysticism* is based on these lectures.

given in November or January. I hope to be able to go from Europe to England and to sail from there sometime in the late summer. I hope also that Mrs. Scholem will be able to join me in New York by coming over directly from Jerusalem as she cannot accompany me on my mission. Thus we will have an excellent opportunity to meet again, to talk over everything and specifically to put the final touch on your *Hekhalot* translation. I am sending you one of the copies which are not yet corrected (I thought I could do this during March when the University business appeared out of the blue. I would, therefore, suggest to wait with the publication until we can discuss the whole matter together. As soon as I will have a European address I will let you know. I am putting aside a copy of the Hebrew text in order to have it sent over with other papers to New York as soon as I know that I am parting there. Please, be so kind and confirm the receipt of the *Hekhalot* to my wife, anyhow everything you write to her, will find its way to me. We are very interested to see something of the States and I hope to be able to finish there my Sabbatian Studies.

A second edition of my *Major Trends* has just gone to press in U.S.A., some kind of revised edition. I have written another 150 pages for this edition but no decent translator from the Hebrew could be found and I had to resign myself to some minor changes and additions.

Please, don't be angry with me for being so short, but I hope to make up for all shortcomings by longer talks with you, wherever I can find you in the U.S.A.

Therefore, *au revoir*, cher Monsieur, and many regards from

Yours sincerely,

G. Scholem

5

248 S. 8th St.
Philadelphia 7 Pa.
August 30, 1946

Dear Professor Scholem,

I should begin by apologizing for my long delay in answering your letter, and so am led directly to my activities of the past months, which must serve as my excuses. My work at the mission in Philadelphia continued – and continued to take every moment of my time – until the end of May. I found, by the way, that the study of rabbinical and patristic literature was an excellent preparation for the management of parish dances and adolescent athletics; it enabled me to find interest and relief in work which, after other studies, might have seemed comparatively stupid. By the end of May, however, I was ready for the rest, and drove to Illinois with my father to attend a family reunion. While there I met a cousin who invited me to visit her in San Francisco. While in San Francisco I took the opportunity of writing to a college friend in Los Angeles, who invited me there for a week, so it was the middle of July before I returned to the East – specifically, to Baltimore, where I am employed as assistant in charge of a chapel attached to one of the larger Anglo-Catholic parishes of the city.[76] My trip across the United States has left, as its dominant impression, that of the physical emptiness of the country, which so well suggests the intellectual condition of its inhabitants. The chief virtue of the great plains, in particular, is that one can cross them at 200 miles an hour, in the air, at night, asleep, and be sure of having missed nothing. It seems a pity that, while we have here so vast a geographical and educational vacuum, the Zionists should devote their effort to squeezing another 100,000 Jews into Palestine.[77] We could use a million, and we probably would be happy to have them if they would settle in rural districts in *kibbutzim*. My hosts

---

[76] Smith served as Curate in 1946–7 at St. Katharine's Chapel, Mt. Calvary Parish, Baltimore.

[77] Following the end of the Second World War intense efforts were made to bring as many Jewish refugees as possible to British Mandate Palestine, with the hope of creating a Jewish State.

in Los Angeles were violently anti-Jewish – on investigation it turned out that their only grievance was the real-estate situation in the *city*. But I mustn't write you hearsay.

My work in Baltimore is much lighter than it was in Philadelphia, and I intend to keep it so, but, *per contra*, I must travel to Philadelphia each week, on Wednesday afternoon, to see my father, and return here each Thursday evening. I should be happy if I could extend my trip some week and see you on a Thursday in New York. I have received the translation and text of the *Hekhalot*, but done nothing about them, excusing myself to myself on the grounds that I didn't know just what was wanted, but having as my real reason too many other concerns. I keep plugging away at Plato, I am obligated to perform the Liturgy and want to take the opportunity to learn something of its history and present laws, I have half-in-my-head-and-half-on-paper several articles on the New Testament, and I am getting more pleasure from and giving more time to people than ever before. But whenever you can spare time to discuss the work with me I shall be glad to have the translation of the *Hekhalot* as an occasion of returning to Hebrew, which of late I have too much neglected, and thereafter, if you should want a translator for the supplementary material of your *Major Trends*, I should be glad to undertake that in return for the knowledge I should gain by it – but I suppose that at the Seminary[78] you will find translators on every corner. At all events I look forward to the work on the *Hekhalot*.

I trust that your European trip was satisfactory and that Mrs. Scholem will be able to join you here as you hoped. Best wishes to her and to you.

Sincerely,

Morton Smith

[78] The Jewish Theological Seminary (JTS), founded in 1886, and located in New York City, is the intellectual and religious center of Conservative Judaism.

6

248 S. 8th St.
Philadelphia 7 Pa.
January 22, 1947

Dear Professor Scholem,

Early in the fall I sent you a letter, addressed to the Jewish Theological Seminary, excusing my summer's silence and asking what you wished done with the translation of the *Hekhalot*. Having received no answer I stopped at the Seminary when in New York a few weeks ago, and was told that you were not lecturing there this year, and now I have received a letter from Singer which tells me that you are still in Jerusalem and attributes the cancellation of your trip to health. Whatever the reason for the cancellation, I am sorry if it has disappointed you, and sorrier if illness has been the cause of it, and I hope this will find you well, or, at least, recovering. Had I followed your directions and acknowledged the receipt of the manuscript to Jerusalem, I should doubtless have done better, but it happened that the manuscript came just in the last days before my departure for California, and by the time I had returned to the East and got myself settled in my new work (at a chapel in Baltimore) I thought you would be already in New York and consequently decided to write you then.

I do hope you are well and trust that if you are you will presently write me your wishes as to the revision of the translation. In case, that is, there is anything I could do here without your immediate direction and later submit to you for correction. My Hebrew reading during the past year has been small, but I keep up to schedule in the Old Testament, and, when I return to Rabbinical literature, do not notice any change except that I have occasionally forgotten the meanings of technical terms. Now Professor Schwabe[79] writes me that the read-

[79] Moshe (Max) Schwabe (Halle, 1889–Jerusalem, 1956). Founder of the Department of Classics at the Hebrew University. Schwabe was the supervisor of Smith's Ph.D. thesis, *Tannaitic Parallels to the Gospels* that Smith wrote in Hebrew during his stay in Jerusalem (1940–5). The English revised version of the thesis was eventually published by the Monograph Series of the Journal of Biblical Literature: M. Smith, *Tannaitic Parallels to the Gospels* (Philadelphia, 1951).

ers have decided my thesis will be acceptable if corrected under the supervision of Professor Lieberman and to his satisfaction, so I must begin again my daily reading of that fascinating work, the Mishna. What price glory?

Please remember me to the Samburskys and to Professor Polotzky, and especially to Mrs. Scholem, whose farewell dinner I still remember with reverence. I trust she has been well, and hope the joy of living in Jerusalem will have made up to her for the annoyance of living in New York.

Sincerely,

Morton Smith

7

28 Abarbanel Road
Jerusalem
March 23, 1947

Dear Mr. Smith,

I was awfully glad to have your letter of January 22, 1947 and I apologize for having delayed my answer so long. The cause was an honorable one: I did not feel well, and on the other hand, I wanted very much to write you some suggestions as to *Hekhalot* translation. I have read with greatest interest what you are telling about your work and my wife and I wish you much success and, moreover, satisfaction in all these meritorious doings. I heard from Lieberman (who was here for a short time, just when I returned from Germany in a rather shattered state) about your dissertation, and I am fully confident that you will work out the whole thing to your mutual satisfaction. It will be very awesome to have our first Christian Ph.D. of our branches, in Talmudicis. And if you satisfy Lieberman who is a great scholar and a very keen mind, you may be justly proud of it. So – our best wishes.

My European journey was no holiday affair and has left its imprint on me. I mean spiritually, for physically I have now more or less recovered (and I hope only to Heaven they will not send me a second time on that business which I am afraid is not altogether out of question; but I think I will refuse). It was, indeed, very interesting and even exiting (Paris, London, Prague, Frankfort, Berlin, [You would have been laughing quite a bit meeting me there in an American uniform!][80] Munich, Vienna and 'surrounding villages'!). But most depressing in almost every aspect except that one of which was important for my mission, i.e. to find out the *facts* about the Jewish Libraries in Naziland. This I could easily do, more or less, as I still found some of the people (in Berlin) who had had to work for the Gestapo's Library department.[81] There is so far no political decision about the final disposal of the Jewish books in Germany, but a satisfactory solution seems to be under consideration in Washington. I don't know if this is of any interest to you but it may be! Of my own work: there is the second (revised) edition of *Major Trends* which should have been promoted to *General Trends* but it seems civilians get no promotion; furthermore there is a new book with the printer. It is called *Reshit HaKabbalah*[82] and if it ever appears you will get a copy! It deals with the first hundred years of Kabbalah 1150–1250, which is precisely the part which is lacking in my English book, and for which I could find no suitable translator into English. A lot of my small stuff has appeared both in the Kabbalistical and Sabbatian Heretical field, and if you tell me you are interested, I will be glad to send you some of it...I am sending you by same mail (but regular mail!) my memorial address on our friend Dr. Lewy[83] which may be a little to high – flown Hebrew for you – nevertheless TRY as Madame Blavaltsky[84] used to say, in capitals.

[80] Added as a footnote in the margin.

[81] During the war the Gestapo was put in charge of amassing a collection of books in Berlin relating to Judaism. Jewish intellectuals were forced to work there. Professor Erich Grumbach was one of the main librarians, and was probably one of the people whom Scholem met in Berlin.

[82] In Hebrew characters. The book was published in 1948 under the title: *Reshit Hakabbalah*, Jerusalem and Tel Aviv. Scholem published a revised German edition, Ursprung und Anfänge der Kabbala (Berlin, 1962), from which the French edition (Origines de la Kabbale [Paris, 1966] and the English one [*Origins of the Kabbalah* [trans. A. Arkush, Philadelphia, 1987] were made).

[83] Scholem's address was published as part of a booklet in memory of Hans Lewy: J. L. Magnes, M. Schwabe and G. G. Scholem, *H. Lewy, 1901–1945* (Jerusalem, 1946).

[84] Helena Blavatsky (Ekaterinoslav, Ukraine, 1831–London, 1891). Founder of the Theosophical Society. Author of *Isis Unveiled* (1877), and *The Secret Doctrine* (1888). Letters she wrote to her students often contained the exhortation: 'TRY'.

Now about the *Hekhalot*. I am of course, very much interested to see your translation in a finished state. It would be a very fine thing to have. Wirszubski (who has returned lately with a Ph.D. in Classical Philology from Cambridge)[85] has gone through your translation and made a number of remarks but it is written in a handwriting that even I find difficult to decipher, so I want him to copy them in a readable way and *I will send them to you by airmail for your consideration*. There are two kinds of possible improvements. a) Some positive mistakes in the translation, b) parallel or identical passages which you have translated in a different way and which should be straightened out. I was not able lately to work on the *Hekhalot* edition but I hope it will be possible to finish it about 1948. Of course, my idea was to have it attached to a critical edition of the Hebrew text but there may also be a way to have it published separately. In both cases the honors would be yours.

It may have been a mistake to cancel my invitation to Stephen Wise for a new set of lectures but I saw no other way when I came back, I was too much 'down'. Maybe I would have recovered just the same in America and we could have done some work together as I so confidently hoped when I last wrote you. But I hope there will be some other opportunity to come over with Mrs. Scholem and we will enjoy it all the more. Our friends and everybody remembers you in Jerusalem.

With kind regards,

Sincerely,

Gershom Scholem

[85] The Dissertation for the degree of Doctor of Philosophy was submitted to the University of Cambridge in 1946. See n. 35 to Letter 3 above.

8

248 S. 8th St.
Philadelphia 7
Pa. U.S.A.
May 9, 1947

Dear Professor Scholem,

Thank you for your letter. I delayed this answer till I should see Professor Lieberman, and delayed seeing him by reason of previous engagements, but at least the great day arrived, and now is yesterday. He expressed himself as very well pleased with the thesis – on the whole – but said it needed a number of minor improvement and corrections, general stylistic improvement, and eliminations of the polemic. So these we shall undertake. Professor Lieberman had not brought a copy with him, so I am writing Professor Schwabe to send me two of the typewritten copies (which I hope the University will let him have) and when these come we shall try to review a chapter every two weeks or so and finish in the course of the summer. Meanwhile I have my work cut out for me, for I have scarcely looked at Rabbinical Hebrew for a long time – though fortunately I have kept up my reading in the Old Testament – and have completely forgotten things like the order of the *Massekhtaot*.[86] Also, I have undertaken a book, two big articles, and a book review which should be almost an article, on strictly New Testament subjects; and of course, parish work goes in as usual. So I am in no great hurry to receive Wirszubski's corrections. Nevertheless, send them on, when he has them ready. And as soon as I can I shall try to correct my translation accordingly and send it back for a further reading, for I think the text is a fine one and ought to be translated, and I am, of course, not averse to the sort of *Kavod*[87] which is reflected on me from your company – even as second hand.

Thank you also for the pamphlets you sent me. Mrs. Lewy had previously sent me the one on her husband, and your article had interested me, especially by reason of the influence it attributed to Stephan

[86] Plural of *massekhet*: Hebrew for 'a tractate of the Talmud'.
[87] In Hebrew characters: honour.

George,[88] of whom I had hitherto heard only as a sort of crank who wrote poetry and was vaguely connected with the rise of Nazism. Such are reputations! Please continue to send me such Kabbalistic and Sabbatian things as you think will interest me, remembering that my concern is the ideas and I am content to learn the bibliographical details to experts.

Best wishes for you and Mrs. Scholem,

Sincerely,

Morton Smith

9

3216 N. 16th St.
Philadelphia 40
Pa. U.S.A.
December 12, 1947

Dear Professor Scholem,

I am to-day sending Dr. Wirszubski the corrected text of my translation of the Hekhalot. I am sending it by registered mail to him at the New Stern House, Kiryath Shmuel, and hope it will reach him safely. There are quite a lot of corrections in it, since I went over it carefully to get it as close to the Hebrew as I could and also to smooth out the English and make the punctuation (etc.) consistent. I'm sorry it's taken such a long time, but I have been very busy not only with parish work, but also with reading for my projected book on the lives of Jesus,[89] and with correction of my interminable thesis.

---

[88] Stefan George (1868–1933). German lyrical poet and man of letters. He was considered a national poet by the Nazis.
[89] Such a book was never published.

Professor Liebermann[90] read and approved it this summer, and I hoped then that all was over but correction and printing.

However, Professor Schwabe wrote me that I was required to send 6 typed copies of the corrected version to the University for rereading by the original referents, since all must approve the thing in its final form. Sisyphus should have gone to the Mount of Olives. However, it gives me something to do. When are you coming to the States to lecture?

Lighten our darkness, we beseech this, *kurie*.[91]

Best wishes, and regards to Mrs. Scholem,

Morton Smith

P.S. Please remember me to the Samburskys.

10

The Hebrew University
Jerusalem
August 6, 1948

My Dear Mr. Smith,

One hour ago I received your gift, Selig's magical tract on the use of the Psalms.[92] Many thanks to you. That such a book – I have the first edition, in German (1788) – should still be reprinted, is cause for wonder. I am very glad to know about this state of magical affairs in the U.S.A., in case I should proceed to open a magical shop thereover.

---

90 *Sic.*

91 In Greek characters: Lord.

92 First edition: G. Selig (trans.), *Sepher Schimmusch Tehillim, oder, Gebrauch der Psalmen zum leiblichen Wohl der Menschen: ein Fragment aus der praktischen Kabbala, nebst einem Auszug aus einigen andern kabbalistischen Schriften* (Berlin, 1788). Second edition: G. A. Selig, *Use of the Psalms* (Boston, 1943).

How are you? Your *new* address since your last letter (December 12, 1947 – this one I received at last and answered but Heaven knows what becomes of the mail these months) tends to show that you are at Harvard. We should like to know about your progress. Is your Ph.D. (Hebrew University) finally come home?

You may be interested to hear that there is a very good chance (if negotiations come to a good end) that my wife and I should be coming to the States for a new course of Strook lectures[93] in spring time 1949. This time it seems to be fairly serious. I am waiting only for the formal letter of invitation.

The last months have been *most* eventful and we could go on and on talking about our experiences.[94] It was a great time. Of course, no academic work could proceed orderly, but everybody has had his fill of excitement and work, building fortifications, standing up to shelling and sniping, it was all very much (a little too much, perhaps) "Historic". I was some kind of porter *honoris causa* with the Jewish H.Q.[95] and have spent some time on Mount Zion when we took over the 'Dormitio' of the Benedictines.[96] The good *patres* had fled and we had to guard the place. You would not have recognized Jerusalem these days! The shelling (very much English-made) was disagreeable, distasteful and exceedingly noisy. Some fell around our house, but no damage was done. Nobody knows whether the whole thing is going to start anew, and both sides are preparing themselves. The optimism which greeted the second cease-fire has vanished.[97] Wirszubski is educational officer in the Haganah and Mrs. Hans Lewy, the widow, is a soldier and can be observed guarding the Agency building with a stengun.[98] Some of

---

[93] Scholem was scheduled to give another set of the Hilda Strook memorial lectures in the winter of 1947 but ended up canceling them.

[94] Scholem is referring to the Arab-Israeli war of 1948–1949 following the United Nations partition plan of Palestine and the creation of the State of Israel.

[95] Headquarters.

[96] 'Dormitio Mariae'. Benedictine Abbey on Mount Zion, just outside the Old City of Jerusalem. Built as a monastery for the German Catholic community in the years 1906–1910, it became an abbey in 1926. At the point at which Scholem is writing, the Old City is fully in Jordanian hands while Mount Zion, at the Old City's Southern tip, is in Israeli hands.

[97] Scholem writes during the tenuous 'second truce': July 18, 1948–October 15, 1948.

[98] Scholem refers to the Jewish Agency for Palestine building, on King George the Fifth street in Jerusalem. The Stengun was a British submachine gun, created in 1941, and very popular among the Allied Forces and the Resistance groups. A local version was also manufactured by the Jews of Palestine.

our best friends are no more, the toll has been considerable. Samburskys are well, and you may have heard the story that the Arabs have given up Safed because they were told by some of their people that the Jews had a small atom bomb.[99] If they had asked Sambursky they would be still there.

Everybody has become tall and meager and since the end of the siege[100] we are living on food parcels from every corner of Israel. Everybody wanted to do something for us. To which we could not object reduced as we were in physical strength. Let us hope that the tribulations of Israel are soon over. And that we meet again in peaceful employment.

With kind regards,

Gershom Scholem

11

3 Divinity Hall
Divinity Ave.
Cambridge 38, Mass.
August 17, 1948

Dear Professor Scholem,

I just received your letter of August 6th and write at once to express my pleasure at hearing from you and learning that you and Mrs. Scholem and your library are all safe. I sincerely hope you will remain so. Here the newspaper reports are beginning to represent the chances of a long truce as at last good. It seems that the Arabs are beginning to realize that they have bitten off more than they can chew and would be happy to make peace if only they could get some face – saving moderation of the Jewish demands. So, at least the *New*

[99] Safed, a town in the Western Galilee, was conquered by the Haganah on May 9–10. Its Arab population of 10,000 fled the city on May 10–11.

[100] Jewish Jerusalem had been under Arab siege in the months March–July, 1948.

York Times and *Time*, in chorus. Whether or not this represents wishful thinking, I wonder. Yesterday I got a letter sent about a fortnight ago from the American School,[101] which suggests that the Arabs are actually in pretty bad state. Ramallah and the country beyond are overrun with refugees, most of them destitute; they are very short of water and food and their situation is becoming critical. I don't know whether or not you have news from the other side of Jerusalem, so shall summarize what I have heard, at the risk of repeating the familiar: the Greek Monastery[102] and the courtyard of the Holy Sepulcher have been hit and several persons killed, but the main building has, so far, escaped serious damage. So has the Dome of the Rock, except that most of the windows have been blown out. The Dominican Monastery[103] was hit several times but no one was killed and, as nothing was said of damage to the library, I suppose that was not the part hit. Shells have landed all around the American School and blown out all the windows, but so far the building itself has escaped unhit and nobody has been hurt. You presumably know more than I do about the shelling of the Hebrew University buildings.[104] I can only hope that the contents of the library and the records – including the priceless manuscript of the Smith thesis – escaped.

Mention of the Smith thesis brings me back to my own affairs, which have been as tranquil as yours have been stormy. Last February I came back to Harvard to work for the degree of Doctor Theology,[105] for which I am to make a special study of the New Testament and of Church history down to 400 and, for a thesis, probably produced,

[101] Founded in 1900, the American School of Oriental Research (ASOR) in Jerusalem, has been known since 1970 as the W. F. Albright Institute of Archaeological Research. The School leads scholarly research projects in archaeological, textual and historical studies of the ancient Near East.

[102] The Great Greek Orthodox Monastery adjoins the Church of the Holy Sepulchre on the west.

[103] The Dominican Monastery of St. Stephen, which hosts the Ecole Biblique et Archéologique Française, is located outside the Damascus Gate.

[104] The Hebrew University campus was established in 1925 on Mount Scopus. Between 1948 (the War of Independence) and 1967, it was isolated from the rest of Jewish Jerusalem and the university was relocated in West Jerusalem. After 1967 part of the university was reestablished on Mount Scopus.

[105] Smith received the Th.D. from Harvard in 1957; his dissertation: *Judaism in Palestine I: to the Maccabean Revolt*, was eventually published as: *Palestinian Parties and Politics that Shaped the Old Testament* (New York, 1971).

under Jaeger's[106] direction, an edition of one of the minor works of Gregory of Nyssa.[107] For the past six months I have been working on the background – giving half my time to classical literature and half to the early Fathers, especially Clement of Alexandria.[108] To keep my hand in Hebrew I keep reading at the Old Testament and the Mishna and, this summer, have been making a translation of my thesis. Also I have been reading a little Syriac, and working hard at my health, which again has been rather bad and which I have undertaken to doctor with large doses of tennis, the pleasantest treatment I know and one which has proved very successful. As you see, a pleasant tranquil life. I hope that after another year of it I shall be ready for my general examinations, and shall finish my thesis in yet another year.

Certainly, I should not care to have this degree drag on as my Ph.D. has.[109] No doubt I wrote you that Professor Lieberman had read and approved the thesis, but suggested a number of minor corrections. The Secretariat of the University ruled that those corrections must be inserted in all the copies and the copies, as corrected, approved by the other readers, before the degree could be awarded. Accordingly, I prepared a list of corrections and sent it to Professor Schwabe early this spring, with the request that he arrange to have the copies in Jerusalem altered accordingly. Since then I have heard nothing. *If Professor Schwabe is still in Jerusalem I should be very grateful if you would find out, and let me know whether or not he received my letter and whether anything has been done and whether there is any prospect that any thing will be done in the future.* Frankly, I am sick of the whole affair. The indefinite withholding of the degree has seriously discredited me in the eyes of the Harvard faculty (who, as they can't read Hebrew, have been unable to judge the thesis for themselves) and materially lessens my prospects of getting a job in a university. I shall see Professor Lieberman shortly after the middle of September and hope then to have the translation of the thesis complete and to discuss with him what disposition had best be made of it. (The *Journal of Biblical Literature* has a fund for the publication of such material, and I am reasonably sure that I could get this accepted for

[106] Werner Wilhelm Jaeger (Lobberich, 1888–Boston, 1961). Classical philologist, editor of the writings of Gregory of Nyssa.

[107] One of the fourth century Cappadocian Fathers.

[108] Clement of Alexandria (d. *circ.* 215). Christian theologian and head of the catechetical School of Alexandria.

[109] Smith's Th.D. was awarded seven years following the completion of his coursework; his Ph.D. only four years (A.P.).

publication). So I should be only glad if, before meeting Professor Lieberman, I could have some news from Jerusalem as to what has been done and what prospects there are of anything being done. I know, of course, that in the present state of affairs information of this sort must be highly speculative and problematical, but any information, at this moment, would be better than none, and I should regard it as great favor if you could get some word to me as soon as possible.

I was very glad to hear that the Sambursky's and Mrs. Lewy are well. Do give them my regards if you see them soon again. It is very good news that you may soon come again to this country. I am anxious to see you again and to talk of all those things which are too long to write.

With best wishes for yourself and for Mrs. Scholem.

Sincerely,

Morton Smith

P.S. what has become of the *Hekhalot*?[110]

12

Jerusalem
August 29, 1948

Dear Mr. Smith,

Is this a sign of better times? Letters are beginning to arrive, some of them even without delay, as did your long letter of August 17 which Mrs. Scholem and I have been reading, or should I say studying with great interest. Your news about the other side of Jerusalem was, indeed, partially news to us. We do not get any papers from the U.S.A., Heaven knows why, and our political education and information is six months old. On the other side, for people who have to put up without *New York*

[110] In Hebrew characters.

Times and *Time*, we are not doing too badly. If there is actually peace around the corner, we don't know although we have been praying for it very whole-heartedly. But from our angle the picture does not look very peaceful, and as I am writing these very lines, shells from the Arab lines are falling around our quarters, and during the last week shelling has been so heavy that – *o tempora, o mores!*[111] – the inhabitants of the old Orthodox quarters North of *Mea Shearim*[112] have had to leave and have been moving into *Katamon*[113] which you would scarcely recognize these days. The Hebrew University has taken a lot of shelling but no really serious damage has been done, and everything could be repaired in six or eight weeks (except one or two of the laboratories), if only we could get our people there to do the repairing in peace.[114] But this is plainly impossible under the present 'truce' conditions[115] and we will have to wait. If the war drags on as it threatens to do now, we will have to move temporarily to some place in town, but there may be few students anyhow what with mobilization and all kind of services abounding.

The Library is not damaged, only the windows are broken (as everywhere) and some shells have landed in the walls of the building without penetrating them. Books, manuscripts and foremost the Smith thesis are therefore intact, although they are not, of course, in current use.

Regarding the matter of your thesis I have at once enquired into that and also spoken to Schwabe who has received your list in May and has written to you then but the letter, as so many others, seems to have been lost. He is going to write you these very days again. As far as I understand, the truth of the matter is very simple: the trouble lies with Professor Lieberman who to this day has never given a written statement to the University authorities expressing (as, according to Schwabe, he was several times asked to do) his formal approval of your thesis and his considered opinion with regard to it. He alluded to it in several private letters which cannot be used as formal statements, and Schwabe who is exceedingly willing to help you in this most regret-

---

[111] Latin for 'What times, what customs!'

[112] Residential neighborhood in North-West Jerusalem. Ever since its establishment in the late 19th century it has been populated by Orthodox Jews.

[113] Upper-class Christian Arab neighborhood in South-West Jerusalem. It was abandoned during the battles of 1948 and then repopulated by Jewish refugees from other parts of the city.

[114] See note 102 to Letter 11 above.

[115] The tenuous 'second truce'.

table matter says that he *needs* such a statement and cannot proceed here without it. I suggested at once that the University send a cable to Lieberman requesting him to do his part of the official requirements in order to enable the people here to do theirs. (Such a cable was to be sent today.) If we would have received Lieberman's formal approval last fall as we expected, the whole affair might have been brought to a speedy and happy end, and you would not have to face the difficulties to which your letter alludes. I certainly believe that your proper place is in a University and I should like to help you if opportunity arises, by my word here or thereover.

I hope this will reach you in time for your meeting with Professor Lieberman to whom I should wish you to convey my kindest regards. About everything else – at another time. The *Hekhalot* are on my table as I am writing. The final edition of your translation should certainly be published, it is wonderful, but our edition is not yet ready.

With all good wishes and kind regards from both of us,

Bevirkat Shalom,[116]

Gershom Scholem

13

38 Divinity Hall
Divinity Avenue
Cambridge 38, Mass.
September 26, 1948

Dear Professor Scholem,

Thank you very much for your intervention in the question of my thesis. I saw Professor Lieberman last week and he told me he had

[116] In Hebrew characters. The phrase is a play on words, meaning both: 'with the blessing of peace' and 'with the blessing of Scholem'.

received the University's cablegram, which you suggested be sent, and had answered by air-mail, sending a formal statement of his approval. He was confident that on the reception of this statement the award of the degree would soon follow – presumably this fall. Professor Schwabe, who wrote me the day after you did, was, though optimistic, by no means so confident. But his letter encouraged me to hope at least that the matter will now soon be brought to a definite conclusion, and this I owe to your kind offices on my behalf. I hope that I may some day have an opportunity of making myself useful to you in partial repayment.

Such a sea of rumors surrounds the Palestine problem since the murder of Bernadotte,[117] that I can't tell what is worth repeating and what not. My guess is that the United States will make a determined effort to use the man's martyrdom for the justification of his proposals, but heaven knows what is really afoot. From the other side of Jerusalem: Some Arab vandals planted a bomb in the doorway of the American School and blew out the front door but did little more damage. The Dominican Convent[118] has had a good many direct hits from Jewish mortars but the library was practically undamaged two weeks ago.

Once again, my thanks for your kindness, and best regards for you and for Mrs. Scholem.

Very sincerely,

Morton Smith

[117] Count Folke Bernadotte (Stockholm, 1895–Jerusalem, 1947). Swedish diplomat who was murdered in Jerusalem in September 1947 by members of the Jewish terrorist group Lehi.

[118] The Dominican Monastery of Saint Stephen.

14

The Hebrew University
Jerusalem
November 25, 1948

Dear Mr. Smith,

I was very glad to receive your letter of September 26. I hope indeed that your doctorate will be settled in the next meeting of the Faculty before which the reports of Professors Lieberman and Schwabe have to come. Of course, you have every reason to be angry about the delay, or skeptical of the final outcome, but I think that as far as I am able to judge there is reason to be confident. The pity is only that the doctor may be conferred to you now after you have already been appointed to a professorship I do not know where. The only consolation I can offer is that this state of things would be in the best French tradition where the 'great' doctorate is mostly given long after you have got your academical appointment.

If there should be an opportunity to use what little influence I have as Chairman of the Institute of Jewish Studies[119] you may count on me.

Your news about the state of the libraries on the other side of Jerusalem were very interesting since we do not know anything here.

I hope that we shall meet again in spring as Mrs. Scholem and I intend to accept the invitation of the Jewish Institute of Religion[120] to deliver a new series of lectures on the beginnings of Chassidism. If everything goes smoothly you may find me in New York in March. I certainly hope that we shall be able to arrange for a visit in Harvard if you do not put in an appearance in New York. I hope also to be able then to discuss with you the question of the translation of *Hekhalot.*

In the meanwhile – with kind regards from Mrs. Scholem and me,

Yours sincerely,

G. G. Scholem

[119] The Institute of Jewish Studies at the Hebrew University. Founded in December of 1924, several months before the official opening of the university itself.

[120] Non-denominational rabbinical seminary founded in 1922 in New York by Rabbi Stephen Wise; it later merged with Hebrew Union College.

15

The American Friends of the Hebrew University
9 East 89th Street
New York 28, N.Y.

Dear Dr. Smith,

I am glad to convey to you our heartiest congratulations on receipt of the Ph.D. degree conferred upon you by the Hebrew University.

I would have written you from Jerusalem but I was so taken up with the last-minute preparations for my journey that I couldn't do it. Now that Mrs. Scholem and I have arrived here and we are settled we would be very pleased to hear from you and possibly to see you, after all those trying years since your departure. I do not know at the moment if and when we can come to Boston although I intend to make it possible.

I will be busy with my lectures at the Jewish Institution of Religion[121] throughout March. At any rate I do not know whether you intend to remain at your present address or if you have any other plans for the future. If you have occasion to come to New York during March this would be fine. You can imagine how eager we are to talk over many things with you.

I hope you have had official announcement regarding the award of your degree from the University authorities. Everybody was very pleased and I really consider it a great pity, and in a way an injustice to you that this matter was not settled a year ago.

Looking forward to hearing from you and possibly seeing you soon, I am with cordial regards to you from both of us.

Sincerely,

G. G. Scholem

P.S. My private address is: Hotel Park Plaza 50 West 77th St., New York City (Please write there).

---

[121] *Sic.* Scholem means the Jewish Institute of Religion, i.e., the Hebrew Union College, the intellectual, academic and spiritual center of Reform Judaism.

16

38 Divinity Hall
Divinity Avenue
Cambridge 38, Mass.
March 10, 1949

Dear Professor Scholem,

Your letter gave me great pleasure and I very much look forward to seeing both you and Mrs. Scholem. Hitherto I had been planning to come to Philadelphia for the week of April 3, which is vacation week here: I should come down on the afternoon of the third and return on the afternoon of the ninth. I could easily stop over in New York, so it would be most convenient for me to see you there either on the fourth or on the eighth, if either of those dates should fit your plans. Should you plan to leave New York before that time, I can arrange to come down sooner, best, perhaps, during the week of March 13. And, of course, I hope very much that you will be able to come to Boston and that I shall have the privilege of entertaining you here.

News of the award of the degree reached me early in January, and made me particularly happy because, just at the moment of its arrival, I was asked to submit a *vita* to Bryn Mawr College, which is looking for a potential Professor of the Philosophy of Religion. The place is very desirable, so they are able to look at leisure and the appointment is still pending, but at least the timely arrival of the degree has assured me of consideration which otherwise I could hardly have hoped for. Needless to say I am very grateful to you for all your assistance in securing the award.

Please remember me to Mrs. Scholem; the thought of you both brings back the most agreeable memories, and I close, as I began, with the happy anticipation of seeing both of you again, and soon.

Very sincerely,

Morton Smith

17

Hotel Park Plaza
50 West 77 Street
March 16, 1949

Dear Dr. Smith,

My wife and I were so glad to hear from you and we hope that you will be successful in your application at Bryn Mawr College. It is indeed a career that you are extremely well fitted for and it would be good to think that your work with us in Jerusalem should have helped you a little on your way.

As to our meeting, we must have it on about April 1 or later on. On April 3–5, I am supposed to be in *Rochester* and perhaps Buffalo. If we are in New York about April 9, we would love to see you, but I am not sure of this as I have given my friends some days to arrange for some lectures. But we shall *certainly* be here during the week of Pessah (April 14–20), and could fix some of the *Chol HaMo'ed*[122] days for your visit.

We should like to come to Boston. I am awaiting the outcome of an invitation tendered to me by some Jewish body there. (Possible end of May.) We would then be about 3–4 days in Boston. My last lecture here at the Institute is at March 28.

With kind regards from Mrs. Scholem and me,

Yours sincerely,

G. G. Scholem

---

[122] In Hebrew characters. These are the five days between the first and last day of Passover.

18

38 Divinity Hall
Divinity Avenue
March 19, 1949

Dear Professor Scholem,

Thank you very much for your letter. I am almost glad that the dates I suggested were not feasible, since that gives me an excuse to come down on the 28th and hear your lecture, and I shall – unless I hear from you in the meantime – look forward to a visit with you and Mrs. Scholem on the afternoon or evening of that day.

Best wishes,

Morton Smith

19

March 22, 1949

Dear Dr. Smith,

We are very pleased to hear that you are planning to come down next Monday, March 28. We will be in the Hotel (50 West 77 Street) from 3 in the afternoon and are looking forward to seeing you.

After the Lecture, we will go to some place with the Dean Dr. Slonimsky[123] and it will be fine if you go with us. In the afternoon we will have a chance of talking between ourselves.

Sincerely yours,

G. G. Scholem

20

38 Divinity Hall
Divinity Avenue
Cambridge 38, Mass.
March 30, 1949

Dear Professor Scholem,

Yesterday in Philadelphia I talked with Professor Nahm[124] of Bryn Mawr and he told me that the appointment to the Rufus James Professorship there had not yet been made, and that he would like very much to have a letter from you concerning my work in Jerusalem. I should be grateful, therefore if you would write him about me; though I have no great hope of getting the chair, which seems likely to be reserved for someone with an 'inspirational message'. The address is simply Professor Milton C. Nahm, Bryn Mawr College, Bryn Mawr, Pa.

I am writing Goodenough[125] today to inquire about the Yale funds for Hebrew publications and also about this occasional lectureships

[123] Henry Slonimsky (Minsk, 1884–New York, 1970). Professor of Philosophy of Religion and Dean of the Jewish Institute of Religion in New York. Author of *Heraklit und Parmenides* (Giessen, 1912) and editor of Judah Halevi, *The Kuzari* (trans. H. Hirschfeld, New York, 1964).

[124] Milton Charles Nahm (1903–1991). Professor of Philosophy and Department Chair at Bryn Mawr College. Author of *Selections from Early Greek Philosophy* (New York, 1964).

[125] Erwin R. Goodenough (1893–1965). American historian of religions, author of *The Politics of Philo Judaeus* (New-Heaven, 1938) and *Introduction to Philo Judaeus* (Oxford, 1940). Most widely known for his 13 volume work, *Jewish Symbols in the Greco-Roman Period* (New York, 1953–1968).

and I shall ask Pfeiffer,[126] here, about the same subjects when I see him on Friday.

Let me again thank you and Mrs. Scholem for a delightful afternoon and evening in New York. It was very good to see you again and see you so well and talk of all our friends in Jerusalem and learn that they and the city itself had escaped with so little damage. And it is always a pleasure to hear you lecture – the imposition of a lien form on obscure material approaches very much to Platonic 'creation'.

With all best wishes

Sincerely,

Morton Smith

21

Jewish Institute of Religion
West Sixty-Eight Street
Near Central Park
New York 23, N.Y.

Hotel Narragansett
2510 Broadway
(Riverside 9 – 5100)

Dear Dr. Smith,

It finally appears that we are not going up to Boston. The day I had set aside for the visit, was taken away by some official function of my Institute where I must take some sort of Ph.D. *honoris causa*.[127] This leaves us in the desert, as far as Boston and Harvard are concerned.

---

[126] Charles F. Pfeiffer. Biblical scholar who did postgraduate work at New York University.

[127] This doctorate *honoris causa* was from Hebrew Union College.

Have you heard from Bryn Mawr? I wrote them a nice letter about you.

Now, do you think you may pass through New York before we leave? This would be on the 27th of June, for Southampton.

Up to this day, we expect to stay here and I hope to do some work. We would be delighted to see you here once again. We have been around for some four weeks.

Please note the new address!

Cordially yours,

G. Scholem

22

Hotel Narragansett
June 6, 1949

Dear Dr. Smith,

Thank you for your letter. I should very much like to come to Boston in a 'private' capacity but I am not at all certain whether we will be able to do it. Anyway, we will be very pleased to see you on Wednesday afternoon (June 15) as you suggest and I have made a note of it. Could you come to our Hotel between 3 and 4? (It is between 93rd and 94th street, on Broadway 2510?)

With Kind regards, also from Mrs. Scholem,

Sincerely yours,

Gershom Scholem

23

38 Dinivity Hall
Divinity Avenue
January 6, 1950

Dear Professor Scholem,

Thank you very much for the copy of *Commentary* which was sent me at your recommendation. I suppose your iconoclastic contribution to the history of aniconic religion must have stirred up a hornet's nest of opposition, but I very much enjoyed it, and should have acknowledged the receipt of the magazine long before this had it not come just as I was preparing for my general examinations. Those I took just before the Christmas vacation, passed, and spent the vacation traveling, so this is really the first moment of leisure I have had for several months.

During my travels I saw Professor and Mrs. Schwabe in New York: his work is going well, but he is troubled by the arrangement of books in the Columbia library, which requires him to hunt all over several buildings in order to assemble the things he wants.

Both he and Mrs. Schwabe are well, and send you their regards. I also saw Jonas, at the Convention of the American Philosophical Association at Worcester,[128] where he read a rather interesting paper on the suppression of causality by sensible perception (i.e. the fact that, though sensations are results, they are not perceived as such. Apparently he has been studying Whitehead.[129] He talked, among other things, about conceiving the universe as an organism, so I tried to persuade him to attempt on this ground, a gnostic or kabbalistic interpretation of Whitehead (whose rather muddled Platonism is only waiting, I think, for its neo-Platonic interpreter). I hope he will attempt it – the results might be interesting and certainly would be curious, which is more than can be said for most American philosophy: to judge by these meetings a dreary bash of symbolic logic and semantics, with a little impractical pragmatism thrown in.

---

[128] The American Philosophical Association (APA) was founded in 1900 and is still active.

[129] Alfred North Whitehead (1861–1947). British mathematician, logician and philosopher. Worked on mathematical logic and the philosophy of science.

Now that my examinations are over I must begin work on a thesis, but the subject has not yet been decided, and as it will probably be the edition of some classical text I shall have in any case to begin by learning something about palaeography. Beside that I want, this spring, to hear Wolfsons' lectures on Aristotle and Nock's[130] on the history of Greek religion, and to read some more Plato, so I don't think the thesis will get on too fast. Also I have been asked by Obermann[131] to prepare a translation, with introduction etc. of *Aboth de R. Nathan*,[132] for the Yale Judaica series, and that will take time.

Have you any suggestions?

I should be grateful if you would transmit to Bamberger and Wahrmann[133] my order for your *Reshit HaKabbalah*[134] and for Yaari's *Torat HaZohar*.[135] Rabinowitz has not imported the first, does not know anything about it, and won't inquire; at least, that was his attitude when I last heard from him a month and a half ago. And on the second, he has simply doubled the price. As for Grun, the best Hebrew book store in Boston, it has gone down hill dreadfully and now seems to be run by an old man who can speak nothing but Yiddish and will stock nothing but service books.

I should write to Bamberger and Wahrmann myself. But I understand that one has died, and don't know which, and don't want to write a letter which, by reason of its address, might be painful to the

---

[130] Arthur Darby Nock (Portsmouth, England, 1902–Cambridge, Mass., 1963). English classical philologist and historian of religions. Author of *Conversion, The Old and the New in Religion from Alexander the Great to Augustine of Hippo* (Oxford, 1933); *Essays on Religion and the Ancient World* (Oxford, 1972). Smith studied under Nock at Harvard and served as his research assistant for three years, and later dedicated to him his *Clement of Alexandria and a Secret Gospel of Mark* (Harvard, 1973) (Nock died in January, 1963 and Smith completed the first draft of this book that summer. [A.P.]). Nock, however, could not be convinced of the Letter's authenticity.

[131] Julian Joel Obermann (Warsaw, 1888–U.S.A., 1956). Professor of Semitic philology at the Jewish Institute of Religion, the Hebrew University and Yale University.

[132] Smith did not end up issuing a translation of *Aboth de R. Nathan*; it was translated by Judah Goldin, *The Fathers according to Rabbi Nathan* (New Haven, 1956).

[133] Bamberger and Wahrmann were well-known Judaica publishers and booksellers in Jerusalem.

[134] In Hebrew characters.

[135] In Hebrew characters. Abraham Yaari (Tarnubjeg, Galicia, 1899–Tel Aviv, 1966). Hebrew writer, translator and bibliographer. The book referred to was not written by Yaari but by Isaiah Tishby. The book was also published in English: F. Lachower and I. Tishby, *The Wisdom of the Zohar: An Anthology of Texts* (trans. D. Goldstein, Oxford, 1989). The *Zohar* (the Book of Splendour) is the most influential work of the Jewish Kabbalah, published under the name of the first-century Rabbi Simeon bar Yochai.

recipient. Please ask the survivor to write me, also, letting me know if there are any new volumes of Kassowski's *Tosephta Concordance*,[136] or of *Otzar HaGeonim*,[137] and I should be glad if he would list any other new publications he thinks I might find interesting.

I hope that you and Mrs. Scholem are well and that your trip through Europe this past summer was both pleasant and profitable.

I know you are busy, but I should be very glad to hear from you whenever you have time. Please remember me to the Samburskys and to Tishby,[138] and also, if you happen to see them, to Mrs. Spingel, Mrs. Bloomentald and Miss Jerusalem, I think of them often and remember with pleasure their kindness to me during my stay on Jerusalem.

With all best wishes.

Sincerely,

Morton Smith

24

January 17, 1950

Dear Dr. Smith,

My double congratulations: to your Doctor diploma from the Hebrew University which was handed to you *in absentia* at the last commencement ceremony on Hannukah, and to your first step towards the second doctorate which you have accomplished. Your expanding scholarship makes me wonder – where will all that lead to? The gentlemen at Bryn Mawr had apparently no use for an intelligent man. Meanwhile

---

[136] By the time of this letter three out of the eventual six volumes of Haim J. Kassowski's *Tosephta Concordance* had been published. The *Tosefta* is an early compilation of Rabbinic traditions that had been excluded from the Mishna.

[137] In Hebrew characters. Edited by Benjamin Menashe Levin. The work is a multi-volume publication of the Gaonic commentaries on the Talmud.

[138] Isaiah Tishby (Sanislo, Hungary, 1908–Jerusalem, 1992). Professor of Jewish Mysticism and Medieval Hebrew Literature at the Hebrew University.

you will know much too much for America, too much of the Fathers of the Church and out of sheer boredom with this world will become a Manichean.

Your news about Schwabe and Jonas was very interesting to us. Of course, everybody in this generation is haunted by Whitehead and I have just the same problem of Whitehead and "American Kabbalah" to an American postgraduate student who has come to study with me here. (There are quite a number of them right now – the boom will not last, be sure!).

Bamberger has died, Wahrmann "ist noch am Leben"[139] and is expected back in Jerus alem with 15,000 valuable books next week – after eight months of European pilgrimage (or pilfering?) He is very clever and we are looking forward to a very hot time in trying to buy some of the new treasures! I shall ask him to send you Tishby's (*not* Yaari's) book on the Zohar. My own book *Reshit HaKabbalah*[140] shall go to you as a gift from me – as a matter of fact, I dream of tempting you into translating it into English. You are the one man who could do the job well (in case it interests you enough). And if not – I am glad to have a serious reader.

The European trip was rather interesting but I hope to have seen the last of Germany (where I had to spend a whole month). We are now bringing over from Germany quite a number of valuable books left by the Nazis.

I am teaching Zohar, Cordovero[141] and Shabbatianism at the University and Hassidism in Tel Aviv. Thus little time is left for my private enjoyment i.e. the reading of the 250 volumes I have brought from abroad. Now that Mt. Scopus is closed to us, the real value of my library is revealed, and even Mrs. Scholem who used to grumble about the budget has been silenced! You cannot imagine what a pleasure it is to sit in the study and to have almost everything at hand. I have always liked my books, now I love them. I am busy writing all the articles I should have written last year; the weather is dreadful (*shanna geshumah*)[142] which has a very great advantage, namely, that nobody disturbs you.

---

139 Is still alive.

140 In Hebrew characters.

141 Moses Cordovero (1522–1570). Rabbi and philosophically-bent Kabbalist in Safed. Highly instrumental in the systematization of Jewish mystic thought.

142 In Hebrew characters: 'a rainy year'. The phrase is taken from a prayer which, according to the Talmud, the High Priest would say in the Temple on the Day of Atonement (*Babylonian Talmud, Yoma*, 53b).

Sambursky has become a great man,[143] as head of the Scientific Research Council[144] of the State of Israel, and is supposed to produce another atomic bomb (or its equivalent) every other week![145] He will be delighted to hear about you.

Kind regards from my wife and me,

Sincerely yours,

G. Scholem

25

Divinity Hall
Divinity Avenue
Cambridge 38, Mass.
March 16, 1950

Dear Professor Scholem,

Thank you very much for your letter, for your transmission of my order to Wahrmann, and, above all for your book,[146] which I have read with great interest. The history is really a fascinating one, and the book is a most valuable completion to your *Major Trends*. The argument concerning the Gnostic elements in the *Bahir* interests me especially,[147] since Wolfson, in his great campaign for the Judaizing of Judaism, is, I think, determined to prove the Kabbalah basically

---

[143] Scholem may be translating from the Hebrew *Ish gadol* which has a clear connotation of metaphorical stature.
[144] Sambursky was in fact the initiating force behind the creation of the Scientific Research Council.
[145] Israel indeed became engaged in nuclear activity as early as 1952.
[146] *Reshit HaKabbalah.*
[147] The *Sefer ha-Bahir* (Hebrew for *Book of Illumination*) is a pseudepigraphic mystical work, considered one of the earliest Kabbalistic books. Scholem had written his doctoral dissertation on the *Bahir* and further developed his claim about the work's Gnostic trends in his *Reshit Hakabbalah.*

Jewish, and, while I haven't talked with him about the matter, I have praised your book to him and I shall be interested to see what he does with the evidence when he reaches it, two or three years from now, in his fifth (?) volume. You and he are as like and as different as fire and moonlight, and I look forward to seeing how the subject changes with the change of illumination. As for translating your book, I am honored that you should offer me the opportunity, and shall be very happy to make use of it. However, it is only fair to warn you that the work I have now on my hands will keep me busy at least till the beginning of the summer, and there is a possibility – though a slim one – that I may meanwhile get a scholarship for travel in Greece, in which event I should be gone for a year.

If you think it worth while to wait till the summer, good; if you think better to get another translator and proceed forthwith, by all means do so. Certainly the book should be translated. (Though what I should most like to translate would be a volume of your essays in Sabbatianism and Frankism: Could you and would you send me a suggested list of titles and places of publication?)[148] (And, speaking of translation, could you build a fire under Wirszubski? It would be a great help to me just now, when I am looking for work, to have my name on the title page of a demonstrable edition of the *Hekhaloth*).

Apropos of that subject, my thesis (English version) has now been definitely accepted for publication by the Monograph Series of the *Journal of Biblical Literature*, I am correcting the text for the printer, and it should be out in the fall. That will be a help.

Schwabe was up to Boston for a week, with Mrs. Schwabe. He spoke at the Hebrew Teachers' College,[149] made a good many visits in Harvard and in the Jewish community in Boston, and was successful in starting a local group of the Jewish Palestine Exploration Society, which may raise some money, I don't know. Unfortunately, at the end

[148] Frankism, a direct outgrowth of Sabbatianism, is a Jewish mystical and messianic movement founded by the libertine Jacob Frank (Podolia, 1726–Offenbach, 1791) in 18th century Poland. This antinomian and messianic cult did not survive very far into the nineteenth century as its adherents gradually merged with the Catholic Church. In his essay 'Redemption through Sin' (1st ed. [Hebrew]: 1937; English version in *The Messianic Idea in Judaism and Other Essays on Jewish Spirituality* [New York, 1971]), Scholem laid the foundations for his magisterial 1957 monograph (in Hebrew), later translated as *Sabbatai Sevi: The Mystical Messiah.*

[149] The transdenominational Hebrew College was founded in 1921 and is located in Boston.

of the trip, he slipped on an icy walk and broke his right arm, not badly, but he will have to wear a cast for several weeks and that will rather spoil the rest of his stay. Doubtless you have already heard of the matter from Miss Wilenski. She told me of our treasure-trove of Hebrew manuscripts and of the photographs she was sending you, so I suppose that most of the big doings in Boston accompanied them. Otherwise there is no news.

Do remember me to my friends in Jerusalem, with best wishes for you and for Mrs. Scholem.

Sincerely,

Morton Smith

P.S. Can you recommend any books (in western European Languages) on numerology, especially numerology in the Zohar and the Kabbalah generally. I have met a professor here who thinks 'there's something in it,' and who asked me to ask you for recommended reading. (His field is political philosophy, so I suppose he will find numerology as useful for his research as he would anything else. I had always wondered where they got it – now a great darkness begins to dawn. M.S.

26

15 Benevolent St.
Providence, R.I.
December 4, 1950

Dear Professor Scholem,

It's a long time since I heard from you, but I hope no news is good news. In my case, it certainly has been: I've had a very happy six months. When I last wrote you, I think, I was considering going to Europe. That didn't come off, but my summer in Providence was extremely pleasant. I played a great deal of tennis, and got myself in the best physical condition that I've ever enjoyed in my life. Being really healthy is a great – and for me a rather new – pleasure, and I've been making the most of it. One of the nice things about it is that it enables me to work really hard without immediately catching cold, or breaking down in some other way, and since school started I've been shamelessly capitalizing on this advantage and giving myself less sleep than I've hitherto dared. This has been necessary, because I've been teaching the Old Testament and the course has been one long demonstration to me of how much I didn't know. But the most important things I've learned from it are that I like teaching – both the contacts with individual students and the lecturing – and that students like me and my lectures. Beside getting up a course, I've finished the revision of the English translation of my thesis and sent it off to the printer – it will come out in the Monograph Series of the *Journal of Biblical Literature* – written about 2/3 of an article on the tradition of the early Church concerning the apostles and the 'twelve', and am now writing an article on the systematic theology of the Old Testament[150] – which, I hope, will be a surprise to the people who deny that there is any. Of the other things I've done most important has been to help organize a corporation to try to find funds for the Orthodox Patriarchate of Jerusalem.[151] About half their people are refugees, and most of their land is in Israel, and money cannot be transferred from Israel to Jordan, so they have great need and little funds. Therefore we are trying to find some money here to carry them over till some equitable arrangement can be made for their lands. A good many American Biblical scholars and clergy have joined up and correspondence has taken a good deal of my time.

With all this miscellaneous activity I've done nothing on my new thesis – a proposed edition of the funeral orations of Gregory of Nyssa,[152] for the Th.D. – nor, alas, on the translation of your book, which, however, I have read, and admire with the sort of complete admiration which always results from my utter incapacity to criticize your work. That incapacity, I suppose, wouldn't make me the ideal translator, and if you've meanwhile made or begun other arrangements for the translation, don't hesitate to cancel my proposal, in favor of them.

As a matter of fact, I'm very much in the air as to what I shall or should try to do in the near future. The only thing clear to me is that

---

[150] Probably: 'The Common Theology of the Ancient Near East', *Journal of Biblical Literature* 71 (1952), 134–47.

[151] This was an "American Friend's" group; Smith served as its Treasurer (A.P.).

[152] Smith never published these orations.

I must get time for a great deal of reading in both Greek and Hebrew, in order to consolidate and somewhat extend my present bridge-heads on those languages. How this had best be done, I'm in doubt. On the one hand, I might stay here, teach, and have a good deal of spare time for reading – though there would be an increasing burden of administrative work, and also I should be expected to turn out a lot of scholarly papers, which would mean wasting a good deal of time on secondary material. On the other hand, I have good reason to expect a fellowship for study in Greece, at the end of this year, and *that* I should like very much – but it probably would do no immediate good to my knowledge even of Greek, let alone Hebrew. And there is yet another possibility – Goodenough has interested the Bollingen people[153] in establishing a fellowship with a big stipend, tenable for a period up to five years, for the purpose of training in the techniques of psychiatry and sociology a man with some knowledge of traditional scholarship. What I am working on now is the question whether or not it is possible in some way to fuse these opportunities – and on this I should like to have your opinion. I know your interest in psychology and remember your references to its relevance to Kabbalistic studies. Do you think it would be worth my while to attempt to marry psychology and philology, or would the result be only a *mamzer*?[154] I have been turning over in my mind the possibility of a psychiatric study of the disciplinary works of Greek monasticism – or, perhaps, of the basic texts of Greek monastic mysticism, e.g. Dionysius Areopagita[155] – as a starting point. That would give me an excuse for combining the two fellowships and going to Greece in my first year of the joint tenure. My present schedule calls for an edition of Gregory of Nyssa's two short funeral orations before the end of this year, then the trip to Greece to photograph the

---

[153] The Bollingen Foundation was founded in 1945. Its main activity was the publication of the Bollingen Series, but it also awarded financial support for various scientific initiatives. The Bollingen foundation provided support for the publication of both the Hebrew, and later, the English versions of Scholem's *Sabbatai Sevi: The Mystical Messiah.*

[154] Hebrew for 'bastard'. On Smith's early views of psychiatry and religion, see his "Psychiatric Practice and Christian Dogma," *Journal of Pastoral Care* 3.1 (1949), 12–16. Smith then thought that psychiatry and dogma were opposed to one another. I thank Albert I. Baumgarten for providing me with a photocopy of this article.

[155] Dionysus the Areopagite (also known as Pseudo-Denys) is the pseudepigraphical identity adopted by the fifth century Christian author of a body of mystical compositions in Greek, which exercised much influence in the development of medieval mystical theology. He is described in Acts 17:34 as having been converted by Paul.

manuscripts of St. Isidore of Pelusium,[156] then either the edition of that ancient worthy (all 1600 pages of him) or at least a study of – say – his textual tradition.[157] But I don't see how I can finish the funeral orations before June (especially since I haven't yet been able to read one through without falling asleep), and after reading a couple of hundred pages of St. Isidore my private opinion is that our knowledge of his text is altogether as good as its content deserves. I am therefore tempted to substitute a short thesis on a New Testament subject, which I could get out of the way in six months; to limit my contribution to Isidorean studies to the photographing of the manuscripts – which I have promised to do if I get the fellowship; and to spend my time in Greece trying to find out just what, in psychological terms, was effected – or intended to be effected – by the traditional monastic 'spiritual training'.

I should be very glad to have your comments on this. Please don't hesitate to say so if you think the study would be unprofitable, either because of difficulties inherent in it, or simply as out of my depth. If you think there might be some profit in it, I should be especially happy if you would comment further on the possibilities of complementary study of spiritual discipline in Jewish writers – Abraham Abulafia[158] for instance – of the psychological foundations of their proposals. For one thing, do you think I could ever surmount the linguistic difficulties of the problem?

Excuse me for writing a letter altogether about myself, but since I've heard nothing from Jerusalem for the past six months I have no basis even for inquiry about your work. Needless to say, I hope it goes on as usual, and I do hope you will send me word of your new publications, and such reprints as you have to spare. Please remember me to Mrs. Scholem. I trust you both are well and shall hope to hear from you soon.

As ever, with best wishes,

Morton Smith

---

[156] Isidore of Pelusium. Egyptian monk who lived in the mid-fourth–mid-fifth centuries. Over 2000 of his letters, but none of his other works, have survived.

[157] Three years later Smith published an article entitled: 'The Manuscript Tradition of Isidore of Pelusium', *Harvard Theological Review* 47 (1954), 205–10. (This paper grew out of a lecture Smith delivered at Oxford in 1951 during his one year leave of absence from Brown in 1951–1952 [A.P.]).

[158] Abraham Abulafia (Saragossa, 1240–Comino, Maltese Archipelago, *circ.* 1291). Vagabond Kabbalist and visionary. Founder of the school of prophetic Kabbalah. Scholem dedicated to him a chapter of his *Major Trends*. See now: M. Idel, *The Mystical Experience in Abraham Abulafia* (trans. A. Chipman, New-York, 1988).

27

28 Abarbanel Rd.
Jerusalem
December 30, 1950

Dear Mr. Smith,

I was very much pleased to hear from you. Your letter found me with a bad cold and unable to answer immediately. Having recovered I take at once to my pen. Let me say that something must have gone wrong with your last letter, for I never had any knowledge of a lot of things you quote or seem to presuppose as known to me from that letter. I was in Europe for some time, and returned in October, but your letter should have been received here long before I left.

That you have taken to tennis is a very agreeable surprise to your friends. If that could happen to you, some more surprises should be in store for them.

As to your question concerning the Bollingen scholarship, I presently proceed to giving you my opinion. Before giving it, let me say that I happen to know Mr. Barrett,[159] who, if I am not mistaken, is the secretary and *spiritus movens* of the Bollingen Foundation. In case you have any dealings with them, you might therefore give (if needs arise) my name as a reference without being hurt by that. We met [in] 1949 and 1950 at the Eranos meeting in Ascona,[160] and he professes to be some sort of admirer of me. I might be able to help you.

I think it would be a fine idea to avail yourself of the possibility of a double scholarship such as you mention. I am not a psychologist

[159] John D. Barrett was the second editor of the Bollingen Series, in the years 1946–1969. He succeeded Mary Mellon, the first editor, who had founded the series with her husband, Paul Mellon in 1943. The series was initially dedicated to the dissemination of C. G. Jung's works (it was named after Jung's Swiss retreat village), but it soon came to publish many other works in psychology, the humanities, and religion.

[160] An annual interdisciplinary gathering of scholars first established by Rudolf Otto and Olga Froebe-Kapteyn, in 1933. It is held on the shores of the Lago Maggiore near Ascona in Switzerland. Scholem was very involved in the Eranos gatherings throughout most of his scholarly career, and many of his publications began as presentations at Eranos. On the Eranos gatherings see: H. T. Halk, *Der verborgene Geist von Eranos* (Bretten, 2001).

myself, and even in Ascona (where the influence of C. G. Jung[161] is very much felt, he himself being the moving spirit of those congresses called 'Eranos') I did refrain from psychological excursions. But I felt that much could be done in this field by somebody with a sound philological training and not given to the more extreme forms of psychoanalytical fantasies for which I cannot arouse much sympathy on my part. I feel that much of the amateurish character of psychological researches into the History of Religion, especially of both the Freudian and Jungian brand, is caused by the lack of a sound philological basis for their contentions. I am sure that somebody who would combine both modes of approach should be able to do most valuable work. In principle, I would therefore urge you to try and get that Bollingen scholarship. As to Hebrew, *besides* Greek, as a possible basis for such studies, it would not be too simple but it may be done. For instance, if you would make a study of Pseudo-Dionysius, which is a very important topic, you need no further kabbalistic embellishments (although a comparison to some curious Zoharic passages might be useful). But if you turn, let us say, to Gregorios Palamas,[162] and the Athos group, a comparative study of Abulafia might be very interesting and revealing (as would, as a matter of fact, be a study of Indian theories expounded best in John Woodroffe's[163] "Shakti and Shakta")[164] and should give excellent results (Certainly for the Jewish mystic!! But perhaps for the other too, as it would reveal the essential character of this mode of thought as *not* bound to its *Christian* ways of expression). Therefore, I am all in favor of *trying*! Whether you find in those five years of further study time to surmount the *linguistic* (and considerable) difficulties of analyzing Hebrew texts preserved and to be it studied in manuscript form only, this my dear friend would be up to you. I certainly would not call it an easy enterprise, even with

[161] Carl Gustav Jung (Kessewil, Switzerland, 1875–Zurich, 1961). Psychiatrist and founder of analytical psychology. He took a special interest in religion, mythology and magic. The Eranos meetings in Ascona were indeed deeply influence by the psychological spirit insufflated by Jung.

[162] Gregory Palamas (Constantinople, 1296–Thessaloniki, 1359). Monk, theologian and chief defender of Hesychasm (from the Greek *hesychastes* [quietist]), an ascetical and mystical technique based on the methodical repeating of the name of Jesus, practiced by his monastic community of Mount Athos.

[163] John G. Woodroffe (1865–1936). British scholar of Indian law and Sanskrit and Hindu philosophy. He was especially instrumental in introducing the West to the esoteric Tantric Shakti system. Also known under his pseudonym Arthur Avalon.

[164] Arthur Avalon, *Shakti and Shâkta Essays and Addresses on the Shâkta tantrashâstra* (London, 1918).

the amount of Talmudic and Midrashic knowledge that you have acquired and which will be very helpful and indeed, invaluable in such connection. But I do not think that you could not do it. Maybe you leave that as a *possibility* of expanding your study – in case you make any statement to the Bollingen people – without committing yourself. If it suits you, you may, of course, tell Goodenough of my opinion (give him my best personal regards; I consider him a very decent and fine man). In short, you would have a great many difficulties, but at the same time you would most effectively widen your horizon and deepen your knowledge. Please, let me know what becomes of this plan.

If you find no time to do the translation of *Reshit HaKabbalah*,[165] it would be just too bad for me, as I have no other translator in sight. But, of course, you must do what is most convenient to you, and no offense will be taken! If you still find the time to do it, it would be of course most pleasing to me, as you write very clear and precise English: As to your remark about criticizing my work, I would say that if your supposed incapacity in this respect *survives* an attempt at translating me – a translator is by necessity the most deadly critic one can imagine – then I should be a very good author indeed.

What kind of teaching have you taken up? History of Religion? Philosophy? Theology? It will be very nice to see your thesis in the English version. Why, considering the obvious suffering it causes you, have you taken up St. Isidore of Pelusium (of whom I have never heard before)?[166]

My own work, alas, has slacked too. I have done a lot of reading and studying in Oriental religion, in connection with my study of religious nihilism. Then I had to go to Europe. The matter of the Jewish books and libraries in Germany is slowly nearing its end. We have brought over quite a lot, and I hope that after this visit, I will be under no further obligation to go to Germany where I found the atmosphere, in September, most sticky. This time, my wife did not accompany me to Europe which enabled me to send her some parcels. In Amsterdam and Berlin I bought a lot of books and feel now well prepared for the third world war although to tell the truth this is no laughing matter and we are already feeling the impact of the general uneasiness. People

[165] In Hebrew characters.

[166] Evidently the topic of Isidore, like Gregory of Nyssa, was the influence of Warner Jaeger (A.P.).

who had accepted positions at the University cancel their plans and stay where they *are* and we will have to do very largely without additional new blood from abroad.

If there is more you want to know in connection with your plans please write and I shall be delighted to give whatever advice I can think of.

My wife joins me in kind regards to you and in best wishes for the success of your activities in help of the Orthodox Patriarchate.

Cordially yours,

G. Scholem

28

15 Benevolent St.
Providence, R.I.
March 31, 1951

Dear Professor Scholem,

Thank you very much for your letter of December with its discussion of the possibility of combining psychology and philological method in the study of Abulafia. I was extremely glad to have your opinion on the matter, and that most of all (though perhaps I should not say so) because it confirmed my own. Not, of course, that I know anything of Abulafia beyond your account of him, but what you said made me think at once of Palamas[167] and the later developments of Greek monasticism, and I was particularly happy to have your letter suggest the same thing which had been in my mind.

Whether or not I shall ever get to the point of undertaking such a study is just as dubious now as it was when I last wrote you. (Incidentally, my letter contained one mistake which perhaps Professor Goodenough has already corrected in conversation with you – he is in the Near

[167] Gregory Palamas.

East and plans to visit Israel in the course of his trip, – the fellowship of which I wrote turned out to be, not from the Bollingen Fund, but from the Ford Foundation, via the Institute of Human Relations, at Yale. It is Goodenough's grant for travel that came from the Bollingen Fund; he told me of that and of the fellowship at the same time, and somehow I got them twisted).

Anyhow, I have still three applications pending – *one* for the fellowship, which would carry with it a year of psychology and sociology at Yale, a year or more in Greek and Syrian monasteries, two years on the documents of Greek and Syriac monasticism from 200 to 600, and a year of writing; *a second* for a Fulbright for study in Greece during this coming (academic) year only – my excuse for wanting to go was my *ad hoc* desire to photograph and study the manuscripts of St. Isidore of Pelusium, so if I get the fellowship I suppose I'll have to do something of the sort, but I shall take the grant principally as an opportunity to visit Greece and Turkey; *a third* for a renewal, on more favorable terms, of my appointment here at Brown, where I am teaching Old and New Testament to small classes of undergraduates and am responsible for the introduction of some more advanced students to patristic Greek. I expect that all three applications will be granted, but which I choose will depend on the exact terms of the grants. After much thinking I have decided that the best thing for me would be to spend four or five years here on general reading, especially in the classics and the Talmuds, but it remains to be seen whether or not Brown will give me generous enough terms to make that worth my while. If it will, I shall probably take the Fulbright as a last sabbatical fling, then put in five years of pretty solid reading here, and then try to find financing for special research; if it won't I shall go to Yale just for spite.[168]

One of the unexpected advantages of working at Brown is that there is in the neighborhood a Rabbi[169] who not only reads Hebrew but is really a devoted reader of the midrashim.[170] He is about 10 years older

[168] This question is resolved in letter 29: after agreeing to come to Yale, Smith was convinced to stay at Brown by its Provost; part of this agreement included a $500 dollar salary increase, an appointment as Assistant Professor – he had been an Instructor, and permission to take a 1 year leave of absence from 1951–1952 to travel to Greece with funding by the Fulbright (A.P.).

[169] William G. Braude (Telz, Lithuania, 1907–Providence, Rhode Island, 1988). Reform rabbi and scholar.

[170] Plural of the Hebrew word *Midrash*. Smith refers here to the various exegetical collections of the Rabbinic traditions of Late Antiquity.

than I – I should judge, perhaps less – took a Ph.D. from Brown (under Casey,[171] for a study of proselytism in Rabbinical Literature)[172] and is now making a translation of *Midrash Tehillim* for the Yale Judaica series.[173] He is a very earnest student and Wolfson and Lieberman both admire him highly. I have been seeing him once a week or so, all winter, to read the Hebrew text along with his translation, which I find remarkably sensitive. If I stay here I shall be able to go on studying with him, and we might even – he has suggested it – undertake a translation conjointly. At all events, there are not many places in America where I should have so good an opportunity to go on with reading in Rabbinical literature.

Rabbi Braude (for that is his name) is actually my reason for writing to you now, while my plans for the future are still undecided, rather than putting this letter off, as I had intended, till a decision should be reached. He will have this summer free and thinks of coming to Israel. Some sort of Institute for American Rabbis is being organized at a place called Beit Beryl (?)[174] and the organizers have been after him and his wife to go there. The program of the Institute will consist largely of addresses by prominent political figures, mostly, I suppose, on investment opportunities in Israel. Since he is not interested in politics and leaves the finances of his Temple to a financial committee (so successfully that they are just about to build a new million-dollar edifice – if the gossip I hear is true, he never talks about it and I don't ask him) he does not think that a summer of intensive indoctrination would interest him, but he would like very much to live in Jerusalem for a couple of months, meet you and Buber and some of the other people at the University, look around the country for himself, and do some quiet reading. (He speaks Hebrew, with a not-very-heavy Ashkenazic accent, and American Yiddish). The question is whether he and his wife could find comfortable rooms and get food at reasonable rates in Jerusalem during July and August. I wonder if Mrs. Scholem would be

[171] Robert Pierce Casey (1897–1959). Succeeded to Millar Burrows at the head of the Department of Biblical Literature at Brown University in 1934.

[172] William G. Braude, *Jewish Proselyting in the First Five Centuries of the Common Era: the Age of the Tannaim and Amoraim* (Brown University Studies 6; Providence, 1940).

[173] *The Midrash on Psalms*. Translated from the Hebrew and Aramaic by William G. Braude (New Haven, 1959). Smith's review of this book is to be found in *Religion in Life* 29 (1960), 161.

[174] Smith means the Beit Berl Institute, established in 1946 in memory of Berl Katznelson (Belorussia, 1887–Palestine, 1944), the central figure of Socialist Zionism and founder of the *Histadrut* labor federation. The institute trained teachers and youth leaders mostly from among the labor settlement movement.

so kind as to make inquiries and let me know – either through you or directly – what sort of rooms could be had for such-and-such a price, and how the prices of food run at pensions and restaurants. I know it is more a question of getting food than of paying for it, so perhaps (unless Israel has changed morally no less than it has politically since I was there) the real questions may be the ones that can't be answered. Anyhow, I should be very grateful if you would send me what answers you conveniently can, and very happy if they could be such as would encourage Rabbi Braude to try to see Israel for himself.

I suppose you have quite given up hope about my proposed translation of *Reshit HaKabbalah* but the book is still in my desk drawer and the purpose is still in my head. If only Brown will be generous I shall get my Th.D. thesis out of the way in the early summer and have a couple of months free, in which to do all the things I have been wanting to do for the past five years – and it will have a high place on the list. (Meanwhile, however, should any other opportunities turn up, please don't sacrifice them for my sake).

Are there any new kabbalistic (or other) publications that I ought to have?

Has Wirzubski given up the *Hekhalot* for good, or is his text of that in the same desk drawer as my copy of *Reshit HaKabbalah*?

Please remember me to Professor Schwabe if you happen to see him. I haven't heard from him for the past year, and should be glad to know how he is.

With all best wishes for you and for Mrs. Scholem,

Sincerely

Morton Smith

P.S. The enclosure will give you a picture of what has taken up most of my time during the winter – unless you have ever tried something of the sort you can't imagine how much time must go into interviews, letters, more interviews, more letters, and so on *ad infinitum*, but at last arise beginning to make some progress

Respectfully yours and with peaceful blessings[175] M.S.

[175] In Hebrew: *BeKhol HaKavod u-BeVirkat Shalom.*

29

May 6, 1951

Dear Dr. Smith,

We thank you very much for your letter of March 31. Shortly after your letter (which was received here about midst of April) we had the visit of the Goodenoughs, with whom we have spent a very pleasant time. He is a most lively man and quite intelligent. Of course, we have talked a lot about you. I am sure that you have in him a real friend who is interested in you, your work and your career. He was quite convinced that your Yale scholarship would be granted and he seems to hope that you would take it. He told us about the way he came to know you and about some of your difficulties. As all of us spoke with much feeling you should have felt it beyond the ocean, through Kabbalistic TV. I think Goodenough left Jerusalem quite satisfied. We were scheduled to speak both of us at the Eranos meeting in Switzerland this August, but I shall have to stay behind, this year, and Goodenough shall be the Jewish expert this year!

My wife (who sends you her kind regards – she has gone for some days to Tel Aviv) has looked into the matter raised by you as to the possible costs of living for your rabbinical friend Braude. First of all, it may well be that *Beit Berl*[176] (Beth Berl – called after our late friend Berl Katznelson, the Rebbe in a hasidic sense, of the Zionist Labour movement) might not all be a bad or inconvenient place for him to go. But, of course, Jerusalem is incomparable! My wife thinks that if he makes arrangements *now*, he can get reservations for July and August. Pension Grete Ascher[177] would cost him about 2 LI[178] each person pro day (without supper which is not provided) – in case he is *not* Kosher, this would be a most agreeable and convenient place for him (Ibn Ezra Street). Otherwise, there are some decent Kosher places – a little more expensive. But it is very possible that until summer, *there will be a general*

---

[176] In Hebrew characters.

[177] Pension Grete Ascher in Scholem's neighborhood, Rehavia, was one of the new hotels of West Jerusalem. It was founded in the 1930's.

[178] Israeli pounds (*lirot*), the Israeli currency in use prior to the introduction of the Shekel in 1980.

addition of 20% in *all* hotels, pensions and restaurants. This has just now been authorized. The prices are strictly controlled and there are no big differences – except for those who wish to use the special facilities made for tourists who wish to enjoy themselves, and who by paying in dollars, can get everything they want. But this is a very expensive thing and I doubt whether your friends would like to avail themselves of these facilities. In short, Mrs. Scholem thinks that for about 5 LI Rabbi and Mrs. Braude might be decently accommodated (if the increase is enacted: 6 LI). This, of course, cannot include traveling and any other special expense. Tourists get special food rations (about three times as much as we get).[179] If your friends decide to come here, we shall try to assist them in our modest way and as far as possible.

Now about the *Hekhalot*: it is *myself* alone who is to blame, not Wirszubski!! I have not got around to do *my* part in the edition, namely the commentary! *He* is O.K. and no reproach attaches to him. I am very much to blame, indeed: instead of writing, writing and writing, I am sitting, and thinking over the whole bunch of problems again and again. They quite well can bear to be thought over from a fresh angle. Meanwhile, I am doing nothing for posterity. Maybe, they should send me to hell, were it not for the good of the students who profit by my indecision! By the way – Goodenough (who did not know of your *Hekhalot* translation and was very excited to hear that such a thing is available) thought the Bollingen people might be interested in that piece of work, if it can be done without prejudice to the critical edition.

I have, therefore, no right to steal your time for my *Reshit HaKabbalah*.[180] You just do what you like best.

Schwabe is now the Rector for two years and has a very busy life. He sends you his best regards. You cannot imagine, how difficult his job is these days.

Could you do me a favour and send me a copy of Millar Burrows' publication of the *Serekh HaYachad*[181] (the last scroll)? I cannot get it here,

[179] Due to meager natural and financial resources and to major waves of immigration the government of the newly created State of Israel enacted an austerity program of stringent price controls and rationing. The limitations were gradually eased in 1951 and repealed altogether in 1959.

[180] In Hebrew characters.

[181] In Hebrew characters. *Serekh haYachad* (*Serech Hayahad*) is Dead Sea Scroll 1QS. Burrows entitled it *The Manual of Discipline*, and it subsequently came to be known also as *The Rule of the Community* for it lays down the communal rules of a certain Jewish sectarian group. Millar Burrows (1889–1980). American Biblical scholar who taught

I will be glad to send you something else in exchange, it seems to me a most important and interesting text which I want to *study*.

With kindest regards and good wishes from both of us,

Sincerely yours,

G. Scholem

30

15 Benevolent St.
Providence, R.I.
June 13, 1951

Dear Prof. Scholem,

Thank you very much for your letter of May 6th – it was especially good of you and Mrs. Scholem to get and send me such accurate information on behalf of the Braudes. I am sorry to say that they have finally decided to stay in the United States for the summer – transportation costs are so high, and their children are a little too small to be left behind with confidence. In a year or so, however, Rabbi Braude hopes to persuade his congregation to give him a sabbatical six months, and they think seriously of coming to Israel then.

I wrote Millar Burrows to check on *Serekh HaYachad*[182] and mentioned your interest in it. He wrote back, offering to ask the American School of Oriental Research to send you a complimentary copy, because of the interest which would attach to your observations on the material. I accepted in your behalf, and hope his opposition to Zionism[183] will

at Yale University. He was the first to publish this scroll along with two others, which were brought to his attention when he served as director of the American School of Oriental Research in Jerusalem in 1948. M. Burrows (ed.), *The Dead Sea Scrolls of St. Mark's Monastery*, 2 vols. (New Haven, Conn., 1950–1).

[182] In Hebrew characters.

[183] Millar Burrows was ardently opposed to the establishment of a Jewish State. He sets forth his view in *Palestine is our Business* (Philadelphia, 1949).

not make you disown my action. The gift will be that of the ASOR, anyhow, though it will act on Burrow's request. The pages of *Serekh HaYachad*[184] constitute the first half of the second volume, of which the second half – the *Book of Lamech* will probably not be out till some time next year, at the earliest.[185] More of the same material is in the Habbakuk commentary in the last pages of the already published vol. I ($5 – mostly Isaiah).[186]

My plans have worked out rather differently than I expected when I last wrote. After accepting the Yale scholarship I was persuaded to change my mind and stay in at Brown for security's sake; since here there is a full professorship in the offing and there, after finishing the research, I should be out of work and still on the level of an instructor. So I decided to stay here, but got leave of absence for the first year, in order to accept a Fulbright grant for work in Greece. This brings me back to Isidore of Pelusium, but I am willing to put up with a minimum of work on that ancient worthy in exchange for a year's travel in Greece. I shall leave in September, and travel via Beirut, going up to (Arab) Jerusalem to get some letters of introduction from my Greek friends there. If it's at all possible I shall try to get across the line[187] and call on you.

As for the *Hekhalot*, I just wanted to know what had happened to them. So long as they're in your hands I'm quite satisfied to have done with them whatever you think best.

With regards to Mrs. Scholem and with the hope of seeing you both this fall,

Sincerely yours,

Morton Smith

---

[184] In Hebrew characters.

[185] The *Book of Lamech* – also known as the *Genesis Apocryphon* – did not appear in Burrows' publication. This composition is one of the seven original scrolls discovered in 1947. It relates, in Aramaic, stories of the patriarchal period down to Abraham.

[186] The first of the two volumes of M. Burrows (ed.), *The Dead Sea Scrolls of St Mark Monastery* (New Haven, 1950) includes two texts: *The Isaiah Manuscript* and the *Habakkuk Commentary*.

[187] Following the 1949 armistice, Jerusalem was divided between Jordan and Israel. Israel controlled the Western half of the New City and Jordan controlled the Eastern half along with the entire Old City.

31

Brown University
Providence 12, Rhode Island
15 Benevolent St.
January 26, 1953

Dear Professor Scholem,

I think I wrote you two years ago of Rabbi Braude, of Providence, who was then planning to visit Israel. The trip didn't materialize at that time, but now it has finally been arranged for, and he and his wife will be in Israel during March and early April. I am giving him a letter to Schwabe and one to you, but I want to supplement the latter by this note, since decency prevents me from saying in a letter sent by him how much I like both him and his wife – not only are they unusually kind and friendly people, but both of them have genuine intellectual interests and the capabilities necessary to pursue these. Mrs. Braude's interests lie in the field of modern art, but Braude himself has a very deep affection for Rabbinical literature and quite considerable knowledge of it. He has just finished a translation of *Midrash Tehillim* (which will come out in the Yale Judaica, but that should not prejudice you against it, for he made it under the supervision of Wolfson and Lieberman, both of whom have praised it to me very highly, and I myself know that it was a real labor of love) and he has every intention of going on with other work in the field. Since he very much admires your work I am sure he deeply appreciates any time for conversation which you can give him, and since he is not without influence (he is one of the directors of Hebrew Union College,[188] etc.) you might find him an effective apostle of Kabbalism to darkest Reformed Jewry.

I owe him a particular debt of gratitude, since it is largely his interest in Rabbinical literature which has kept mine alive. Since my return from Greece – which took place only in September – I have been going with him to Boston to hear Rabbi Savitsky[189] expound the

[188] The Hebrew Union College was founded in 1875. At the time of the writing of this letter the institution had two campuses: in Cincinnati and in New York. Later campuses were established in Los Angeles and Jerusalem as well.

[189] Rabbi Mordechai Savitsky (Poland, 1911–New York, 1991). An authority on the Talmud and Jewish law.

Talmud. Since Savitsky, whenever he gets excited, bursts into Yiddish, I am now learning Yiddish – so one thing leads to another. Believe it or not, I have not abandoned my plan of translating *Reshit HaKabbalah*. A month or so ago I got around to putting it on my desk, and it will stay there now till it gets translated. Perhaps by that time Wirszubski will have got around to his proposed edition of the *Hekhalot*.

I can't recall whether or not I wrote you about my year in Greece. It was pleasant and reasonably profitable. I brought back about 5,000 photographs of manuscripts (i.e. about 10,000 pages) out of which I hope to get an account of several minor collections of manuscripts hitherto unstudied, my Th.D. thesis on St. Isidore of Pelusium,[190] an edition of St. Maximus' *Centuries on Love*,[191] and some studies of patristic catenae[192] – all in good (or bad) time. But even if the photographs should by some accident go up in smoke, the magnificent scenery and the peculiarity of places like Patmos and Mount Athos would have made the trip worth while.

Life in the University is agreeably tranquil – after Greece. If I didn't try to keep up with new publications in the fields of Judaism and Christianity it would be even more tranquil, and I might get my own work published. As things are, I feel something like an intellectual butterfly with a time-clock on every flower.

Having said this much I shall add, Good-bye, and hurry off to read another periodical.

Do give my best wishes to Mrs. Scholem and to the Samburskys.

With kindest regards,

Morton Smith

P.S. If you have time to write I should be very glad to hear from you. What's new in the Holy Kabbalah? MS

---

190 This project was never completed. Nevertheless, Smith published several articles on the subject as: 'the Manuscript Tradition of Isidore of Pelusium', *HTR* 47/3 (1954), 205–10; 'An unpublished Life of St. Isidore of Pelusium' in H. Alivisatos (ed.), *Eucharisterion* (Athens, 1958), 429–438.

191 Maximus the Confessor, or the Theologian, was a seventh-century Constantinopolitan mystic and ascetic. Smith did not end up publishing Maximus the Confessor's writings.

192 The *catenae* ('chains' in Latin) are commentaries on the Bible that are arranged according to the order of the Biblical verses.

32

15 Benevolent St.
Providence, R.I.
June 7, 1953

Dear Professor Scholem,

The Braudes are back, enchanted with Israel and especially with the Scholems; whenever I visit them I come away full of your praises. Bill[193] at once gave me your gift, the *Kabbalot of Rabbis Jacob and Isaac*,[194] and I thank you for it very much indeed. The story of my request to him, that he try to find me a copy, is this: Glancing through Bamberger's silly *Fallen Angels*[195] I saw how angry this particular strain of the Kabbalah made him, so I said to myself, "*This* must be worth looking into." – and I'm particularly glad to have it now because I think it should form a valuable complement to *Reshith HaKabbalah*. For the latter, I still have nothing more to report than my good intentions, but they're still good. For the time being my struggle with my Greek essay on the concept of incarnation goes on.

It was very pleasant to have greetings from you and Mrs. Scholem, and I send you mine in return, Bill tells me there is some hope of your coming to the States again and, of course, I'm all for it. As for him, he is already making plans – or, at least, daydreams – of going back to Jerusalem. I can see that a shuttle service will have to be established.

Again with thanks, and with best wishes to both you and Mrs. Scholem,

Sincerely,

Morton Smith

---

[193] William Braude.

[194] Jacob and Isaac the sons of Jacob the Cohen belong to a circle of late 13th century Castilian kabbalists; they were engaged, according to Scholem, in a 'Gnostic' reaction against the more philosophically-bent mainstream Kabbalah of the day. G. G. Scholem 'The Kabbalah of Rabbi Jacob and R. Isaac, the sons of R. Jacob the Cohen: Sources for the Study of the Kabbalah before the Appearance of the Zoahr', *Ma'adei haYahadut* 2 (1927), 244–64 (Hebrew).

[195] B. J. Bamberger, *Fallen Angels: The Soldiers of Satan's Realm* (Philadelphia, 1952).

33

28 Abrabanel Road
Jerusalem
196

Dear Dr. Smith,

Many thanks for your kind letter. If I didn't answer yours of February earlier, it was because I thought I might *a*) send you much information about us by the way of the Braudes and *b*) have an early opportunity of meeting you again. As for the second – nothing, exactly nothing, has materialized, which means that the official in the state Department who deals with exchange or guest professors to be financed under some new or special funds, has just left the file on his desk and done *nothing* about it. Therefore, this year 53/54, nothing will happen. I might suggest that if your department of Religion in Brown should be interested in getting one for one academic year *free of charge*, you try something from your angle since it might then be possible to arrange something for the year after (1954/55). If only somebody would be able to locate the man in the State Department who is responsible for these invitations on State Department allocations, it should be not too difficult to put the thing over. I did *not* mention Brown in my remarks where I might be willing to go (and they in Washington definitely did *not* ask at all those places like Yale and Chicago which I did mention). It would be a good idea if your place takes the initiative. Personally I would quite like to spend another nine (or eight) months in a place where I would teach Rabbi Braude a 'Blättl Zohar'[197] – auf Staatskosten – as the Germans say.[198] And *we* would do something together about the *Hekhalot*! Think it over – perhaps you find a way, and it certainly is not too late to plan it now. Do you or your dean know the right people in Washington?

[196] No date is given for this letter, but it is postmarked July 14, 1953.
[197] Literally, a little page of Zohar, i.e. a bit of Zohar.
[198] Auf Staatskosten: at public cost.

About angelology there is the further very rich material in my second book on the Cohens: *LeCheker Kabalat R' Yitzhak HaCohen*[199] which appeared [in] 1934. These texts are very precious indeed.

It was a great pity that we have missed you in Jerusalem. Thereafter we expected to hear from you from Greece but we did not know where you were. Now we hope you will be satisfied with your work at Brown. If you are publishing something please put us on your mailing list.

This summer we are going (on the 2nd of August) to Switzerland for a couple of weeks, but will be back about October 1st.

[The] Braudes are very friendly in their exaggerated praises. But we liked very much to have them and we are glad that they went away from Israel with a feeling of having been at home.

Please give them our kind regards (and thanks for the Lindt-chocolates from Zürich which we rascals have eaten very well but not even acknowledged which is sheer impendence on our side. We ask to be forgiven!)

We hope to hear from all of you.

All good wishes and kind regards,

Sincerely yours,

Gershom Scholem

[199] In Hebrew characters. This book was actually a reprint of a series of articles on the Cohen brothers that Scholem had published in the newly created Hebrew University periodical of Jewish Studies, *Tarbiz* (vols. 2, 3–5).

34

Brown University
Providence 12, Rhode Island
15 Benevolent St.
August 2, 1953

Dear Professor Scholem,

I have had your letter for a month or so, and should have thanked you for it sooner had not I been waiting for an answer to my inquiries as to the possibility of our getting your services here during 1954–5. When your letter came I inquired of the Provost,[200] he asked me to write a man in New York, and now that the answer has come back it is a reference to another man, this time in the Department of State. It appears that since Israel does not participate in the Fulbright program, you will have to get a Smith-Mundt grant-in-aid.[201] 'Smith-Mundt grants are intended by the government to cover minimum expenses (in addition to travel costs); additional supplementation by universities... is encouraged'. Unfortunately, I'm in no position to ask Brown for any supplementation, since only last year they gave me an extra $2,000 to cover the cost of making prints of the photographs (of manuscripts) which I brought back from Greece. Your chances of getting a grant would be much stronger if some institution would be willing to supplement it – and I think Brown would be willing to request you on the understanding that you would be shared with some other institution. Do you think any group in New York would be willing to put up some money to help out the grant? I shall go ahead and inquire of the State Department, anyhow, and shall also take the liberty of writing to Lieberman and asking him if he has any suggestion as to where supplementary funds might be found. You are leaving for Switzerland to-day – or rather, left yesterday, since it is after 5 here which makes it after midnight in Israel – so this, even if it is not forwarded, will be

[200] Samuel T. Arnold, dean of Brown University, was the first provost at Brown.

[201] As the Fullbright grant, the Smith-Mundt grant is given by the state department. The Smith-Mundt Act was passed by the U.S. Congress in 1948 and provided, among other things, grants for international educational and research exchange programs of teachers, students, lecturers and other specialists.

waiting for you when you get back. By that time you may find another letter with more news, but I doubt it – my experience with governments leads me to believe they resemble the mills of the gods in speed rather than efficiency.

I enclose also a sample translation of the first chapter of *The Beginning of the Kabbalah*. You will quickly see that it's not literal – it wasn't intended to be, but I have penciled question marks in the margin wherever I felt uncertain as to the exact sense of the original. I didn't know what to do about transliteration, titles, etc. and you will find that the treatment of these is not consistent. I should be grateful if you'd not only correct this chapter so as to make it an example, but also send me a handy list of rules which I can keep in the book and refer to as occasion arises. In a good many cases, especially in the notes, I've simply left out titles when I didn't know whether you'd want them transliterated, printed in Hebrew, or translated with the notation (*in Hebrew*) after them. Personally, I'm against the last device, but of course, I'm prepared to follow any plan you prefer. When I left out the title I sometimes left out the rest of the note, too. Also, I couldn't find Foscaire[202] (if that's how you spell it) on any atlas I had in handy. All this looks sloppy and is, my excuse is that the only time I have for translation is the last hour of my day, when I'm too tired to do much hunting around in reference works. However, I like to translate then – it's restful – and I find I can do a page or so every night, which, with due allowance for interruptions, should get me through the rest of the book by the beginning or middle of next summer – if you are willing to have the process go on in this way. Incidentally, I'm not making any carbon copy (because I type as I go and make so many mistakes in the process that a carbon would either take an impossible amount of time to keep clean or be quite illegible) so this copy which I'm sending you is the only one there is. I don't expect you to think much of it as it stands, but I hope it will prove sufficient to serve as a basis for revision and correction.

My life during the summer has been pleasant and uneventful: I'm trying to get myself in good physical condition and have been playing tennis daily, with fairly satisfactory results. I bought a car and that has kept me sufficiently impoverished to stay out of mischief. I've been

---

[202] The reference should be to Posquières (today Vauvert), a small town in Provence, the home of Rabbi Abraham ben David, a famous twelfth-century Talmudic authority. The mistake is easily explained from the unvocalized Hebrew alphabet.

writing an article on Taylor's commentary on Mark,[203] and as soon as that is out of the way hope to get down to the long-delayed editing of my photographs, but current business and the preparation of my coming courses take up so much time that I wonder if I shall.

The Braudes send you and Mrs. Scholem their best wishes, and to theirs I add my own.

Sincerely,

Morton Smith

35

The Hebrew University
Jerusalem
March 22, 1954

Dear Dr. Smith,

I am greatly in your dept and I hope you will forgive me for writing hastily just at the moment when I am about to leave Israel on my sabbatical leave. It was a great, although most agreeable, surprise to receive the official invitation to come to Brown University. It is obvious to me that you were the prime mover in this. The invitation, however, came too late for me to do anything about it now. When you wrote to me in August I expected to hear shortly afterwards from the State Department. Since no word came from them, I thought that nothing would come of the matter. Your activity, however, seems to have been successful, although up to this moment we have not yet had official notification from the State Department. I am enclosing for your private information [a] copy of my letter to your president, which explains itself. However, I wish to add something for your personal information: Next year is, of

[203] M. Smith [rev.], 'Comments on Taylor's Commentary on Mark', *Harvard Theological Review* 48 (1955), 21–64.

course, out of the question, but the year following is also problematic. There exists an obligation towards Dr. Tishby who wishes to leave that year. It would be very difficult to imagine both Tishby and myself being away for a whole year at the same time. I seems to me, therefore, that if there is some way of making a proposal to the Hebrew University asking that I be granted leave for one of the two following years, at my discretion, it may work out. It should stand to reason that there is nothing lost by my coming at a later date. I assume that the money which Brown University has offered as a special stipend would also be available for the same purpose at a later date. Let me only say that I am very grateful for your kind efforts and that I would appreciate seeing things arranged in a way suitable to both sides. It would be very helpful for my own work to be in a quiet place like Providence. I do not know the requirements which would be asked of me with regard to teaching. I assume that there would be about two hours lecturing and two hours reading texts. I also assume that I would be free to lecture in my own field of research despite the fact that I have been made over into a Visiting Professor of Biblical Literature.

When your last letter came, I was abroad for several months and returned only towards the end of the year. This is the reason why I am so late in answering your letter and in expressing an opinion on your translation. I thank you *very* much for your undertaking such a tremendous effort. I have gone over it for a first reading. I can see that it can serve certainly as a basis for a final translation, and I should indeed be very happy to meet with you in person to discuss various matters about this translation. I am leaving your manuscript behind with the secretary of the Institute of Jewish Studies at the Hebrew University. If you want it back before I return to Jerusalem, I can at any time ask that it be returned to you. Please inform me of your wishes.

I have been working very hard during the past few months and I expect to work even harder during my sabbatical year in London[204] and possibly in Switzerland. Perhaps I shall be able to complete my book on Sabbatianism which is already ripe to be born, without my being ashamed of it. It might be quite a voluminous work, if I do not decide to cut it down.

---

[204] Scholem spent the academic year of 1954 at the Warburg Institute of the University of London, an interdisciplinary research institute dedicated to the study of the classical tradition and its reception.

Mrs. Scholem is going with me and expects to become an expert in English and in some other good things as well. If you write me about the developments at Brown and about your own work and welfare, I promise you speedy reply.

London, as you know, is a much easier place for mailing letters than Jerusalem!

How are our friends the Braudes? I suspect Dr. Braude of having had a hand in helping with the invitation extended to me. Is his translation of the *Midrash on Psalms* already published? Please give the Braudes our kind regards. We still remember the wonderful Seder we had together.

Tomorrow we are flying to Amsterdam and from the 1st of April you will find me in London, c/o Friends of the Hebrew University, 237 Baker Street, London N.W.1.

With many thanks and all best wishes to yourself,

Very sincerely yours,

Gershom Scholem

36

15 Benevolent St.
Providence, R.I.
U.S.A.
May 14, 1954

Dear Professor Scholem,

This reply to your letter of March 22 has been delayed thus long by the hope that I would have some more definite news to send you than I yet have. But since nothing continues to happen, it seems best to write and let you know the general state of affairs here, which, I fear, you will find disappointing.

Both Braude and I regretted very much that you were not able to accept the University's invitation for the coming year, but we perfectly understand (as, of course, do the officials of the University) that you could not wait indefinitely and had to make other arrangements in the meantime. I think you do me too much credit in supposing that I was the chief mover in securing the invitation: What really turned the scales was Braude's willingness to raise the salary by contribution from his wealthy friends. The University here has been running into debt and has no money whatever for luxuries, so that, had not Braude's friends been willing to contribute your salary it could not have considered inviting you: It was negotiation over this point which held the matter up so long. I have every confidence that Braude can get the money for later years and I am sure that if he can the University will be willing to extend the invitation: it is of course happy to have on the campus, *gratis*, a scholar of your standing.

It therefore should not make much difference to the arrangements that after next year I shall no longer be at Brown.[205] They are "letting me go" allegedly because the teaching here is almost entirely of undergraduates and they think me better qualified to teach graduate students. The real reason, however, seems to be that the University, because of financial difficulties, depends heavily on current contributions from alumni and the religious group among the alumni have therefore been able to press the administration to support a religious revival. (I don't think it took much pressure, really, but the capacity for pressure was there). One step of this revival requires that a dynamic popular preacher of Christianity be placed in the Department of Biblical Literature. There are only two chairs in the department, and the man[206] in the other one has "tenure" – i.e. has been employed so long that he can't be fired except for grave scandal – so out I go. Where – I don't know yet. If no decent position appears by the end of this year, I shall apply for an annual professorship at the American School in Jerusalem and so may soon have the pleasure of seeing you again.

In spite of my good intentions, I have not been able to go on with my translation of *Reshit HaKabbalah*.[207] I broke it off in order to read the *Bahir* before translating the chapter on it, and one thing and another prevented my resuming. At the moment I must finish off this semester's work and then move, during the month of June, to some other address

[205] Smith had been notified two or three months earlier (A.P.).
[206] *I.e.* William Robbins (A.P.).
[207] In Hebrew characters.

in Providence. (Letters to the Department of Biblical Literature, Brown University, Providence 12, will continue to reach me). I haven't found an apartment yet and the thought of moving my library gives me cold chills, but move I must, for the house I occupy is to be made over to house undergraduates.[208] After June perhaps I may again find time for extracurricular activities: if I were to come to Jerusalem, of course, the opportunity to translate under your immediate supervision would be ideal. At present, however, all is uncertain.

With best wishes for Mrs. Scholem and yourself,

Sincerely yours,

Morton Smith

37

[209]

Dear Dr. Smith,

I am using Whitsunday[210] to take a little rest and to thank you very much for your letter. It is bitterly disappointing to hear that you are leaving Brown, and I wish you find a place where your tenure is not dependent on the churchmen's interests. That's a bitter pill and I understand how you must feel. When I thought of a year in a place like Providence, it was of course because I thought I would have you as a good neighbour on the faculty. This is indeed very distressing news. Please let us know when you have definite other plans or arrangements.

---

[208] At this time, Smith had amassed a book collection of 3,000–4,000 books; it would eventually become a collection of more than 10,000 books, donated at the time of his death to the Jewish Theological Seminary in New York (A.P.).

[209] Despite the lack of date in the heading, the letter testifies to having been written on Whitsunday, June 6, 1954.

[210] Whitsunday is a British designation for Pentecost, probably derived from the White robes worn by the festival's baptismal candidates.

We will stay here until 15th August and possibly even until [the] end of October, but it is possible that we [will] go for the last three months of the leave to Zurich where I can also do a quiet piece of work. I am working hard at formulating my final views and analysis of the Shabbetai Zvi movement and it will be, I am afraid a rather long affair.

I have worked in this field now for so many years that I am overwhelmed by the new look the whole thing gets [to be] if you go down to write your "final version". But I doubt whether I will be able to finish it, but there is nothing wrong in trying. In case you really come to Jerusalem you will find us back as from the 1st of December, scarcely before. I need every day I can take out.

I am not quite sure what to do about that year at Brown. The Hebrew University have now decided (and written to the President of Brown) that they would grant me leave for the year 1956/7. But I have never been able to understand what that provision of my own application for a Mundt act grant actually means. Have I to make a personal application? In that case, the whole thing may another time linger on in some file and two and two will never be put together. It seems to me that the scheme of Brown has nothing to do with the original demand from Washington for an exchange professor.

Since you are leaving Brown and would not be there to smooth things: is it quite clear, that the invitation for Biblical Literature means just that I can give courses in *my* field of study and do not have to pretend to be what I am not? As I know I was not coming the next year I did not take up the point with anybody but I assume you know pretty well what was the idea behind the scheme and whether they would have been willing to let me do what I am really able to do.

I am sending you a reprint of my paper on the Golem[211] and hope you receive it. Another paper on Christian Kabbalism[212] is to follow shortly.

---

[211] G. G. Scholem, 'Die Vorstellung vom Golem in ihren tellurischen und magischen Beziehungen', *Eranos Jahrbuch* 22 (1953), 235–289. Reprinted in *Zur Kabbalah und ihrer Symbolik* (Zürich, 1960) (trans. R. Manheim, *On the Kabbalah and its Symbolism* [New York, 1969]).

[212] G. G. Scholem, 'Zur Geschichte der Anfänge der christlichen Kabbala', in *Essays Presented to Leo Baeck* (London, 1954), 158–193. (trans. D. Prager, 'The Beginning of the Christian Kabbalah', in J. Dan (ed.), *The Christian Kabbalah: Jewish Mystical Books and their Christian Interpreters: a Symposium* (Cambridge, Mass., 1997), 17–51.

My wife and I wish you a good end to the anxiety into which you have been thrown.

With many kind regards,

Very sincerely yours,

G. Scholem

38

Morton Smith
102 Bowen St.
Providence, R.I., U.S.A.
June 19, 1954

Dear Professor Scholem,

This is merely a note to acknowledge and thank you for your whitsuntide epistle and for the article on the Golem, which I read with great interest. The subject is certainly fascinating and your treatment of it, in particular, leaves me interested to know what the function of the Golem was in the mediaeval rites of making a Golem. That is to say, *if* these rites – as you report, and, I am sure, correctly – give no indication of the purpose which the Golem is to serve, and the whole process which they report is reducible to a meditation on the creative powers of the Name, by which the mystic is gradually elevated to a state of ecstasy in which he feels himself to participate in those powers, and then gradually brought down to earth again: *if* all this, then why the Golem? Surely the mediaeval mystics (especially after Abulafia) were able to exalt themselves to ecstasy and become aware of their participation in divine powers by the meditative recitation of combinations of letters (which seems to have been the actual means used by the Golem recipes also). If so, why the addition of the Golem? One cannot say that it *objectively* justified their conviction of participating in God's creative powers – it didn't actually come alive, and anyhow, the certainty produced by the mystical experience should have made objective justification quite unnecessary. It might be suggested that the whole ritual was produced by the stories in the tradition, particularly in the Talmud, i.e. Some mystics felt a need of casting their experiences in the traditional form; they were convinced that in their experiences they attained perfect righteousness; now when Rabha attained perfect righteousness he proved it by creating a man;[213] therefore they developed a ritual way of doing the same thing. Possibly – but this sort of demonstrative, almost competitive, imitation, does not seem to me a very plausible motive. My guess would be that there must have been some magical rite in which the figure was symbolically made alive (probably for symbolical sacrifice) and that this rite has been taken over by the mystics and in the preserved recipes appears merely as a means to mystical ecstasy, and the *raison d'être* for its distinctive elements has therefore disappeared. As to the *psychological* reasons for which the mystics would take over such a rite, you might turn the Eranos associates loose on the trail of those. I hope you will take all this guess-work – which has no more basis than your essay and my ignorance – not so much as a criticism of the present essay, as a bait to lure you into writing another. I look forward to your account of Christian Kabbalism with great interest.

Here, it has been settled that I am to stay on for 1954/5. Where I shall go thereafter, I have no idea. Jerusalem is still a possibility and the knowledge that you will be there in 55/6 makes especially attractive – if I can get the annual professorship at the American School for that year. As to Brown's offer to you, I have no further news. I am now completely out of things at Brown (their employment of me for another year is merely a financial courtesy, I shall have almost no pupils and hope to get some of my editing done). So everything now rests with Braude and the University and you. I think that if you came here you could have a quiet year of work in comparative comfort, at the cost of delivering six or eight popular lectures on Jewish mysticism to an audience which would be composed largely of members of the city's Reformed and Conservative congregations. If you wanted to augment

[213] The Babylonian Talmud, *Sanhedrin* 65b, reports that Rabah (or Rava or Rabha), a Talmudic rabbi from the fourth century, created a non-speaking man (*gavra'*, in Aramaic) of clay, a golem, and sent him to rabbi Zera, who reduced him to dust. In his *Clement of Alexandria and a Secret Gospel of Mark* (Cambridge, Mass., 1973), 220, Smith argues that the holy spirit, by communicating to Rabba its creative powers, enabled him to create this homunculus.

your income (and $4,000 is certainly not much) you would have to do some additional lecturing, for which Boston, New York and Philadelphia would probably provide opportunities. (And there are lots of small cities, near at hand, which contain sizeable and wealthy Jewish groups). The present head of the Department of Biblical Literature is an academic and intellectual non-entity who would give you no trouble.

Bill Braude has talked to Arnold (the Provost) about the matter, and Arnold says the University is waiting for word from the State Department, to which it has applied. I think Bill's continued interest will count a lot with the University, and he is undoubtedly the person through whom you should work, since I have definitely become *persona non grata* (chiefly for financial reasons, I think: Since they were so late in firing me, their sense of decency compelled them to keep me on for another year, and they now find themselves paying me a year's salary for almost no teaching, a fact of which they don't like to be reminded, and the sight of me is a reminder of it). Be that as it may, I certainly don't think that my further prominence on the scene would be likely to help you, so I advise you to keep Bill Braude on the trail of the matter. He has the greatest respect for your scholarship and would be extremely happy to have you here, so I am sure you can count on him to do all he can and get you any information which you think desirable.

With best wishes for yourself and for Mrs. Scholem,

Sincerely,

Morton Smith

39

London
September 21, 1954

Dear Dr. Smith,

I have been so glad over the news of your last letter which indicates that you will be able to dedicate yourself more or less to your own research work for the next year. This is always a good thing, and you can look around, without undue haste and trouble. If you can come over to Jerusalem for 1955/56 that would be very fine and your friends will stand ready to receive you – only there will be the nasty frontier through the city[214] which you will be able to cross only by very good "protekzia"[215] as we call that happy gift to know the right people who can get you over the barriers.

During next year, I shall try to find out what will become of the year at Brown, if I get a Smith-Mundt grant, *plus* those $4,000 from Brown in addition, the plan will be workable; otherwise it would not do, as I have no intention of doing additional lecturing, just to earn some more money for a living. The whole attraction of the scheme is just the quiet prospect of sitting down with one of my unwritten books. Of course the plan was much more attractive as long as we thought you might be there for discussion and guidance to American scenery. So now we will have the one really pleasant help and companionship of Braude who will have to put with me or both of us if we come.

I am writing but I do not see [that] I will be finishing my book here. It is much too long, as I do not want to summarize but to present the evidence at least in the more important and unknown chapters, it will require 500–600 pages.

Your remarks on the Golem have interested me very much. There is, of course, a problem. But I do not believe it has to do with a kind of sacrifice, of which I find no trace in the documents. (It is some kind of Kabbalistic satyr,[216] perhaps?)

We will be here another month, and then go off to Paris and Zurich. After the *20th [of] November* you [can] reach us again at our old Jerusalem address.

I have still to receive the reprints of my paper on the early Christian Kabbalism – they always tell me: just another 4 weeks! There is some sabotage by the publisher, it seems. I [will] send it as soon as possible,

---

[214] See note: 'division of Jerusalem'.

[215] 'Protekzia' is a word of Russian origin which in modern colloquial Hebrew means 'connections'.

[216] Scholem adds an illegible word.

in the meanwhile I am sending you a very curious letter by Cardozo[217] which I have unearthed.

My wife and I are sending you our kindest regards,

Sincerely yours,

Gershom Scholem

40

102 Bowen St.
Providence, R.I.
August 1, 1955

Dear Professor Scholem,

I am ashamed of having put off so long my answer to your letter from London, but I kept hoping that I would have some definite news, either of your affairs or of mine.

To day I had dinner with Braude, who told me he had received a completely non-committal letter from the State Department: The application on your behalf had been received and was being considered and you would be notified as soon as a decision was reached. Braude, who has done everything possible in this matter, was quite indignant at the delay, and at the indefinite tone of the letter, and told me he would soon be seeing Abba Eban[218] and would ask him to use his influence to hasten a decision. I said I thought that was a good thing, but I also think the letter a good sign. I got such a letter about a month before notification about my Fulbright grant, and was told at the time, by the

[217] Abraham Miguel Cardozo (1626–1706). Sabbatean leader and theologian. For Miguel's letter (MS. Oxford 2481, fol. 4b) see: G. G. Scholem, *Sabbatai Sevi: The Mystical Messiah*, 1626–1676 (Princeton, 1973), 4 n. 1.

[218] Abba Eban (Cape Town, 1915–Herzlia, Israel, 2002) was an Israeli diplomat, a government minister and member of Knesset (Israeli parliament). During the years 1950–1959, he was ambassador to the United States.

University authorities, that this meant that I had reached the final group under consideration. Apparently the people eliminated in the earlier rounds get no notification until the end. Of course, the Smith-Mundt grants may be run differently, so there's no justification for relying too heavily on this news, but at least I'd be inclined to think it a good sign rather than a bad one. I hope that all this delay has not forced you to make other arrangements, so that if the grant does come through you will still be able to use it. Braude told me, by the way, that he'd seen Arnold again, and that the University had received a letter of the same content as the one sent him.

For my own affairs: I got a Guggenheim[219] for a study of the text of the letters of St. Isidore of Pelusium, and am settled here for a year's study.[220] The house I'm living in is up for sale, which may mean that I'll have to move (which would involve the loss of at least a month), but it's in such ratty condition that no sale is likely, and otherwise there's no cloud to be seen as far as the horizon. The horizon is, however, June of next year. For the period after that, I have an invitation from the Archbishop of Athens,[221] to spend six months studying the manuscripts in the Meteora,[222] and I shall ask for a renewal of my Guggenheim to enable me to take advantage of the offer. (Since work in the convents, high and unheated, would be practically out of question during December, January and February, I should have to spread my six months over two visits, and should require a year's grant). The manuscripts collection is one of the largest yet uncatalogued, and nothing approaching even an adequate check list has as yet been published, so it's a worthy cause and I have good hope of getting a grant for it. Six months of life in the monastery would probably ruin my stomach but perfect my Greek, but for the chance of the Greek I'm willing to risk my stomach. I hope, also, that there should be some important manuscripts of the hesychasts,[223] who have always seemed to me, from the very little I know of them, a most interesting and unjustly neglected

[219] The Guggenheim Foundation offers fellowships in various fields of the humanities, the sciences and the arts. The Foundation has been active since 1925.

[220] In fact Smith used the opportunity of the Guggenheim to do research that formed the topic of his Th.D. and later was published in 1971 as *Palestinian Parties and Sects that Shaped the Old Testament*. See the Introduction of that work (A.P.).

[221] Theocletus II. Archbishop of Athens during the years 1957–1962.

[222] Meteora, in northwest Thessaly, is a group of monasteries.

[223] See note 158 to Letter 27 above.

group. They also have an accidental importance in ecclesiastical politics. If the Orthodox Church is to be saved from becoming an intellectual province either of Protestantism (which is extremely unlikely) or of the Church of Rome (which would be a cultural catastrophy for western civilization) it must be saved by a revival of its native theology, of which the last vigorous form was that given it by the hesychasts. So when I am done with St. Isidore – which I hope to be sometime next Spring, I look forward to a little exploration of the holy jungle of mediaeval mysticism. Of course, if you can come here this winter and if I can translate *Reshit HaKabbalah* under your direction, that will hasten me along the left hand path.

This, however, is looking rather far ahead, for just at present I haven't even reached St. Isidore. I've bogged down in the task of writing an extra chapter for a book on Mark which I finished last summer.[224] I thought I'd found considerable evidence for Mark's use of a collection of miracle stories like those (collections) put together by the devotés of Asclepius,[225] and some evidence indicating that the group which put together this collection conceived Jesus as a healing god, by analogy with Asclepius and Sarapis.[226] Nock objected, on reading it, that the miracle stories unquestionably come mostly from Galilee, and that the Galilean Jewry of Jesus' time was so thoroughly cut off from gentile influence that any such conception or influence was highly improbable. This goaded me to writing an additional chapter on Paganism in Jewish Palestine,[227] and for this chapter (which I haven't yet started writing) I now have about two hundred pages of notes. And I haven't begun to exhaust the scholarly material. But at least I've read the most important books, and I've read just about all I'm going to. After about

[224] Such a book was never published. See Smith's further references to this book in his letters 43 (October 27, 1955) and 45 (February 28, 1956).

[225] Asclepius (Greek Asklepios) belongs to Greek and Roman mythology, first as physician, and then as a god of medicine and healing. His cult was widespread and very popular, mostly during the Roman period. The manifold accounts of his miracles (aretalogies) were widely distributed and showed him not only as a miraculous healing god, but also as a saviour and a benefactor.

[226] Sarapis (or Serapis) is originally an Egyptian god who was the object of a popular worship in Greece and Rome. He was considered as a saviour and a healing god. His cult shares some features with that of Asclepius.

[227] See M. Smith, 'Palestinian Judaism in the First Century', in M. Davis (ed.), *Israel: Its Role in Civilization* (New York, 1956), 67–81.

three more volumes I shall begin to write, ready or not, from sheer necessity of release.

With all good wishes for your self and Mrs. Scholem

Sincerely,

Morton Smith

P.S. Braude sends you his regards. All his family are well and thriving.

As ever, M.S.

41

The Hebrew University
Jerusalem
August 10, 1955

Dear Dr. Smith,

I received your very interesting letter yesterday and as I am about leaving for Europe (for 2 months) I hurry to write you at least a short notice. I hear with pleasure that you will be another year free for your scholarly work and congratulate you upon your Guggenheim fellowship. And in case you will be able to make a study of the Hesychasts, that should prove a very interesting subject. Your journey to Athens during 1956–7 would of course mean that even in case the matter with Brown comes through I would miss you, as I could be there only in September 1956 – precisely when you will be in Greece. Whether anything will come of the Braude plan, I do not know and I can do nothing about it. In any case, the application is only for 1956/7 and I can wait until the end of the present year. My main interest in going to Brown is to be able to concentrate on writing one of my volumes.

I hope that even in the case of a positive answer, I would not have to undertake heavy duties, but could give a course on one of my subjects for advanced or graduate students who may have some smattering of

Hebrew. Otherwise the attractive feature of the scheme would be lost. Up to this day, I do not even know, what the amount of the Smith-Mundt grant would be. But let us face the future with equanimity.

From Switzerland I will go to London where the University has invited me to give a series of lectures in [the] Fall, but I expect to be back by the 25th of October. Last year I almost finished one volume of my opus on Sabbatianism[228] which will be a lengthy affair, and I hope to write the second one in America or to take out another special leave for this purpose, in case I do not come to the U.S.

Don't ruin your stomach, even for the Greek Orthodox Church! We try to keep in good health, and I at least succeed quite well. My wife has suffered from various minor afflictions but she feels much better lately.

Both of us send us our kindest regards and best wishes,

As ever,

Yours sincerely,

Gershon Scholem

My wife is staying here and letters reach me through Jerusalem

42

102 Bowen St.
Providence, R.I.
October 27, 1955

Dear Professor Scholem,

Rabbi Braude last week told me that he recently had a conversation with Arnold, the Provost of Brown, who told him that it seemed very

[228] In Hebrew characters.

probable that you would get a Smith-Mundt grant to enable you to come here in 1956–7. I had an opportunity to speak to Keeney, the new President of Brown,[229] to-day, so I asked him about the report and he confirmed the likelihood of the grant. Congratulations. I hope that your stay at Brown will prove agreeable and will provide you with the opportunity for work which you desire. (Brown, I understand, is to pay $4,000 and Smith-Mundt the transport, which should get you through).

The more I think of it, the more I regret that I shall not be able to be here during your stay. I should like very much to take up again the study of the Kabbalah and particularly to do so by making a translation of your *Reshit HaKabbalah*. I have therefore been trying to think of some foundation which might be willing to give me a grant to enable me to do research under your direction during the coming year. The only possibility which occurs to me is that the Bollingen Foundation might be interested – at least it might if you wrote to it about the desirability, for the comparative study of religion, of introducing kabbalism a scholar familiar with gnosticism and the New Testament, and recommending me as a suitable beneficiary, for this purpose, of one of their fellowship grants. I am sure that if the question were once raised, Goodenough, Lieberman, Nock *et al.* would be glad to recommend me, and I think that there would be much greater likelihood of the award's being made if the question were initiated by a recommendation from you that there would be if I were simply to write directly to the Foundation and apply.

My plan to try for a grant to enable me to study, the manuscripts at the Meteora has been going on smoothly. The Archbishop of Athens has granted permission for the study and for the stay at the monastery necessary to make it. Jaeger, at Harvard, is much interested in the scheme, and I think that his interest alone would suffice to put it through. However, since you are going to be here only next year, while the manuscripts will be there for all predictable time to come, I should prefer to use the opportunity of your visit here while it lasts, and to leave the manuscripts for the following year.

There is always, too, the almost unpleasant possibility that I may be offered a good teaching job which I'll have to take in self interest, and which will put an end to these more exotic possibilities. As yet,

---

[229] Barnaby C. Keeney, a Medievalist, was the twelfth president of Brown University, from 1955 to 1966. He is well known for his expansion of the campus.

however, the threat does not seem imminent. I'm going down to Yale next month to be interviewed by a committee there, but Goodenough has warned me that they're a committee of preachers, so the probability of their liking me is small. (This, of course, is not to be repeated. I really need a job very badly, and I'm deeply grateful to my friends who are trying to get me one, but, strictly *entre nous*, I hope that before success crowns their efforts I'll have one year's work on the *Kabbalah* and another's in Greece).

This year's work has not been going at all as I planned. I got involved in the study of Hellenistic influences in Palestine and am still at it, though now at last about to give it up and simply write an account of my results to date, which fill about 300 file cards. Some I shall use for some lectures which I must give this winter in Boston[230] and New York, some will make an article,[231] some will go into the chapter of my book on Mark, for which the whole study was started and which is still awaiting its completion, and then, with unspeakable relief, I shall be able to get on to St. Isidore, whose constant occupation of the horizon is beginning to get on my nerves. Fortunately, nothing else has got on them. The summer has gone by so quietly and so fast that I scarcely noticed it. My health is almost back to normal and there is nothing to disturb my days. I hope that your trip to Europe was pleasant and your lectures in London were successful. Please remember me to Mrs. Scholem.

With best wishes for you both,

Sincerely,

Morton Smith

P.S. the Braudes are both well and send you their regards. Braude is working on a new translation, this time *Pesikta Rabbathi*,[232] and is already about a third of the way through it. His translation of *Midrash Tehilim*

---

[230] Smith gave three lectures at Hebrew Teachers' College in Boston, in early 1955. The text of these lectures forms the basis for his "The Image of God: Notes on the Hellenization of Judaism, with Especial Reference to Goodenough's Work on Jewish Symbols," *Bulletin of the John Rylands Library* 40 (1958), 473–512 (A.P.).

[231] Probably: M. Smith, 'Palestinian Judaism in the First Century' in M. Davis (ed.), *Israel: Its Role in Civilization* (New York, 1956), 67–81.

[232] *Pesikta Rabbati: Discourses for Feasts, Fasts and Special Sabbaths* (Yale Judaica Series 27; New York, 1968).

will come out in the Yale Judaica as soon as Obermann[233] is out of the way, which should be some time this winter. Will the volumes of your book on Sabbatianism come out separately, or shall you hold over the first one until the second is also ready for publication?

Please remember me to the Samburskys.

Regards, M.S.

43

November 7, 1955

Dear Dr. Smith,

I was very pleased to hear from you and about you and your plans. As for my coming to Brown, nothing has as yet been decided and the piece of information about Smith-Mundt paying only transport (contained in your letter) has somewhat alarmed me, as I had received from the Hebrew University authorities quite different information about the Smith-Mundt grant. I wrote about this at once to Braude to clear up possible misunderstandings. On $4,000 I could never agree to go for 10 months to the U.S., and I always took that sum to be the additional pay put up by Brown's benefactor, in addition to the Smith-Mundt grant. (Maisler and Polotsky got $3,000 + transport, from Smith-Mundt funds).

As to your Bollingen scheme, I am afraid it would not work and I do not think I could propose it even if the matter with Brown is settled after all. They do not make awards of this kind (for introducing somebody into a new field of research under somebody else's direction). In order to qualify you have to show that you are already an authority in your field and want to do some specific research. It would not do to say that you want to be a specialist in Kabbalistic matters too, or

[233] Julian Obermann was the editor of the Yale University Press. He died that same year.

translate my book, (if I were there and could speak to them *personally*, I might be able, in a favorable hour, to cajole them into such a scheme of translation. But certainly not from here and by writing. As I know the responsible man,[234] I do not think it would be wise). It would be, of course, a *very* good thing, if by some favorable turn you would be at Brown when I came and I am, therefore, not overeager to congratulate you on your possible trip to Greece just at that time. In case the Yale committee should prove better than its reputation, we would be not too badly off for some reunions!

I hope to have the first volume of my Shabbetai Zvi ready for press next spring. I write and rewrite, and during my last journey have made some very interesting new discoveries of unknown material. Maybe I should give my course in Brown not about the *Kabbalah* but on Sabbatanism?

I am very curious to see your book on Mark. My best wishes for its completion, and kind regards from my wife and me,

Sincerely yours,

G. Sch.

44

The Hebrew University
Jerusalem
December 27, 1955

Dear Prof. Smith,

Many thanks for your letter of December 5th. I am still without any intimation as to the decision in Washington about my invitation, and this delay begins to get on my nerves. By the way, I have since found that my basic assumption about the Smith-Mundt grant was based on a letter of yours, August 2nd 1953 where you wrote me that these

[234] Scholem obviously means here: 'the man responsible (for the matter)'.

grants "cover minimum expenses *in addition to* travel costs; additional supplementation by [the inviting] University is encouraged." This was the basis for my understanding that the $4,000 which Brown put up on Braude's initiative were meant as that "additional supplementation."

As to your question regarding Hans Lewy's book on the Oracula, I can tell you, that the book has been set in print during the last three years – in Cairo, where the manuscript was sent by Lewy (to the French Institute), and they had managed somehow to sabotage their own decision to publish it. (Only when a new director came in, things moved after all). One of our colleagues has read the proofs (via London and a relay system) and he tells me, that two months ago he had seen the last proof. Actually the whole book is finished, at least in proof, but we do not know how much has already been printed and when the whole will be published. It is a large volume of nearly 600 pages, and if only a little better luck prevails, it should be on the market during 1956.[235] Maybe you will know about it before us. Only the collection of the Greek fragments is lacking in the book – we have not been able to locate the manuscript of this appendix. But still it will be a very substantial work and a monument to the author whose 10th year of death has just been remembered in a very fine memorial meeting we arranged last week.

We have a very rainy winter.

With best wishes for the New Year and kind regards from both of us,

Yours sincerely

Gershom Scholem

---

[235] H. Lewy, *Chaldaean Oracles and Theurgy: Mysticism, Magic and Platonism in the Later Roman Empire*, was eventually published in 1956 but many copies were lost during the Suez Campaign. A new edition, much enlarged with indices and a series of appendices, was published by Michel Tardieu (see n. 23 to Letter 1 above).

45

102 Bowen St.
Providence, R.I.
February 28, 1956

Dear Prof. Scholem,

First I must thank you for your letter of December 27, which I haven't answered because I've had no definite knowledge, either of my plans or of the prospects for your grant. Braude now tells me he has received from Brown a copy of a letter sent you, informing you of the grant by the government and the other, supplementary, sums which would be available. I hope this information will reach you in time for you to take advantage of the offer, and I hope the offer will be sufficiently attractive to persuade you that to take it would be advantageous. My hope, in this matter, is not purely altruistic. I have been assured that if I choose to remain in Providence for the coming year I shall be given a grant for research, so I hope that I shall be able, again, to do some work under your direction: I think especially of translating *Reshit HaKabbalah*, and doing some supplementary reading. Perhaps I might also try to put the *Hekhalot* in shape for publication. If you have any suggestions as to preparatory reading which I might do to advantage in the course of the summer, I should be glad to have them. (My main work during the year will be the study of the text of St. Isidore – long overdue as a thesis for the Doctorate of Theology from Harvard – and I hope, besides, to do a good deal of reading in Greek, especially on the Gnostics).

Quite apart from the pleasure of seeing you again, and the hope of working under you, I'm happy for social reasons that the grant came through: Governments do so many stupid things that when, occasionally, something good gets done, it has the effect of the unexpected relief. I very much hope that in this instance the saying, 'Better late than never.' will hold good.

Thank you for your information about Lewy's book; I shall look forward to seeing it in the publications of the French Institute.

I've been working quite steadily, and a number of articles and my perennial book on Mark are actually now completed or on the very verge of completion. One advantage of the consequent pressure is that I haven't time to write about them, but I trust you'll see them in due course.

Please remember me to Mrs. Scholem and to the Samburskys.

With the happy expectation of seeing you and Mrs. Scholem this fall,

Sincerely,

Morton Smith

46

The Hebrew University
Jerusalem
March 11, 1956

Dear Dr. Smith,

Many thanks for your letter of February 28 which reached me together with Braude's one. Today I cabled Braude because the official letter of Brown's invitation which must have been sent two weeks ago, has *not* reached me. They may have sent it by mistake to "Palestine" (meaning that it would have gone to Jordan) or by surface mail (meaning that it would reach me after 2 months). This is of course very regrettable, because I to this moment do not know what precisely I have been offered. This Friday I am to see Mr. McGrail, the cultural attaché in the U.S. Embassy. I hope to get a cable through Braude's intervention, informing me of all the details. If, as Braude writes, my income would be $ 7,000 (but what about taxes?) I shall *accept* the offer, and it is very pleasant to hear from you that you will stay on with us. I do not know how the traveling expenses will be calculated and whether I can manage to get my wife there by traveling cheaper. She has now decided that in case I accept she would come with me.

Could you give me good advice as to I) the *division* of the academic year at Brown; two or three terms, the exact dates, are courses calculated to be given during the whole year, or for one term? And II) the number of hours I should give. I should like to give *four* hours weekly, two for lectures and two for reading texts with students, who have some command of Hebrew. Do you think that would do? I should like to give teaching for graduate students, principally, or possibly I may give *two* courses, each of one hour lecturing. And in addition two hours reading texts (I thought also of the *Hekhalot*, and of some sources on Sabbatianism. *Zohar* may be *too* difficult?) But the first thing is to know the framework into which my courses belong. Would there be 3, 5, 10 or more students? Could there be a lecture of one hour weekly on general outlines of Kabbalah (or its Messianisim) designed for a wider audience? It all depends on the number of hours and I will appreciate your advice. I thought four would be fair.

The information about the grant given me so far by the Embassy is very imprecise and contradictory. I wish to clear it up this Friday.

I hope to do a lot of work in Providence, and we can think of something to do together. Beside my little book on *Reshit HaKabbalah*,[236] there will be the big volume on Sabbatai Zevi which I have finished – Hebrew, I want to write the second volume if possible, in Providence.

Are they giving an 'office' or study to people like me on the campus buildings? I hope your good tidings will be confirmed if I get the full text of the invitation. These technical difficulties are silly.

Please give my kind regards to the Braudes. Show him this letter if you want and tell him that I shall write him after returning from Tel Aviv.

All the best to you and, I hope *au revoir*!

Yours sincerely,

G. Scholem

[236] In Hebrew characters.

47

102 Bowen St.
Providence, R.I.
March 16, 1956

Dear Prof. Scholem,

I have just received your letter of the 11th and shall answer at once before passing it on to Braude who, since he is the source of the money, is the party who should make the official inquiries of the University. Since I am no longer on the staff, I do not wish to seem to intrude myself. Consequently, I can give you only opinions, but they will probably be fairly correct.

Braude reported to me the matter of the cablegrams (after he had acted). I hope his action was satisfactory to you and I trust that the official offer has now arrived and been officially accepted.

Arrangements about travelling expenses will have to be made with the US government, since they will come out of its grant. It undoubtedly has a set (probably two, contradictory sets) of rules governing the matter and the consulate will no doubt be able to misinform you about them.

The academic year will begin about the 20th of September and conclude about the 30th of May. It is divided into two halves, by a two weeks examination period, beginning about the first of February. There is one long vacation in the first half (from the Saturday before Christmas to the Monday after New Year's – usually about two weeks), and a week's vacation (in early April) in the second half. Courses normally run for one half-year only, but if you wish you may offer one course for the full year. I doubt that you will be expected to teach any courses, unless you wish to. What Arnold proposed when I first talked to him about the matter was a series of evening lectures – probably about eight (i.e., one a month) – on some topic likely to interest local religious groups – e.g. *Kabbalism and Christianity* or *The study of Mysticism and the Religious Life* or *Mysticism and Abnormal Psychology* or something of the sort (double-barrelled titles are good for such series, since they attract people interested in both the subjects mentioned). This is not to imply that the lectures need to be trash.

A considerable number of people in and around the University are sincerely interested in religion and some of them have done some reading about Christian mysticism. Braude and the local Protestant clergy will recommend your lectures and you should get a sizeable audience, perhaps 100, about half Jewish. Brown has money to publish works produced by its faculty, and this might be an opportunity to produce quite a valuable little book of reflections on your study and insights derived from it, if you can find some popular theme on which to hang them.

If you decide to offer a course, beside this series of lectures, I think one session a week, of two hours, should be sufficient. The university will probably have no students capable of reading any of the texts in the original, but I am sure Braude hopes to do some reading with you, and so do I, and perhaps some other persons here or in Boston may wish to. Whether you arrange a private reading group, or offer a course and open it to outsiders, does not, under these circumstances, make much difference. The university will furnish an office, I understand.

Taxes are a complicated problem, since your income will come from several sources. Whether or not the Smith-Mundt grants are taxable, I don't know. You should find out from the consulate and, if it says they're not, ask it to put that statement into writing (I've just been through a pitched battle with the Internal Revenue, which wanted to tax my Fulbright grant, although I had been assured, when I took it, that it was not taxable. Fortunately, I won). For the other money, the rule is that earned income is taxable, free gifts are not. Since all your income will be grants, it would be to your advantage to have only the smallest of the grants made to the University and paid to you as salary (which would then be your taxable income), and the other grants given to you directly. Unfortunately, the individual donors must give not to you directly, but to recognized charitable institutions (otherwise they cannot deduct the gifts from their taxable incomes) so we must try to arrange to have the charitable institutions grant directly to you, and not to the university. Perhaps the synagogue can do it. I'll speak to Braude about this when I give him your letter. *If* your government grant is not taxable and *if* the 'salary' paid you by the university can be kept down to a couple of thousand dollars, the taxes will be negligible. (*Negligible* is certainly the wrong word; I mean, $100).

I hope that things will go smoothly from now on and that you and Mrs. Scholem will arrive this fall and have a pleasant and profitable year at Brown. I look forward with the greatest pleasure to seeing you both again.

With all good wishes,

Morton Smith

P.S. I see a book announced 'The Physical World of the Greeks' by Samborski. Is this *the* Sambursky?[237] If so, my congratulations, and anyhow, my regards. MS.

48

102 Bowen St.
Providence, R.I.
March 26, 1956

Dear Professor Scholem,

Braude thought it would be better for me to talk with the University officials about the questions you asked, so to-day I saw Arnold, with the following results:

As to the periods and divisions of the academic year, they are as I wrote in my former letter. The year will begin on the 17th of September and end on the third of June, but the University would be quite happy provided you arrived within a week or so of that date, and would be willing to grant permission for you to leave in May. Exact dates for the internal divisions of the year are not yet available, but they will be approximately those I indicated.

As to teaching, one of the donors – a Jewish charitable organization – worded its gift 'to enable him to conduct a seminar' or words to that effect, so the administration feels that the acceptance of the gift with

[237] The author of this book is indeed Samuel Sambursky. The book was originally written in Hebrew but was translated and published the same year as this letter: S. Sambursky, *The Physical World of the Greeks* (trans. M. Dagut; London, 1956).

these terms in it will make some sort of seminar necessary. They had been thinking in terms of a series of public lectures, such as I suggested in my previous letter, and I think they would be happy if you decided to give such a series. Arnold told me he would consult with the other people concerned and would write you within a week or two.

As to taxes, the news is bad. The university specified, in its letter to you, all the money it expected to receive for the purpose, and described it all as 'salary'. A copy of that letter and previous, corresponding statements about the salary it expected to pay you were sent to the State Department and formed part of the conditions on which the grant was awarded. Therefore Arnold thinks that it would be very difficult to change the terms now. The contract on the strength of which the grant was awarded cannot be changed without the consent of the State Department, and State will not give its consent if the obvious reason for the change is to avoid payment of income tax. So probably the whole will be taxable. However, if I understand the form correctly, you have an exemption of travelling expenses plus three hundred dollars per month of residence in this country. This should bring the taxable amount down to $4,600 for an eight month's stay. The taxes on $4,600, at the rates for U.S. citizens, come to about $600. What the rates for non-resident aliens are, I don't know. The university will be required to withhold 30% of your salary. You then send the income tax authorities a form indicating the difference between the amount withheld and the tax you claim you should have paid, and the surplus is paid you in lump. (This, at least, is how it works for U.S. citizens; again, the rules may be different for aliens). My experience with the income tax administration has been that it promptly repays the full amount claimed, adjudicates afterwards, and is, on the whole, quite fair and willing to listen to reason. How the repayment system works with people who are going outside U.S. jurisdiction, and who therefore could not be prosecuted if their claims turned out to be false, I don't know.

The university will provide an office, probably in Wilbour Hall,[238] which is a pleasant old building, recently reconditioned and reasonably comfortable. You will have the Egyptology department above you and

[238] Wilbour Hall, named after the 19th century Egyptologist Charles Edwin Wilbour, is located on the corner of Prospect and George Streets and housed since 1949 the Department of Egyptology.

the department of the History of Mathematics in the basement (the latter means Neugebauer and Sachs, who are excellent people, extremely knowledgeable and easy to get along with).[239]

I hope that all, meanwhile, has gone well with you and that no further hitches have occurred or are occurring in the Plan. The Braudes send you and Mrs. Scholem their best regards and join me in looking forward with the greatest pleasure to your arrival.

With all good wishes

Morton Smith

P.S. As for students, if you offer a seminar entitled 'Reading of Hebrew Kabbalistic Texts' or words to that effect, you will probably get Braude and me and perhaps a stray rabbi or Hebrew teacher from the vicinity. It is barely conceivable that there should be more than five. A seminar which did not require knowledge of Hebrew (or any other foreign language) might draw more, but also might not. The seminars normally offered by the department of Religious Studies usually get between six and a dozen.

Best wishes, MS

[239] Otto Neugebauer (Innsbruck, 1899–Princeton, N.J., 1990). Historian of Ancient Mathematics. Editor, together with his closest colleague and friend, Abraham Joseph Sachs (1914–1983), of *Mathematical Cuneiform Texts* (American Oriental Series 29; New Heaven, Conn., 1945).

49

Institute of Jewish Studies
The Hebrew University
Jerusalem
April 25, 1956

Dear Dr. Smith,

I was very glad to receive your letter of March 26th. I have been waiting now for 4 weeks for the letter of provost Arnold which you said would be written within a week or two of your letter. Nothing has come so far. I am writing therefore to you unofficially about the suggestion for my lectures. I understand that I will give two hours weekly as a seminar called Kabbalistic texts. I think it will be best to read there some parts of the *Zohar*. This would be of course a research seminar, or a seminar for graduate students, or whatever other name you may choose to call it. As to the other course of lectures, there are two possibilities. The first is a course of public lectures such as suggested in your previous letters for a total of 6 or 7 lectures on some aspects of Jewish mysticism. If this would be acceptable to Provost Arnold, I would suggest some topic such as Hassidism or some other facets of Jewish mysticism about which I would like to talk. The lectures on Hassidism would seem to me to have the broadest appeal to a general public (once a month).

If instead of this series of public lectures, preference would be for a course of lectures in the University itself, I would give a course on the general outline of the history of Jewish mysticism, one hour a week.

My preference is a choice between these two alternatives as outlined here. I hope I will not be asked to give both types of lectures. I definitely would prefer the first type of monthly lectures.

As to the days, I would prefer Tuesday or Wednesday afternoon for the seminar. In case the course of public lectures should be decided upon, I assume it will be given evenings on some day of the week.

I am sending a copy of this letter to Rabbi Braude and I hope to hear about the acceptance of my suggestions as soon as possible.

Please give my letters to Provost Arnold who I hope has in the meantime received the official letter of acceptance which I wrote in longhand some time ago.

Very sincerely,

Yours,

G. Scholem

50

102 Bowen St.
Providence, R.I.
April 30, 1956

Dear Professor Scholem,

Your letter of April 25 arrived this morning. I read it to R. Braude by telephone and he agreed with me in thinking that, in spite of your request, I had better not show it to Provost Arnold, since, although the wording was perfectly correct, there was a certain brusqueness in the tone which suggested that you did not realize the amount of trouble to which Arnold has already gone in arranging this matter. (I suppose the basic difficulty was the fact that there are less Smith-Mundt grants than there are applicants. The State Department is naturally anxious to use the grants to further its own interest, which means that it very much prefers applicants from 'strategic' countries and applicants whose work is directly connected with matters of social concern – e.g. economists, sociologists, chemists, agricultural experts, engineers etc.). Be this as it may, the Department certainly delayed this particular award in the most outrageous fashion and I can understand that, as victim of the delay, your annoyance naturally extends to the whole business and to everyone concerned. However, I can assure you that Arnold did his utmost in the matter, and that if he had not paid a special visit to the State Department and made a scene there, the appointment might still be hanging fire. Therefore I hope that you will not be too much annoyed at this delay which has occurred in connection with your question as to your courses. It may be that the letter has been sent you and that it is suffering from the same retarded delivery as the previous one. However, it may also be that Arnold has not yet got around to the matter, since his schedule at this time of year is extremely heavy. On the chance that the latter was the case, I called on his secretary and told her that you had written me, saying you hoped that the University would find agreeable your proposal to give two courses, one a series of popular monthly lectures, open to the public, on some aspects of Jewish mysticism, and the other a seminar for the reading of Kabbalistic texts in Hebrew, to meet for two hours each week – the hours to be arranged by you. I said you wanted an answer concerning this as soon as possible, and she said she would bring the matter to Arnold's attention at once. So I trust you will have your answer within a few days. In any event, I feel certain that the University will make you no difficulties about this matter and that you may count on offering these courses which you propose. So I hope that, should any further delay occur, you will not let it disturb you, but will proceed with your plans as if you had already received the University's approval of this proposal, for I cannot doubt that it will eventually be given.

Let me urge again that you choose, for the monthly lectures, as popular a topic as possible. Rabbi Baude protested when I remarked to him this morning that there were probably half-a-dozen people in Providence who knew what Hassidism was: He thought there might be fifteen or twenty. You must remember that American Jewry has had no Martin Buber. I know that both Buber's works and your own have had considerable sale in America, but that has been almost entirely limited to Jewish circles, and, for a number of reasons, it would be a pity to have your lectures here an exclusively, or overwhelmingly, Jewish affair. Further, the fact is that Providence cannot provide even a Jewish audience of any considerable size capable of following you to appreciate the originality of your solutions of questions historical and literary. If you deal with such questions you will have to give so much of your time to elementary explanations that there will be little left over for anything else. (I should confess, too, that I am anxious to persuade you to speak on the psychological, philosophical or *religionsgeschichtliche* aspects of the material, since I think you are uniquely qualified to do so. Reliable historical scholarship is a fairly common commodity. It is a much rarer thing to find such scholarship at the disposition of a mind of the reflective profundity and psychological insight which yours possesses and which I have never found equalled. Therefore I am really more anxious to learn what you *think* about your subject than what you *know* about it, and I hope I can coax you to use this opportunity to write a great book, not just another good piece of history). I hope you will think the impertinence of this justified by the end.

In any event, let me add to it my sincere respect and my best wishes for yourself and Mrs. Scholem.

Morton Smith

51

Institute of Jewish Studies
The Hebrew University,
Jerusalem
May 29, 1956

Dear Dr. Smith,

Your letter of April 30th reached me on May 11th and I waited with my answer until I had heard from Professor Arnold as indicated in your letter. Only 5 days ago I received a letter from him, but it contained only formal intimation about final action taken by the Corporation of Brown University in appointing me as a visiting professor. About the nature of my teaching he said nothing and I therefore wrote to him today the letter, a copy of which I am enclosing to you. This leaves us where we were, and you will see from my letter to Arnold that I have taken your advice regarding the courses. But please let it be clear that in case there is any difficulty about the second course I am quite willing to give instead of these public lectures a general course once a week "Survey of Jewish Mysticism (Main Points of its History and Teachings)". As for the monthly lectures course I think that your formulation is quite correct, namely that I may speak what I think about the subject more than what I know about it. If it is to contain about 6 or 7 lectures, they could certainly be about topics which will leave ample room for comparative appreciation of the doctrines of the ideas of the Kabbalists and those of other mystics. I would mention some topics which might be interesting just from your point of view: 1. The God of the Kabbalists. 2. The Mystical Meaning of Revelation and the Speculations of the Kabbalists about the Torah. 3. Meditation and Ecstasy in Jewish Mysticism. 4. Myth and Ritual in Kabbalah. (This would certainly be a good topic for at least two of these lectures). 5. The Ideal Figure of the Saint or "Just Man". 6. On the Psychology of the Kabbalists. 7. The Impact of Jewish Mysticism on Christianity during the Renaissance and Later (What is called Christian Kabbalah). Here you have some suggested topics for such a type of public monthly lectures which should not appeal to a Jewish audience alone. I think this would be a fair kind of schedule and I will be glad to have your and Braude's reactions.

I appreciate very much your kindness in writing your last long letter and I am surely very far from being annoyed by it. Never be afraid to speak your mind. If I hear nothing from Provost Arnold, I think I can proceed on the assumption that my suggestions in my letter to him have been approved.

Kind personal regards to you from my wife and myself and from the Samburskys too who remember you with much affection.

Very truly yours,

Gershom Scholem

52

102 Bowen St.
Providence, R.I.
June 15, 1956

Dear Professor Scholem,

I got your letter some time ago, but did not get a chance to talk with Arnold until to-day, the change of presidents which took place at

Brown a year ago[240] has thrown a great deal of work on him, since he is the chief continuing officer from the prior administration.

Your suggestions about courses are quite satisfactory to him. The University has no wish, in this matter, save to leave you in the most complete possible freedom to teach what and when you wish. No announcements will be made until you arrive, and you will then be free to say exactly what you choose to teach, and what you say will go. One fly has crept into the ointment: The present Professor of Old Testament[241] has expressed regret that your seminar will require a reading knowledge of Hebrew. He says he thinks there would be a number of students who would like to take a seminar with you, but who could not meet that requirement. (He is right at least as to one student – himself, and I think his regret is due to the fact that he thinks such a seminar as proposed might call attention to his deficiency in this matter). When Arnold spoke of this with me I said that I thought your time would be wasted in a seminar of which the students could not read the material you would be talking about. Further, Braude's interest in raising the money was his desire to read Hebrew with you and therefore you would be morally obligated to provide an opportunity for that, whatever else you did. Therefore to burden you with a seminar for the illiterate would effectively double your work without greatly increasing your usefulness. At this Arnold recoiled and said. Well, the University had no wish to impose anything whatever on you. He thought this question might be left for you to decide when you arrived and when the actual possibilities could be put before you. So I think you will have only to decide against that suggestion and to explain that a reading knowledge of Hebrew is essential for worth-while work in the subject.

Braude and I are both very happy as to the subjects you propose for your English lectures. I, in particular, am enthusiastic. I think they may well make your most significant book (for, just between the two of us, I think your intellectual profundity is probably greater than that of most of the mystics you study, so what you think is very likely to be more important than what they said). If I might make one suggestion, I should suggest switching the places of lectures 4 and 6 in the list you

[240] Barnaby Conrad Keeney succeeded in 1955 to the educator and statesman Henry Merritt Wriston (1889–1978), who was at the head of the university from 1937 to 1955.

[241] William J. Robbins. A Baptist minister, Chairman of the Department of Religious Studies at Brown since 1950.

sent me – i.e., putting the psychology of the Kabbalists in 4th place and myth and ritual in 6th. The Psychology would naturally follow your lecture on meditation and ecstasy, and would be of more general interest, while myth and ritual would certainly contain a number of technical references to Jewish practices for which the non-Jews of the audience would be better prepared the later they came in the series.

As for lectures at other institutions, Brown will be happy to have you accept as many as you choose. Acceptances will make the State Department happy, since they prove your importance to 'international understanding', and will make Brown happy, since you are a walking advertisement for the university at which you are a visiting professor. However, Arnold hopes you will feel under no obligation to accept anything you do not want, and he said he could understand your refusal of the American Council of Learned Societies[242] offer, since that would, in effect, have tied your hands and subjected you to a program of their arranging. However, you may feel quite free to accept whatever obligations you want. (I hope, by the way, that your refusal was reasonably gentle, since Goodenough[243] is a fervent admirer of your work and a very kind man, and I'm sure he was trying to do you a kindness by negotiating the invitation).

Just now Cornell[244] is considering me for a position, so I may be bought back into slavery before you get here. I scarcely know whether to hope for another year of liberty and insecurity with the opportunity of working with you, or to hope for a job. However, if the job is offered I shall certainly have to take it, so in the meanwhile I try to go on working without wasting time in thought about eventualities which, if they present themselves, will impose their own solutions.

With best wishes to Mrs. Scholem and with the pleasant hope of seeing you both in September,

Sincerely,

Morton Smith

---

[242] The American Council of Learned Societies (ACLS), that has for mission the advancement of humanistic studies.

[243] Goodenough took an active part in the American Council of Learned Societies from 1953 to 1965 and was a member of its Committee on the History of Religions.

[244] Cornell University, in Ithaca, New York. This offer did not materialize.

53

The Hebrew University,
Jerusalem
June 26, 1956

Dear Dr. Smith,

Thank you very much for your last letter. Although it would be certainly sad to lose [you] as an attentive pupil and colleague in my seminar at Brown, I think I should wish you all success for your candidacy at Cornell, and I hope very much you will get the appointment whatever it is. How the American Universities let a scholar like yourself sit around and wait for a good appointment is above my understanding. I hope to hear from you when you know the results of their deliberations. As to your remarks about the Professor of Old Testament, I suppose that is the same gentleman who wrote to me in his capacity as acting chairman of the Department of Religious Studies. I felt I could not possibly let him down if he really had some people who wish to have guidance from me in my field even if they are without an adequate knowledge of Hebrew. I have expressed my readiness to give another hour for readings and discussions of English texts like the *Soncino Zohar*[245] or my book,[246] if there be some takers. I have a feeling that the people at Brown are very modest as to the request they make on my time and I think I should repay their generosity at least by offering myself for an additional hour if it comes to that. It certainly would not require much work on my part.

With cordial regards from my wife and myself,

Very sincerely yours,

G. Scholem

---

245 *The Zohar* (intro. J. Abelson, trans. H. Sperling and M. Simon [London, 1934]).
246 Presumably *Major Trends in Jewish Mysticism*.

54

Brown University
Providence 12, Rhode Island
December 13, 1956

Dear Morton,

This is to inform you that there is a change of address in New York. Since our friend Mr. Schocken is going away, he has kindly offered us the use of his apartment, 67 Park Avenue, on the 15th floor. You can easily inquire the number of the apartment from the Superintendent. Therefore we shall not be at the Westover Hotel, and I shall be looking forward to seeing you on December 26 from 1:30. Our telephone number will be Murray Hill 9-5452, in case you need to reach us before.

Sincerely yours,

Gershom Scholem

55

The Department of History[247]
Columbia University
New York 27, N.Y.
December 9, 1957

Dear Gershom,

This is an apology for having done nothing on your book since I saw you last, and having every expectation of doing nothing for the next

[247] Smith has been appointed as a Professor of Ancient History at Columbia University in New York City since 1957. Although he retired in 1985, he continued to teach there until shortly before his death in July 11, 1991.

twelve months to come. The fact is that my courses and preparation for courses to come are taking every bit of my time.[248] I have some 95 students in my general course on ancient history, and this has meant a great deal of paper work. That course and another, on classical literature, which I am teaching, I had never given before; the subjects covered lie somewhat outside my former field; and consequently I have had to work constantly on preparation for them. I'm standing the strain all right, but by summer I shall be dead tired, so I am planning to spend the whole of the summer in the Near East – from mid-June to mid-July in Jordan, a week in Israel (when I hope to see you and Thanya),[249] a week in Istanbul, a month in northern Greece, hunting for collections of manuscripts in the monasteries of Chalcidice (*ex*cluding Athos), and a week each in Rome, Paris, and London. This means that when I get back I shall have another term of keeping up with my courses, but I hope that by a year from now all will be in hand, and I shall be able to get back to *Reshit HaKabbalah*. If you do not wish to wait this long for the completion of the work (longer, in fact, since if I start it again in January 59 I shall not be through before fall of that year; you know my speed) I shall be quite willing to turn over to you the part completed to date. For myself, however, I should like to go on and finish the translation of the work, and seriously intend to do so as soon as I can get time. I think, too, that it would be easier to get the whole book printed if portions had not previously appeared. However, your experience in these matters is much greater than mine – and, anyhow, it's your work – so I shall be quite content to do whatever you think best in the matter.

For the time being I am a member of the Committee on the History of Religions of the National Council of Learned Societies. They have some money for publication and for financing work on projects thought desirable. In discussion, recently, the question of publishing translations of the Pseudepigrapha[250] came up. Everybody agreed that this was one

---

[248] At Brown and Drew, Smith was teaching Biblical Literature and Religion; he joined Columbia as Assistant Professor in the History Department, which required he lecture on topics he had not previously prepared (A.P.).

[249] Scholem's wife was actually Fania (which Smith usually spells Fanya).

[250] The term 'pseudepigrapha' usually refers to Jewish and Christian ancient writings that were not included in the Jewish or the Christian canon of Scriptures. In his 'Terminological Boobytraps and Real Problems in the Second-Temple Judeo-Christian Studies' (in P. Slater and D. Wiebe (eds.), *Traditions in Contact and Changes* [Waterloo, Ontario, 1983], 295–306), Smith deals, *inter alia*, with the problematic of this term.

of the things most desperately needed – Charles[251] being prohibitively expensive for students, and unreliable anyhow – but nobody had any notion of an adequate editor. Do you think there is any chance that Polotzky – who must be one of the very few competent people – could be interested in the matter? If there were any chance at all of his willingness to cooperate, I would ask the chairman of the editorial board to write him of the matter.

Columbia is pleasant, except for the constant drive of work, and I am well, except for increasing tension.

Regards to the Samburskys, the Braudes, Polotsky, and all my friends in Jerusalem, and especially to you and Thanya.

Sincerely,

Morton Smith

56

Brown University
January 10, 1957

Dear Morton,

Saturday morning at 10:00 on the 19th will be alright and I will be expecting you then instead of the other appointment hour.

Sincerely,

Gershom Scholem

[251] *The Apocrypha and Pseudepigrapha of the Old Testament*, 2 vols. (R. H. Charles (ed.), [Oxford: Clarendon Press, 1913]). Thre have been various reprints.

57

Brown University
February 11, 1957

Dear Morton,

There is a change of address for our meeting on Friday February 22th. You will find me at the home of Dr. Brodski.[252]
14 East 81 Street where I will stay over the weekend.
Could you possibly come at 1:30 instead of 1?

With cordial regards,

Gershom

Please do not forget to bring a copy of *Reshit HaKabbalah*[253] with you – I may be without mine!

58

[254]

Dear Morton,

Please come Tuesday afternoon to my office, at about 3 P.M.
I have a course until 2, and take a short rest. We may not be free [in] the evening.

Cordially yours,

Gershom Scholem

---

[252] Perhaps Ruth Nanda Anshen (Brodsky) (1900–2003). Philosopher, author and a leading editor. She edited several series as 'Religious Perspectives (Harper)', the 'Science of Culture Series (Harcourt)', and the 'World Perspectives (Harper)'.
[253] In Hebrew characters.
[254] This letter was written on a postcard postmarked March 26, 1957.

59

The Hebrew University,
Jerusalem
December 31, 1957

Dear Morton,

Many thanks for your kind letter. I am glad to hear that you are busy with your lectures although I regret that this will delay for the time being your translation of my book. I have not yet made any other arrangements and shall wait and see until we have a chance to talk things over when you come to Jerusalem. Please arrange your trip about which you write in a manner enabling you to be here not later than by the end of July. You will then find me still in Jerusalem and we will be very glad to see you again.

As to your question about the new addition[255] of the Pseudepigrapha, I have talked to Professor Polotsky according to your wishes. Polotsky is very interested and in principle agreeable to the proposal of his co-operation as one of the editors of the proposed new translation. He will be glad to hear directly from your committee if they are interested in his co-operation. He said he considered it a good idea and would be glad to take part in it.

I am back in my old world and have started the new life after this long journey. My wife and I remember you most affectionately and send you our cordial greetings of the holidays and the New Year.

Always yours,

Gershom

Cordial greetings from the Samburskys

255 Scholem probably means 'edition' (see Letter 60).

The Department of History
Columbia University
N.Y. 27, N.Y., USA
January 12, 1958

Dear Gershom,

Thank you very much for your letter of the thirty-first. I shall look forward to seeing you and Thanya again when I get to Jerusalem, which should be about the 19th or 20th of July, supposing I can hold to my present schedule.

I have written Schneider[256] – the editor of the American Council of Learned Societies publications about the history of the religion – of Polotsky's willingness to participate in a reëdition, or, at least, retranslation of the Pseudepigrapha.[257] I suppose that Schneider will write him presently. Since I don't know anyone capable of 'coöperating' with Polotsky on such a project, I suppose Schneider will ask him to take charge of preparing a volume containing the major works, which might then be followed by another volume by another editor, if Polotsky didn't want to go on. The bulk of the material is formidable. I have been thinking of things to omit. Fortunately the New Testament apocrypha are easily available in James' edition,[258] and the Dead Sea material obviously *can* be left for a collection of its own (though I don't know that it should be, at least, not all of it), and the obviously Gnostic works belong in a class by themselves (though not everything which has picked up a Gnostic touch here or there should be forced into such a class), and works of Hellenistic form (like the Sibylline Oracles[259] and the letter of Aristeas)[260] have no proper place in the collection, and so on.

---

[256] Herbert William Schneider (1892–1984) was at the head of this Committee until July 1940. Author, in collaboration with H. Freiss, of *Religion in Various Cultures* (New York, 1932).

[257] This project never came to fruition.

[258] The New Testament Apocrypha are writings written by ancient Christians that were not accepted into the New Testament. See M. R. James, *Apocryphal New Testament* (Oxford, 1924).

[259] The *Sibylline Oracles* are a collection of oracular prophecies, from the middle of the second century B.C.E., to the fifth century C.E. Written by Alexandrian Jews and Christian writers, they consist mainly of *post eventu* eschatological prophecies.

[260] *The Letter of Aristeas*, an Old Testament pseudepigraphical work, is a fictional account relating the translation of the Pentateuch from Hebrew to Greek in Alexandria.

I think that only works which purport to be written by Old Testament worthies should be included, and of this group I'm doubtful whether or not we should try to include Rabbinic, Samaritan and Christian works (e.g. III Enoch,[261] Asatir,[262] Odes of Solomon) or not. (And what about early magical works, like the Testament of Solomon?)[263] So it seems best to start out with one volume of undisputed candidates, and go on to the rest as time and money permit. On this matter I should be glad to know your opinion, as also about form – the notion now is to publish the bare texts of the translations, with an absolute minimum of introductory material, and no notes unless absolutely necessary (e.g., to explain puns).

Please remember me to Polotsky and give my regards to the Samburskys and the Braudes,

With best wishes for yourself and Thanya,

As ever,

Morton

It claims for the authority among the Jews of the Greek new version. The letter was probably written by a Hellenistic Jew in the middle of the second century B.C.E.

[261] The *Hebrew Book of Enoch*, or *III Enoch*, is a Late Antique mystical text.

[262] Pseudepigraphical work also known as *The Samaritan Book of the Secrets of Moses*. It was compiled around the end of the third century B.C.E. In 1927, Moses Gaster published a translation and commentary: *The Asātir: The Samaritan Book of the Secrets of Moses* (London, 1927).

[263] Old Testament Pseudepigraphical treatise describing demons, their form and activities, as well as the various techniques used by King Solomon to counteract them.

61

The Department of History
Columbia University
N.Y. 27, N.Y., USA
December 4, 1958

Dear Professor Scholem,

This summer I promised to make a fair copy of what I have hitherto translated of *Reshit HaKabbalah*[264] and send it to you after the Thanksgiving vacation. I'm afraid you will not be surprised that I have not been able to keep the promise and am now promising to make the copy during Christmas week and send it on after the Christmas vacation. This half year has been very busy. I was in Europe until the last days before the beginning of the term, so my preparation had to be done almost between classes, and I was persuaded to give an extra course – in spite of my better judgment: it was urged on me as a favor I should do for the Department of Religion. And I didn't want to refuse. With the arrival of Christmas vacation the worst will be over, and I really hope then to have the time not only to go over and copy what has already been done, but also to make some further progress.

Meanwhile, I am still terribly busy, but otherwise all right. Bickerman[265] I see often and he is well and sends you his greetings. Lieberman I haven't seen for months, but trust he continues as ever.

Best wishes to Mrs. Scholem and the Samburskys, and Polotsky (who has never written me about the proposed translation of the Pseudepigrapha, so I suppose that he decided against it). Do write if you can spare the time and let me know of your publications; I am especially

[264] In Hebrew characters.

[265] Elias J. Bickerman (Kishinev, 1897–Tel Aviv, 1981). Historian of the ancient world. He taught in Germany and France before the Second World War, and subsequently at the Jewish Theological Seminary and at Columbia University. Upon his retirement in 1967 Bickerman was succeeded by Smith as Professor of Ancient History at Columbia.

anxious to see the lectures on the beginnings of Merkabah[266] mysticism which you gave at the Jewish Theological Seminary.[267]

With kindest regards,

Morton Smith

62

August 3, 1959

Dear Morton,

How are you and what is happening to you? I have not heard from you since long – and I should have liked so much to receive your paper on the Essenes[268] in Hippolytus[269] which I saw in a journal.[270]

I assume that you were very busy with your own work and could not proceed with the translation of *Reshit HaKabbalah*[271] but it will interest you that I now have made up my mind to rewrite it in German on a somewhat larger scale and have signed an agreement to that effect with a very good publishing house in Berlin.[272] From the German text it will be *much* easier to have an English translation.

---

[266] Hebrew for 'chariot'. Merkabah mysticism refers to the vision of God's throne chariot as depicted in the first chapter of Ezekiel. Jewish mystics from the first century B.C.E. to the tenth century C.E. produced prolific literature on this subject.

[267] G. G. Scholem, *Jewish Gnosticism, Merkabah Mysticism, and Talmudic Tradition* (New York, 1961) is based upon the Israel Goldstein lectures, delivered the previous year at the Jewish Theological Seminary of America. See Smith's review: 'G. Scholem, Jewish Gnosticism, Merkabah Mysticism, and Talmudic Tradition', *Journal of Biblical Literature* 80 (1961), 190–1.

[268] The Essenes were a Jewish ascetic sect that flourished between the second century B.C.E. and the second century C.E.

[269] Hippolytus of Rome, a mid-third century Christian theologian and heresiologist, author of the *Philosophoumena*.

[270] M. Smith, 'The Description of the Essenes in Josephus and the *Philosophumena*', *Hebrew Union College Annual* 29 (1958), 273–313.

[271] In Hebrew characters.

[272] G. G. Scholem, *Ursprung und Anfänge der Kabbala* (Berlin, 1962). Smith did not end up translating this book; it was ultimately translated from the German by Allan

Fania and I are going this year to Poland (in search of Jacob Frank) – as long as there is still a visa to be had, who knows how long.[273] And from there to Uppsala, where they are in need of Kabbalah.

Cordially yours,

G. Scholem

63

Prof. Morton Smith
The Department of History,
Columbia University,
N.Y. 27, N.Y., USA
August 7, 1959

Dear Gershom,

Thank you for writing, I was very glad to hear from you. Let me hasten to apologize for my long silence. As you probably know, it was caused by a bad conscience. I sincerely meant to get your chapters transcribed during the spring vacation, and, when that proved impossible, I told myself I would surely do it this summer. But it turned out that Bickerman was going to Europe and thought I should teach the ancient history courses in the summer school (and I agreed with him, especially since I needed the money), so the summer, to date, has been full. Worse than that, I promised to write a short history of Greece, for a series of introductory history books used in a course in Cornell, and I must turn to it as soon as my courses stop.[274] (It is part of my campaign to make the authorities

Arkush: *Origins of the Kabbalah* (R. J. Zwi Werblowsky (ed.), [Philadelphia, 1987]). See n. 80 to Letter 7 above.

[273] Scholem writes during the years of liberalization of the Communist regime in Poland under the initial years of Władysław Gomułka's leadership (1957–1959). By the early 1960's Gomułka changed course in favor of a more oppressive, pro-Soviet policy.

[274] This work would be published the following year by Cornell University Press: M. Smith, *The Ancient Greeks* (The Development of Western Civilization: Narrative Essays in the History of our Tradition from its Origin; Ithaca, 1960).

here think I am really a general historian and not a biblical scholar in disguise. I shall be considered for appointment with tenure this fall,[275] so if you know any particularly powerful charms from practical Kabbalah, please put them to work). Given this state of affairs, I am delighted to know that you intend to prepare an enlarged German edition of *Reshit HaKabbalah* and to have an English translation made from that. I suppose this means there will be no further need for the work I have done to date and I shall accordingly put it into the waste basket on the first of September, unless I hear from you to the contrary before that time. I did it primarily to learn Hebrew and to have the chance of working with you, so it was worth while for its own sake – *Torah leshemah*[276] – and I am not at all disturbed by the apparent waste. (What I still *do* want to see is an English edition of the *Hekhalot Rabbati*).

The material by Clement of Alexandria which I found at Mar Saba last year is turning out to be of great importance, and as soon as I get all minor nuisances off my hands I must work hard at it.[277] Also, the Berlin Academy[278] has asked me to prepare a text of the letters of Isidore of Pelusium for the Griechischen Christlichen Schriftsteller,[279] and this should fill all my spare time for the next five years. Otherwise, no news. I'm honored that you should want a copy of my Hebrew Union College Annual article and am sending one, along with some other recent reprints which may interest you. Of course, I hope to get something of yours in return. In particular, I look forward to the appearance of your Jewish Theological Seminary lectures of last year – now year before last! How time flies!

Regards to Fanya, and best wishes for your trips to Poland and Sweden,

As ever,

Morton Smith

---

[275] Smith was promoted to Associate Professor in December 1959 (A.P.).

[276] Hebrew Expression meaning the study of Torah for the sake of learning and not for any other purpose.

[277] Smith alludes to his discovery of Clement's Letter. See Introduction.

[278] The Berlin Academy, first known as the Königlichen Preußischen Akademie der Wissenschaften zu Berlin, now as the Berlin-Brandenburgische Akademie der Wissenschaften.

[279] The Series 'Griechischen Christlichen Schriftsteller der Ersten Drei Jahrhunderte' (GCS), offering critical editions of Greek Patristic texts, was launched in 1891 by Adolph von Harnack and Theodor Mommsen.

64

Zürich
October 25, 1959

Dear Morton,

Your letter of August 7th was too late to reach me before we left Israel and I regret this very much as I learn from it (now that it reaches me here just as we prepare for our return to Jerusalem in 4 days) that you very unwisely gave a deadline for your destroying the fine translation of *Reshit HaKabbalah*[280] on which we worked so much. I would regret it infinitely if you actually did destroy these papers which still might be very useful. Please keep them!

We are already working on some magical charms for your benefit and should be very happy to learn that you got the promotion which you so fully deserve. I also congratulate you on your plans and the invitation by the Berlin Academy.

We are just back from Poland and Scandinavia where we had a most interesting time. Got some very valuable material in Poland concerning the Frankists and Fanya enjoyed the weeks when I was prevented by my ignorance in Polish to interrupt her in her highly musical and fluent Polish lucubrations. Uppsala was wonderful and I bought a book called *Der gelehrte Narr*[281] (the learned fool) published [in] 1725 in Germany about people like me and you! I enjoyed the title and paid the money.

Now work starts again and the long journey is over. Tonight I am giving my last lecture on this trip. Everywhere we had the most wonderful weather and blue skies, quite extraordinary.

Cordial regards,

Yours as ever,

Gershom

---

[280] In Hebrew characters.

[281] David Fassmann, *Der Gelehrte Narr, oder, gantz natuerliche Abbildung solcher Gelehrten, die da Vermeynen alle Gelehrsamkeit und Wissenschaft Verschlucket zu haben*... (Freyburg: Auf des Autoris Eigene Kosten, 1729).

65

The Department of History
Columbia University
N.Y. 27, N.Y., USA
October 28, 1959

Dear Gershom,

I was terribly sorry to learn from your letter, which reached me this morning, that you wanted the translation of *Reshit HaKabbalah* saved. Your previous letter was so definite as to the fact that there would be a new German edition and that a translation had better be made from that. I supposed the matter was quite settled, and therefore set a date after which I would not keep the manuscript, only because I supposed you would probably be too busy to reply and I did not wish to burden you with an unnecessary letter. So when I got no reply I took for granted that my supposition was correct, and the manuscript is gone. The only consolation I can see is that now we shall certainly (I hope) have the German edition, with your revisions and additions and second thoughts – and of course, for the purpose of saying what you mean, your German will be incomparably better than my English.

Your trip to Poland and Scandinavia sounds as if it had been a pleasant one. I used to think the Scandinavian countries utterly uninteresting – they were identified in my mind with dull respectability and stupid comfort. But as I get further into middle age I become more tolerant of respectability and more concerned about comfort, and I now think I should like to visit them, if only to see what is probably the least disturbed remains of the nineteenth century European civilization.

Life here goes on as usual. Bickerman is away and I am teaching one of his colloquia, as well as two courses of my own. This makes a pleasant program and leaves me some time to myself, in which I hope to make a study of Simon Magus[282] and then get on with the edition of fragment of a letter, allegedly by Clement of Alexandria, which I

[282] Simon Magus, from first-century Samaria, was perceived by the early Church Fathers as the source of all heresies. See M. Smith 'The Account of Simon Magus in Acts 8', in S. Lieberman *et al.* (eds.), *H. A. Wolfson Jubilee Volume*, vol. 2 (Jerusalem, 1965), 735–749.

found summer-before-last, and which contains some amazing information about the Carpocratians[283] and the Gospel according to Mark. Also, the Berlin Academy has asked me to prepare the text of Isidore of Pelisium's letters for the Griechischen Christlichen Schriftsteller (and one advantage of this is that if I do so I shall probably learn eventually how to spell that title), so I have no lack of things to keep me busy.

The question of my appointment should be settled within the next month. Everyone with whom I have spoken of it has been most encouraging, but I shall not permit myself to be optimistic until I have the contract in writing. One good thing, however, is that I am simultaneously being considered for a full professorship at Cornell, and this may persuade Columbia to try to get me signed up quickly on the associate level.

I'm surprised you found the title '*Der gelehrte Narr*' striking. The English equivalent is a stock phrase (not only because it describes a stock object, but also, I suppose, because it expresses the healthy English contempt for learning – so alien to the Germans). I think I once knew where it came from and still have a vague recollection that it's Shakespearean or classical or something of the sort. Did the book live up to the title? (Books with good titles generally don't).

Do give my best wishes to Fanya and also to the Samburskys and to Jonathan Goldstein,[284] who will be spending the winter in Israel before coming back to teach here next fall. He's a remarkably capable student from whom Bickerman expects great things.

With all good wishes, as ever,

Morton

[283] Members of a sect founded by the Alexandrian Gnostic Carpocrates (*fl. circ.* 130–150). According to Clement's Letter, Carpocrates received from a certain presbyter of the church in Alexandria a copy of the Secret Gospel of Mark but added shameless lies and interpretations.

[284] Jonathan A. Goldstein (1929–2004). Professor of History and Classics at the University of Iowa. Author of *I Macabees, a New Translation with Introduction and Commentary* (Anchor Bible 41; Garden City, N.Y., 1976).

66

The Hebrew University,
Jerusalem
December 30, 1959

Dear Morton,

Fanya and I wish you a happy and fruitful new year and I should like to hope that [in] the meanwhile your appointment to Columbia has come through. It is the very least you deserve and you should be able to settle down without having to think every time about the future. And in case you go to Cornell, it might be even better for you, although I think a place like New York should attract you by its treasures and libraries. Let us know sometime the outcome of all this labor!

We had a very interesting trip indeed, and could go on and on telling about our experiences.

If you make a study of Simon Magus do not forget to send it to me if ever it sees the light of publication. I am amazed to hear that there is still unknown information about the Carpocratians to be found. Those are the Frankists of Antiquity. Produce it as soon as possible!

I received your reprints with much pleasure. I did not know about the new Jewish Gnostic Amulet and I am asking Goodenough to send me his paper. Maybe I could try my luck with the Hebrew elements which apparently nobody was able to decipher so far.

My book on *Merkabah* has finally gone to the printer – says Professor Finkelstein.[285] I hope you will find something in it.

Many cordial greetings,

From both of us, yours,

Gershom

[285] Louis Finkelstein (1895–1991). Talmudic Scholar and Jewish historian, longtime Chancellor of the Jewish Theological Seminary of America (1951–1972), and central figure in Conservative Judaism.

67

The Department of History,
Columbia University,
N.Y. 27, N.Y., USA
February 10, 1960

Dear Gershom,

This is chiefly to acknowledge and thank you for your new year's letter. My appointment at Columbia has come through (or, at least, everything is settled that it will come through in May) as you hoped, and I have decided to stay here, at some sacrifice of rank and salary, in order to have the great world within reach, so that I can feel virtuous by resisting the temptation to reach for it. If I buried myself in Ithaca I should never forgive myself for having sacrificed the theater and the opera and the galleries, but so long as I stay here I can indefinitely put off going to them, and feel happy and virtuous about it.

I'd feel more happy and virtuous if I were getting more done. The routine of class work and committees and so on has taken a great deal of time, especially during the past two months, so my research is almost where it was when I wrote you last. I did finish the first section of my study of Simon,[286] read it at the Biblical Society meetings and shall probably publish it in *Harvard Theological Review*[287] – you will get an offprint of course. Conclusion: the story in Acts 8 is best explained on the supposition that Simon had been baptized as a follower of John the Baptist. (There is actually some evidence for this, though admittedly tenuous). I should like to go on – there are some very curious

---

[286] Simon Magus.
[287] The article 'The Account of Simon Magus in Acts 8' was eventually published in S. Lieberman *et al.* (eds.), *H. A. Wolfson Jubilee Volume* (Jerusalem, 1965), 735–749.

traits in the second century evidence – but whether I can find time or not remains to be seen.

Regards to Fanya, and best wishes for you both.

As ever

Morton

P.S. All the Braudes are well, and send greetings.
Remember me to the Samburskys when you see them.
Do let me know when your *Merkabah* book comes out. M.S.

68

Columbia University
In the City of New York
New York 27, N.Y.
Department of History
January 30, 1961

Dear Gershom,

At long last! First I put off writing you till I should finish reading the *Jewish Gnosticism*, then till I should finish my report on the Mar Saba manuscripts, then till I could send my paper on the *Hekhalot* at the same time.[288] Now you have them all at once. (No, you don't. On weighing the package I decided to send the printed things by surface mail). *Jewish Gnosticism*, is even more impressive as a book than it was as lectures. You will see my comments on its importance in my lecture on the *Hekhalot*. Here only a few questions:

I wonder whether the *Visions of Ezekiel* (and, indeed, the make up of the other *Merkabah* texts) may not point to the original existence of

[288] M. Smith 'Observations on *Hekhalot Rabbati*', in A. Altman (ed.) *Biblical and Other Studies* (Cambridge, Mass., 1963) 142–160.

several different mystical groups/traditions concerned, one with the *merkabah*, another with ascent through the various heavens, a third with the entrance of the series of palaces/temples and a central throne. Clearly we have in the pseudepigrapha remains of an ascent mysticism which did not lead to *a merkabah*, and in the visions of Ezekiel the *merkabahs* seem to have been added to such a basic text in a way rather different than they have elsewhere. Conversely, in Ezekiel we have *Merkabah* without ascent, and the heavenly sphere remains *over* the beasts. The heavens, again, are not palaces, and the palace within palace tradition (*cum* throne) can appear without either *merkabah* or spheres (e.g. Enoch 14). Do you think there would be any point in trying to sort out these early separate traditions and trace the synthesis?

p. 21: why don't the translations agree with the Hebrew:
I l.3 utterance*s* – הגיון sing.
II l.2 chorister – מרננים pl.
________ בשיר גילה omitted
p. 22: III l.6 גאון omitted
p. 32: I don't see any hippodrome in the text quoted.
p. 33: l.5 read *tantras*?
p. 64, Should one understand the second אז in the question in note 20 as a pun for עֹז?
p. 95, n. 8 *MacCown*, read *McCown*.
p. 96, l.16, *word* read *world*?
p. 103, § 3, l.1 בגשר read כגשר?
last line לכבודו read בכבודו or לכבדו?

These are all trivia, of course, but for most of the book I have nothing but praise, and why should I praise it to you? I'm sure you know much better then I do how good it is.

About my text on the *Hekhalot*. Which I enclose, there is nothing to say except that I'm sending it by air mail in the hope that you may be kind enough to make some comments (don't bother to return the text, I have other copies) before the proofs reach me, and so save me from my grievous sins – if any (or if remediable).

Both Altmann[289] and Goodenough (Yale Judaica) have asked me for the translation of *Hekhalot Rabbati* and, as you know, I should like to

[289] Alexander Altmann (1906–1987). Rabbi and scholar of Jewish Philosophy, born in Hungary and educated in Germany. He moved to England with the advent of Nazism,

finish it and see it published. If Wirzubski isn't going to complete his work on the Hebrew text, how about turning the manuscript over to someone who will do so?

I'm deeply honored that you asked for me as a reverse Fulbright Professor for next year. Perhaps I can arrange to take my sabbatical by anticipation – but I doubt it. Anyhow, we'll see what the possibilities are when the offer becomes concrete. It would be delightful to be in Israel again, and I could certainly use a year of concentrated work on Hebrew before I forget the language altogether.

There's so much to write about the Mar Saba manuscript – which I'm sending by surface mail – that I just despair of doing it justice. With it I'm sending a summary of my report on the parallelisms to Clement's style,[290] and a couple of other recent publications. I'm in the midst of a history of the collection, which involves a history of the monastery, and have discussions of the allegedly Markan material, and the significance for church history and for New Testament criticism, still to write. If I can do a miracle, all will be in the hands of a publisher by June.[291]

Meanwhile, I hope you'll send me any comments you may have, and I'd request you *not* to show the text around. Above all, I don't want any publication about it before the critical edition comes out, since once the flood starts I shall never be able to keep up with it, and I'd like to have the first edition at least, up to date.

Best wishes to both Fanya and yourself. I hear you're to be in England this spring. Is there any chance of your coming over? I wish there were; I should like very much to be able to talk with you about the problems those new texts raise.

As ever,

Morton Smith

---

and eventually to the USA, where he became Director of the Lown Instiue of Advanced Judaic Studies at Brandeis University. He edited *Biblical and Other Studies* (Cambridge, Mass., 1963) in which Smith published his 'Observations on *Hekhalot Rabbati*'.

290 Eventually, this study will become part of his *Clement of Alexandria and a Secret Gospel of Mark.*

291 It would take a further two years to finish the first draft of Clement.

69

Jerusalem
February 10, 1961

Dear Morton,

Please take my apologies for writing only a short letter. I am working under great pressure in order to finish at least the German manuscript of my book on the origin and the beginnings of the Kabbalah[292] before I leave for London – I have tentatively booked for April 3rd. Instead of translating my old little book which was much too short I have written a full length study and a completely new book. I should have supposed from the beginning that it would come to that. Now I must concentrate and use all my time for I cannot take my books and files with me. I will then read and edit my manuscript in London and I hope it will go to press in June and appear possibly at the end of the year. You will be greatly edified by much of what you are going to read there. The English version will be made, I hope, during the year.

I cannot, therefore, comment at length on your paper. I think you can publish it as it is and the discussion will certainly be helped by it. Only on p. 16 I should like you to state my point of view more precisely. My conclusion was of course that there was a pre-Christian synthesis, as you say, but this means with me the time before Christianity had become a distinct force in Jewish history which precluded Christian influence on Judaism. This is as true for the most part of the first century of the Christian era as for the first century B.C. Therefore, I would not write on line 5 from bottom "in the first century B.C." but "in the first century A.D.". This is the latest date and much of the common stock may be earlier.

I am sure Wirszubski will return to complete his work with me on the Hebrew text.

On p. 33 of my book, the word yantras is correct. Tantras are books, yantras are formulae and mental images. p. 64: I do not think there is a pun in the quotation. Your corrections on p. 103 do not appeal to me.

---

[292] G. G. Scholem, *Ursprung und Anfänge der Kabbala* (Berlin, 1962).

I had a most enthusiastic letter from Nock. I understand that he would be very glad to publish a review article on the new vistas opened up by my book, for the Harvard Theological Review, if it were offered to him.[293] You are obviously the one man besides Lieberman who could do it. Don't you think it would be a good idea? I am of course, interested in having the book brought to the knowledge of wider circles interested in the study of Gnosticism.

My cordial congratulations for your Mar Saba findings and discoveries. Please, do not forget to send me all you publish about these matters. I do not expect to come over to [the] U.S.A. this year.

If you get a Fulbright commission, will you come to us as a visiting professor for History of Religion? I heard that the Committee in Israel sat yesterday but do not know what they decided or recommended.

With cordial greeting from both of us,

As ever,

70

Department of History
Columbia University
N.Y. 27, N.Y., USA
February 15, 1961

Dear Gershom,

Thank you for your letter. I am very glad my paper pleased you, and am making the correction you print out. I'm afraid I can't do a review article for Nock since I'm terribly pressed for time and I've already said what I had to say in this article which will be published by Brandeis[294] (and Nock would not be happy to have me duplicate in *Harvard Theological Review* what I said elsewhere). However, I have

---

[293] No such review was published by the *Harvard Theological Review*.
[294] *I.e.*, Brandeis University.

asked Lieberman to send a copy of *Jewish Gnosticism* to *Journal of Biblical Literature* for review,[295] and have written Enslin,[296] asking that it be sent me when it comes in. I can say in a review what I have said in the Brandeis article and more – and a review in *Journal of Biblical Literature* will reach a considerably wider circle of readers than would an article in *Harvard Theological Review*.

As I wrote last time, if I get a Fulbright appointment I shall be delighted to come out as Professor of the History of Religion; the only question is one of timing. Timing is really getting to be difficult: I'm going quietly frantic and I gather from your reply that you will not only pardon my consequent brevity, but also approve it.

Regards to Fanya and best wishes,

As ever,

Morton Smith

71

297

Dear Morton,

I am writing on the eve of my departure for London (Warburg Institute, Woburn Square, London W.C. 1 – until August 1st!) to thank you for the three reprints especially the two on Clement's letter on the Carpocratians.[298] I received them only five days ago, they have impressed me very much. I congratulate you most cordially on this

---

[295] See: M. Smith [rev.], 'G. Scholem, *Jewish Gnosticism, Merkabah Mysticism and Talmudic Tradition*' *Journal of Biblical Literature* 80 (1961), 190–191.

[296] Morton Scott Enslin (1897–1980). Biblical scholar, President of the Society of Biblical Literature (in 1945) and, since 1952, President of the American Theological Society. Author of *The Prophet from Nazareth* (New York, 1961).

[297] The letter is postmarked March 31, 1961.

[298] *I.e.* the two reports mentioned in the Introduction: the text of his talk at the Society of Biblical Literature and Smith's summary (A.P.).

discovery. Your argument seems very strong indeed, and I am curious to see what valid objections Nock and Völker[299] have to make. I look forward to the book which must surely arouse greater interest. What an unexpected testimony!!

I have finished the German version of *Reshit HaKabbalah*[300] – more than twice the text!! It will be quite an interesting book too.

In [a] hurry – yours cordially,

Gershom

72

Dept. of History
Columbia University
N.Y. 27, N.Y., USA
June 13, 1961

Dear Gershom,

This is merely a note of greeting. I have been busy all spring with trivial tasks, but seem now about to finish them off and hope to be at work on the manuscript by the end of next week. New York is so hot that electric cables have been burning out right and left. We had three failures this afternoon, just as everyone was going home, which left half the city (42nd–80th Sts.) without electricity. Even for traffic lights and subways (to say nothing of air – conditioning and refrigeration and house lights). You can imagine the mess. Tomorrow is to be better. I believe it's a communist plot. (Have you heard, by the way, what the Cubans are calling the White House? The Casa Bu-bu).

Though I haven't been able to work on the letter, I've been thinking a good deal about it, and about the possibility that Jesus may actually

---

299 Walther Völker (1896–1988). Professor of Church History at the University of Tübingen. Author, inter alia, of *Der wahre Gnostiker nach Clemens Alexandrinus* (Berlin, 1952).

300 In Hebrew characters.

have taught a libertine gospel – Libertinism is so widespread in the New Testament, almost every book combats it, it cannot all derive from Paul, there are a lot of libertine sayings in Jesus' mouth (The Law and the Prophets were until John, since then!).[301]

Do you think the body and blood eaten and drunk can be a ritual expression of libertinism? (Eating a human sacrifice was a way of binding conspirators together, Apollonius of Tyana[302] was charged with it). I talked about it with Bickerman the other day and he was rather enthusiastic, saying this background would explain the reaction to the crucifixion, which I think it would. Any comments you may make on *Mitzvah habaa b'avera*[303] in or before the Tannaïtic period will be most welcome.

Best wishes both for yourself and for Fanya.

As ever,

Morton Smith

73

London
July 3, 1961

Dear Morton,

Since you wrote your last letter in the fiendish heat of the great desert of New York I have been through a heat wave too but have

---

[301] *Sic*! Smith's theory claiming that Jesus led a libertine sect that may have included homoerotic practices between Jesus and his disciples will be expounded in his *Clement of Alexandria and a Secret Gospel of Mark* (Cambridge, Mass., 1973) and his *Jesus the Magician* (San Fransisco, 1978).

[302] First century C.E. miracle worker and neo-Pythagorean teacher. In his *Life of Apollonius of Tyana*, the third century author Philostratus sought to refute the reputation of magician attributed to Apolonius and emphasizes his opposition to blood-sacrifices.

[303] In Hebrew characters: a *Mitzva* coming in transgression. Talmudic concept referring to the fulfilment of a commandment during or by means of a transgression.

managed to survive by thinking of the finest things I could imagine. If this goes on in your vacation time, how will you ever be able to finish your paper for which we all are waiting so eagerly. About libertinism in the New Testament I do not feel competent to comment although there may be something in what you say regarding libertine sayings put in Jesus' mouth.

But I admit to an amount of skepticism regarding the hypothesis about the body and blood formula as a ritual expression of libertinism, Bickerman's enthusiasm notwithstanding.

My Shiur Qoma paper from the *Eranos Jahrbuch*[304] has not yet appeared but you shall certainly have it as soon as I get my offprints. A little later there will be my criticism of Buber's Hasidic writings[305] in one of the next numbers of *Commentary* which will no doubt attract your sympathetic attention. Since *Commentary* do[es] not give offprints I must ask you to look out for it in the September or October issue. It is something that was long overdue.

In August I proceed to Switzerland where I hope to meet my wife. In September we both will return for some weeks to London. The Warburg Institute is a paradisiacal place for work and I can only highly recommend it to you if you decide to take refuge in some European scholarly hideout.

Cordial greetings,

As ever, yours,

Gershom

---

[304] Scholem means "for the Eranos-Jharbuch." See G. G. Scholem, 'Die mystische Gestalt der Gottheit in Kabbala', *Eranos Jahrbuch* 29 (1960), 139–182.

[305] G. G. Scholem, 'Martin Buber's Hasidism: A Critique', *Commentary* 32 (1961), 305–316. See further Scholem's response to this article's critics: 'Buber and Hasidism', *Commentary* 33 (1962), 162–163.

74

The Hebrew University,
Jerusalem
Faculty of Humanities
March 25, 1962

Dear Professor Smith

I take the liberty of requesting your advice and assistance in the following matter. This University is considering the promotion of Dr. D. Flusser[306] to the rank of Associate Professor in Comparative Religion. It is our usual procedure in cases of appointment or promotion of senior members of the academic staff to ask also for expert opinion from abroad. I should therefore be grateful for your opinion on the suitability of Dr. Flusser for this promotion.

For your information we enclose Dr. Flusser's *curriculum vitae* and a list of his publications. The question we should particularly like to ask is whether on the basis of his scholarly work he would merit an appointment to a corresponding position, according to the standards prevailing in your university.

Senior teachers with tenure at this university fall into the following categories: Lecturer (roughly corresponding to a Lecturer in Great Britain), Associate Professor (roughly corresponding to an Associate Professor in the United States, or to a Reader in Great Britian), and Professor.

In evaluating the suitability of a candidate we take into account not only his work as a scholar but also such qualities as character, capacity for cooperation with colleagues, teaching ability and administrative efficiency. If you happen to know Dr. Flusser personally, we should appreciate your opinion on these points as well. If you wish to receive any of Dr. Flusser's publications, we shall be glad to forward them to you on request.

---

[306] David Flusser (Vienna, 1917–Jerusalem, 2000). Influential scholar of ancient Judaism and Christian origins at the Hebrew University.

We shall be greatly obliged for as full and detailed a reply as you may care to make. Your opinion will of course be treated as confidential.

Thanking you in advance for your courtesy and cooperation, I am,

Sincerely yours,

With the blessing of friendship,[307]

Gerschom Scholem
Chairman of the Ad Hoc Committee

75

April 24, 1962

Dear Professor Smith,

Thank you very much for your reply to my letter regarding Dr. Flusser. Your opinion will be of greatest value to the official bodies concerned.

Sincerely yours,

G. Scholem
Chairman of the Ad Hoc Committee

[Dear Morton – I hope you received the copy of my book *Ursprung der Kabbala* which was sent to you on my behalf from Berlin, in early April. It is a "vote of thanks" for your efforts on behalf of the Hebrew-English edition!]

[307] In Hebrew: *BeVirkat HaYedidut.*

76

Columbia University in the City of New York
Department of History
October 6, 1962

Dear Gershom,

Since you probably know more about magic than anybody else in the world, I have taken the liberty of giving your name as a reference to the Guggenheim and Bollingen Foundations, along with my application for funds to finance the project of which an account is herewith enclosed. I enclose also a list of publications and an account of my studies. The account does not say so, but I am now full Professor (of History); this appeared elsewhere on the applications, I mention it here since you may want to refer to me by title.[308]

I hope you think the project a good one. Nock and Bickerman, with whom I have discussed it, think it might yield quite valuable results. I hope for those, and I am sure it would enormously improve my knowledge of ancient history on the side of geographical and cultural background, so I shall be happy if it goes through.

The foundations will presumably write you directly; this letter is merely by way of warning and does not call for an answer.

I have been sick much of the summer (persistent bronchitis) and the edition of Clement on the Carpocratians creeps along by inches, but quite wonderful things keep turning up. I am really beginning to think Carpocrates and the sort of things he represented (and especially the ascent through the heavens) were far closer to Jesus than has ever been supposed. What's more, I have the evidence.[309]

[308] See Appendix A.

[309] The passage of the Secret Gospel of Mark refers to Jesus's mysterious teaching at night of a young man, whom he had previously raised from the dead. According to Smith, this nocturnal initiation shows Jesus' practice and teaching of 'Ascent to Heaven'. See for example, Smith's *Clement of Alexandria and a Secret Gospel of Mark*, 251–2 and his 'Ascent to the Heavens and the Beginning of Christianity', *Eranos Yearbook* 50 (1981), 403–89.

I wish you were here so that I could discuss it with you. You must persuade the Jewish Theological Seminary that it needs another set of lectures.

Regards to Fanya and best wishes,

Morton Smith

77

Jerusalem
October 25, 1962

Dear Morton,

I have just returned with Fania from Switzerland where I had to undergo an operation (extirpation of the gall bladder) because of recurring attacks which troubled me a lot during the last year. This took the larger part of our leave and I had to cancel my other plans for Europe.

Now I have fully recovered and am going to start working again. I found your letter of October 6th, but not the list of your publications and an account of your project and studies which you wrote you would enclose. But this is not necessary for I have also received a letter from the Guggenheim-Foundation which contains a description of your project.[310]

You can be sure that I shall do everything in my power to support you and your project. I hope you get the funds and whatever will be the outcome of the studies and research, will be the highest interest to me. You can easily imagine that I am looking forward to your book on the Carpocratians and the discussions on the various scholars which will certainly follow it.

I note with greatest satisfaction that you have finally got what was due to you, namely a full professorship. If my congratulations should

[310] See Appendix A.

be delayed, they are coming all the more from the heart. By the way, I saw Nock in Locarno, where we met by chance. We had a very rambunctious and friendly conversation. The whole Hotel was shocked by the voice of his laughter.

I do not think there is much hope for another visit of ours to [the] U.S.A. before 1965. That year may provide a possible opportunity.

I hope you are again in good health. Please let us hear from you if you get the grant. In the meanwhile, cordial regards from Fanya and me,

ever

Yours

Gershom Scholem

78

Columbia College
Columbia University
New York 27. N.Y.
Department of History
October 31, 1962

Dear Gershom,

Thank you very much for your letter and for your kindness in recommending my project.[311] As you know, your recommendation, particularly to the Bollingen Foundation, will probably count for more than any one else's, so I am particularly grateful for it – and I am also very happy that you approve my work, and I hope to deserve your approval.

I trust you are, as you say, fully recovered from your operation. This summer I had a long lesson in the necessity of taking things easy after sickness.

[311] See Appendix B.

Surly out of vanity, I enclose the forgotten bibliography.

As you probably know, Baron[312] is retiring. We – i.e. he – hoped that Ankori[313] would succeed him (and I shared the hope, for I liked Ankori personally very much, though I think he never forgave me for writing a review which declared his book a thorough work of scholarship and a bore).[314] At all events, Ankori has now decided to stay in Israel, so we must look for someone else. If Baron has another candidate on whom his heart is set, then *Roma locuta est, causa finita est.*[315] If not, I wonder whether Tishby would consider the place? The chair is a very comfortable and influential one, with funds for a research assistant etc. and I think the department would prefer a man in mediaeval Jewish history with interests especially in the Near East or Spain and South France. So Tishby would seem a very strong candidate if, as I seem to remember, he speaks English well, and if he would be willing to come.

Do remember me to the Sambuskys if you see them.

With best wishes for yourself and Fanya

As ever

Morton Smith[316]

---

[312] Salo Wittmayer Baron (Tarnov, Galicia, 1895–New York, 1989). Eminent Jewish historian. He taught for more than thirty years (1930–63) at Columbia University, where he held the first Professorship of Jewish history at any secular Western University. Author of *Social and Religious History of the Jews*, 27 vols. (New York, 2nd ed. 1957–83).

[313] Zvi Ankori (b. 1920). Studied at the Hebrew University and at Columbia University, where he became the Director of the Center for Israel and Jewish Studies and held the Chair of Jewish History, and taught at Tel Aviv University. Author of *Karaites in Byzantium* (Columbia Studies in the Social Sciences 597; New York, 1959).

[314] M. Smith [rev.], 'Z. Ankori, *Karaites in Byzantium, The Formative Years, 970–1100*' *Greek Orthodox Theological Review* (1960), 87 f.

[315] 'Rome has spoken, the case is closed'. Famous saying, based upon a sentence of Augustine (Sermon 131.10).

[316] In Hebrew characters.

79

Jerusalem
November 13, 1962

Dear Morton,

I have your letter of October 31st. My answers, to both [the] Bollingen and Guggenheim Foundations, are already off. I hope you will get what is due to you. I also received the bibliography from which I quite belatedly learn a great deal about your published work.

I am sorry to hear that you too have been sick this summer. I hope everything has turned out well, as it did for me.

As to your question regarding Tishby's possible candidature for Columbia, I have talked to him. There is not the slightest chance, that he would be willing to accept such an appointment and leave Jerusalem for good. By the way, he has had a serious heart attack this summer and has to take things very easy. He will not lecture during the first term. Being a very lively person, and of sanguine character, he is a bad patient. He should not speak or worry, but he does speak and worry. So we have our troubles too.

My private opinion is that Duker[317] in Chicago would be the best candidate for Baron's chair and I do not understand what Baron has against him and why he did not put him forward, especially after Ankori doesn't want to have it. For some reason or other, he has not got a fair deal in the States. I don't know how he is as a teacher, but I have high regard for his abilities in historical research. Of course he is a specialist for Eastern Europe and not for Medieval Jewish History.

With kind regards from regards from both of us,

As ever yours,

Gershom Scholem

---

[317] Abraham Gordon Duker (Poland, 1907–1974). Social historian of the Jews at Yeshiva University (New York). Author of *Jewish in the Post-War World* (New York, 1945).

80

Dept. of History
Columbia University
New York 27, N.Y., U.S.A.
November 17, 1962

Dear Gershom,

Thank you very much for your letter of the thirteenth, of which this hasty note is a mere acknowledgment. I am disappointed, but not surprised, to learn of Tishby's decision. *A good sign is it for the land of Israel*[318] that it creates such loyalty in such men. I am much sorrier to learn of Tishby's illness, and hope indeed that he will learn to take the precautions necessary. Do give him my good wishes and tell him I am slowly working my way through *Mishnat HaZohar II*,[319] to my appropriately unspeakable edification – As for the job, we shall probably try once again to steal Gershon Cohen[320] from Jewish Theological Seminary; say a Kabbalistic prayer for our success, we'll need it.

Best wishes for yourself and Fanya, and sincere thanks for your letters on my behalf.

As ever,

Morton Smith

---

[318] In Hebrew: *Siman Tov lah leEretz Ysrael*. Expression from the *Babylonian Talmud*, *Shabbat* 89b.

[319] I. Tishby, *The Wisdom of the Zohar: An Anthology of Texts* (trans. D. Goldstein, Oxford, 1989).

[320] Gerson David Cohen (1924–1991). Jewish historian and Chancellor of the Jewish Theological Seminary of America. Author of *Studies in the Variety of Rabbinic Cultures* (New York, 1991).

81

March 3, 1963

Dear Morton,

In your manuscript,[321] page 369, you mention a review of *Nock* of my *Jewish Gnosticism* – of which I have never heard or seen anything. Can you look up in your papers and give me the reference as to where I could find this? Is it in the *Bulletin of the Harvard Divinity School*?[322] This would be bad as no copy of this publication is available here!

Cordially yours,

Gershom

82

Chicago House
Luxor Egypt.
January 14, 1964

Prof. Gershom Scholem
28 Abarbanel Road
Jerusalem, Israel

Dear Gershom,

I reached Haifa, Cyprus, Beirut, Alexandria, Cairo and Luxor[323] without any untoward incidents, and have been soaking up sunshine here

---

[321] Scholem may refer to the manuscript of *Clement of Alexandria and a Secret Gospel of Mark*, which Smith had sent him (see Letter 68). A.P. thinks he actually is referring to a draft of a chapter for *Clement of Alexandria* that Smith had asked Scholem to read.

[322] A. D. Nock [rev.], 'G. G. Scholem, *Jewish Gnosticism*', *Harvard Divinity Bulletin* 26/3 (1962), 27.

[323] During his sabbatical study supported by his Guggenheim award (A.P.).

at Luxor for the past two weeks, trying to get rid of a cold I picked up in route and to finish my long overdue book on religious parties in pre-Maccabean Palestine.[324] Now I have made such a progress that I am beginning to excavate my mail in the evenings and have come to your note requesting the reference to Nock's review of *Jewish Gnosticism* it is in *Harvard Divinity School Bulletin*, April, 1962, p. 27. I am sending this to Helmut Köster[325] at Harvard with a note requesting that he forward it to you and if possible send either a copy of that issue of the Bulletin or a xeroxed copy of the page(s) containing the review. I hope all will reach you safely. I could write a book on my travels – particularly my impressions of Egypt – and maybe I shall, someday, but just now I'm falling asleep.

Thanks for a delightful visit,

Regards to Fanya and best wishes to you both,

As ever,

Morton Smith[326]

---

[324] M. Smith, *Palestinian Parties and Politics that Shaped the Old Testament* (New York, 1971).

[325] Helmut Köster (b. Germany, 1926). Winn Research Professor of Ecclesiastical History and John H. Morison Research Professor of Divinity at Harvard Divinity School, where he has taught since 1963. Author, *inter alia*, of *Ancient Christian Gospels: Their History and Development* (London, Philadelphia, 1990).

[326] In Hebrew characters.

83

Columbia University in the City of New York
Department of History
Hamilton Hall
New York, N.Y. 10027
May 22, 1967

Dear Gershom,

Thank you for your note, I'm terribly sorry to hear that Fanya must have an operation, and do hope that all will go well. She knows, of course, how fond I am of her – I wish affection were some practical help in such matters. Do let me have her address in Zürich.

I hope, too, that the Arabs won't interfere with your plans. What makes me most pessimistic about the present crisis is, that I think it indicates the failure of Nasser's efforts to get Egypt on the road to a solution of its internal problems.[327] Russia of course is egging him on,[328] especially in the hope of distracting us from Vietnam, but also in the hope of increasing generally our Afro-Asian difficulties. But I don't think he'd be willing to be egged if he weren't at the end of his resources for keeping his people quiet by other means, and that's a real disaster, since, bad as Nasser is, the imaginable alternatives for Egypt are mostly worse. Needless to say, I have no fears for Israel – save that you may punch so hard you give yourselves a black eye. From what I've seen of the Syrian and Egyptian troops I don't think they could even successfully run away from you.

I'm fine, and Carpocrates is being mutilated by the stylist and should be in proof this fall.

Best wishes to you both,

Morton

---

[327] By the time of this letter the region was the theatre of heavy tensions between the Arab countries and Israel. The 22nd of May, the day of this letter, President Nasser closed the Straits of Tiran to Israeli shipping. Less than one month later, on June 5th, the Six Days War broke out.

[328] In April 1967, Russia encouraged the Egyptians to send their troops to the Israeli border.

84

Columbia University in the City of New York
Department of History
Hamilton Hall
New York, N.Y. 10027
August 15, 1967

Dear Gershom,

Many thanks for your article on the myth of punishment[329] – a wonder of concentration. I was particularly struck by your remark that there is no *Middat HaAhava*[330] comparable to those of *HaDin*[331] and *HaRachamim.*[332] Do you think this may be due to the fact that all such passages are developments of a legal metaphor, and in law the admissible attributes of a judge – or an authority before whom are offender is brought for punishment are *Din* and *Rachamim? Ahava*, is there in rabbinic thought certainly, but it figures in a different cycle of stories where there was no such a *literary* or – better – *dramatic* reason for personification.

You were magnificent in the discussion. The squelches administered to Castelli[333] and Brun,[334] in particular, made me shriek with joy. Why is it that the study of religion attracts so many nitwits? *Per contra*, I was much impressed by Kerényi's remarks,[335] which I thought showed him

[329] G. G. Scholem, 'Quelques remarques sur le mythe de la peine dans le judaïsme,' in E. Castelli, ed., *Il mito della pena* (*Archivio di Filosofia*, 1967), 135–164.

[330] In Hebrew characters: Measure (i.e. divine attribute in Rabbinic Theology) of Love.

[331] In Hebrew characters: Measure of Justice; or the concept of God's power who is judge and punisher (G. G. Scholem, 'Quelques remarques sur le mythe de la peine dans le judaïsme', 141).

[332] In Hebrew characters: Measure of Compassion; or of grace and mercy. Scholem argues that in Rabbinic Judaism the importance of the Love of God is secondary to mercy and grace (*rachamim* and *hesed*), *op. cit.* 142.

[333] Enrico Castelli (1900–1977). Director of the *Istituto di Studi Filosofici* at La Sapienza University, Rome.

[334] Jean Brun (1919–1994). French Philosopher who taught at the University of Dijon. Author of *Héraclite ou le philosophe de l'éternel retour* (Philosophes de tout temps 27; Paris, 1965).

[335] Karl Kerényi (1897–1973). Hungarian Classicist and Historian of Greek Religion. A friend and collaborator of Carl Jung, he published together with him *Essays on the Science of Mythology: the Myths of the Divine Child and the Divine Maiden* (Bollingen Series

at his best (and there are very few writers who seem to me to have so wide range of variation).

I hope Fanya got to her operation on time and without difficulty, underwent it successfully, and is now enjoying a happy and complete convalescence. Do give her my regards and best wishes.

With the same for you,

As ever,

Morton

P.S. if you have my letter which I mailed just before the war, please note the prediction. If I ever come up for canonization I can use that as one of my miracles. MS.

85

Jerusalem
June 30, 1968

Dear Morton,

I owe you a great debt of gratitude for your contribution to the volume in my honor.[336] It has taken some time but I finally received a copy of the book on my return from a little trip abroad. You know how much I am looking forward to your book on the letter attributed

22; Princeton, 1949). His major works are essays on archetypes of Greek mythology, such as *Prometheus, Archetypal Image of Human Existence* (Bollingen Series 65; trans. R. Manheim, Princeton, 1963).

[336] M. Smith, 'The Reason for the Persecution of Paul and the Obscurity of Acts' in E. E. Urbach, R. J. Zwi Werblowsky, Ch. Wirszubski (eds.), *Studies in Mysticism and Religion Presented to Gershom G. Scholem on his Seventieth Birthday by Pupils, Colleagues and Friends* (Jerusalem, 1967).

to Clement[337] into the ambiance of which your article belongs, which of course whetted my appetite even more. I hope it will not take too long to appear. May I, in the meantime, ask you if you have still a reprint of the article on the variety of messianic figures[338] which you quote on page 262, and which I have never seen.

Is there a chance or our meeting in some foreseeable future? It would give me great pleasure. By the way, I saw your letter to Werblowsky[339] about the study conference in Jerusalem and your refusal to attend. It distressed me not a little and I would have liked very much to be able to talk about this matter with you. The situation between the leading spirits on both sides of the International Association for the History of Religions[340] seems to me to be a very unhappy one, since it became clear at the Claremont Congress three years ago, that there was indeed a considerable difference of opinion about the aims and means of this organization, but – leaving aside a clash of rather different personalities – I would venture to think that you would have been very much on the side of the so called Europeans in their view of what should constitute an organization like this. At any rate, let me say that I deeply deplore that you did not accept our invitation.

Fania and I will be in Europe during August and September, mainly in Switzerland. Are you by any chance in Europe too? Between August

[337] Towards the end of the article Smith contributed to the volume in honor of Scholem he mentions his forthcoming edition of a letter attributed to Clement of Alexandria.

[338] M. Smith, 'What is Implied by the Variety of Messianic Figures', *Journal of Biblical Literature* 78 (1959), 66–72.

[339] R. J. Zwi Werblowsky (born Frankfurt am Main, 1924). Founder of the Department of Comparative Religion at Hebrew University and a versatile scholar in the field. He translated into English Scholem's *Sabbatai Sevi: The Mystical Messiah*, 1626–1676 (Princeton, 1975).

[340] The International Association for the History of Religions is a worldwide body of national and regional associations for the academic study of religion. It was founded in 1950 and regularly holds an international conference every five years. In 1965 the international conference was held in Claremont, California and among its topics were 'the impact of modern culture on traditional religions', and 'the role of historical scholarship in changing the relations among religions'. It seems that these contemporary questions aroused fierce debate.

The Jerusalem conference Scholem refers to was a regional conference held in July, 1968 on the topic of 'types of redemption'.

17 and 31 we will be at the Hotel Tamaro in Ascona, where I am making a speech at the Eranos Meeting.[341]

With all cordial regards from both of us,

As always yours

86

Columbia University in the City of New York
Department of History
Fayerweather Hall
New York, N.Y. 10027
July 5, 1968

Dear Gershom,

Thank you for your letter. As you know, it is rather I than you who am honored by the including of my article in your Featschrift, but I trust you will take it at least as an expression of intention – if I *could* do you honor I should gladly have done so.

I enclose the offprint you requested – my last of that article.

The book on Mark[342] goes forward, at glacial speed. But I shall finish revising the stylist's revision this summer (unless something quite unforeseen happens) so it should go off to the press by fall.

I am sorry my letter to Werblowsky distressed you. I hope it made clear, at all events, that my only reasons for regretting my necessary refusal were the facts that the meeting was being held in Israel and that you and he were its sponsors. I wish you had somebody better

---

[341] G. G. Scholem, 'Die Krise der Tradition im jüdischen Messianismus', *Eranos Jahrbuch* 37 (1968), 9–44.

[342] Smith means his *Clement of Alexandria and a Secret Gospel of Mark* (A.P.).

than Bleeker[343] to sponsor and I had money and time to travel. With the latter, I could at least get to see you in Ancona,[344] but as things are I must stay here and write and write and write.

At all events I console myself with the hope that you and Fania will soon be here again and that, when you are, I shall see more of you than before. Do give Fania my regards and my thanks for her invaluable bibliography. I hope she is now quite recovered from her operation and much the better for it.

With best wishes to you both,

As ever,

Morton Smith[345]

87

Columbia University in the City of New York
Department of History
Hamilton Hall
New York, N.Y. 10027
April 18, 1969

Dear Geshom,

Thanks for your letter, I was very glad to hear from you. The man who wrote you about a copy of my translation of *Hekhalot Rabbati* is

343 Claas Youko Bleeker (1898–1983). Dutch Egyptologist and historian of religions. Author *Hathor and Thoth: Two Key Figures of the Ancient Egyptian Religion* (Studies in the History of Religions 26; Leiden, 1976).

344 City of the Adriatic Cost of Italy. Smith is confusing Ancona with Ascona in Switzerland, where the Eranos meetings took place.

345 In Hebrew characters.

Dr. J. Massingberd Ford[346]
University of Notre Dame
Dept. of Theology
Notre Dame, Indiana, U.S.A.

Carpocrates is on the shelf for the moment, but I hope to have the final revision (i.e. my revision of the Press' revision) back to the Press before fall and they will start setting at once.

I might well go to Brown, if they asked me. Columbia is going to be under very strong pressure from Harlem,[347] and it's anybody's guess how the racial relations in America are going to go. The Communists (largely Jewish, I'm sorry to say) and their friends are doing their best to whip up a civil war, and a number of the young negroes are lending themselves to the cause – either from stupidity and ambition or from a deeper self-destructive drive. With such storm clouds on the horizon a quiet port like Providence (negro population negligible) has strong attractions. This is the time for a little practical Kabbalah, if you can spare any.

Best wishes, for both you and Fanya,

As ever,

Morton

---

[346] Josephine Massingberd (Massyngberde) Ford. Professor of New Testament at the University of Notre Dame. Author of *The Pentecostal Experience. A New Direction for Catholics* (New York, 1970).

[347] In April 1968, Columbia University was the theatre of an uprising conducted by students members of the Columbia University Students for a Democratic Society as well as other leftist groups and the Black Panthers. They protested against the construction of a gymnasium in Harlem (perceived as an aggression against the residents) and against the participation of the University in military research. During the protest, the Dean's office was taken over.

88

Columbia University in the City of New York
Department of History
Fayerweather Hall
New York, N.Y. 10027
June 26, 1969

Dear Geshom,

Thank you very much for your letter. I wish I could come to the Congress,[348] but unfortunately it falls at a time when I must be here teaching summer school – a non-luxury I cannot afford to forego. Fortunately, you are as mobile as I am fixed, so I look forward to seeing you – and, I hope, Fanya – in New York this winter, or next, at the latest.

Perhaps by then my article will have generated some retorts worth discussing.[349] To date I've heard only mutterings. If you hear any good criticisms – particularly of the sort which would make specific correction possible – please let me know.

With best wishes for both you and Fanya,

As ever,

Morton

[348] The Fifth World Congress of Jewish Studies, held in Jerusalem on August 4–12, 1969.

[349] M. Smith, 'The Present State of Old Testament Studies', *Journal of Biblical Literature* 88 (1969), 19–35. In this article Smith attacks a tendency in Old Testament scholarship which he calls 'pseudorthodoxy', that is, apologetic and anachronistic scholarship recruited for the defense of certain religious beliefs about the Bible.

89

Jerusalem
July 9, 1969

Dear Morton,

What a pity that you cannot come to the Congress in Jerusalem where no doubt you could have taken up the cudgels in discussing your article with those in Israel against whom your vigorous attack is directed. I find it difficult to believe that people like Malamat[350] or Tadmor[351] should not be able to make a case for using the materials of the second millennium B.C. for illuminating the Bible and even more so the history of Canaan in this period. Such a discussion should be invaluable. Lacking that, I look very much forward to see what kind of replies will be made to your article. For myself, as an historian of religion, I would say that there exists a level on which, seen from the development of later Judaism, one can indeed speak of a biblical theology without being "pseudorthodox". This, of course, refers to the moment, when some of all Books of the Bible were seen as documents of revelation, and therefore could be seen as referring to a common level, as they in fact were in the literature of the Aggada[352] and no less so in the halakhic midrash.[353]

Your point about myth in the Old Testament also needs further clarification, in my opinion. Of course, there are myths, but there is also the question of a struggle between the religion proclaimed in the various documents and the myth. I find it difficult to believe that there is no tension.

---

[350] Abraham Malamat (born Vienna, 1922). Historian of ancient Israel. Author of *Sources for the History of Israel and its Land in the Age of the Bible: the Second Millennium B.C.E.* (Jerusalem, 1964) (in Hebrew), attacked by Smith in his 'The Present State of Old Testament Studies'.

[351] Hayim Tadmor (Harbin, China, 1923–Jerusalem, 2005). Historian of the Ancient Near East and founder of the Department of Assyriology at the Hebrew University.

[352] Aramaic for: 'tales', 'lore'. Rabbinical exegetical teachings of a non-legal (*halakhic*) charater, containing folklore, witticism, mythical stories, etc.

[353] In Rabbinic literature, *Halakhic Midrash* designate an exegetical method of the Bible (*midrash*) having a legal (*halakhic*) character.

I am sorry never to have seen your article on the Common Theology of the Ancient Near East.[354] I must look it up in the library.

There is one point which I fail to understand in your judgments, and this is how, from your point of view, you could say anything good about the life work of Kaufmann.[355] In the context of your article, this seems paradoxical. Perhaps you could enlarge on this if you reprint the paper.

With cordial greetings from Fania and from me,

90

Columbia University in the City of New York
Department of History
Fayerweather Hall
New York, N.Y. 10027
July 15, 1969

Dear Gershom,

Your letter resembles the Epistle to the Hebrews in at least one respect – it leaves me with a lively realization of things to be expected. I didn't say one couldn't speak of biblical theology without being pseudorthodox; I said I thought it *unspeakable*, which I do in two senses (1) the original theology is sometimes atrocious, e.g. Deuteronomy 7 (considered as a revelation of the will of the deity), (2) the bulk of the modern products which go under the name is always atrocious. Given these two subjects for discussion, I hope you'll agree with me that *unspeakable* is the *mot juste*.

---

[354] M. Smith, 'The Common Theology of the Ancient Near East', *Journal of Biblical Literature* 71 (1952), 135–147.

[355] Yehezkel Kaufmann (Podolia, Ukraine, 1889–Jerusalem, 1963). Biblical scholar. Author of the eight-volume work, *The Religion of Israel: From its Beginnings to the Babylonian Exile* (abridged and trans. By M. Greenberg; Chicago, 1960). Kaufmann's work is characterized by the revision of some common scholarly assumptions, such as the gradual development of the monotheistic idea, and the later dating of the Biblical priestly source.

I didn't say there wasn't a strong anti-mythical element in the Old Testament. Of course there is. One of the places in which the Old Testament comes closest to Greek literature is its remarkable rationalism (remarkable by contrast with what the Babylonians and Egyptians were doing at the same time) and the similarities in content and coincidences in date are sometimes astounding (e.g. the attacks on the idolatry by Xenophanes[356] and Second Isaiah).[357] All I said was that there *are* myths in it, too.

As to Kaufmann, of course he's a relentless pleader for absurdities and he must have been Hell to live with, but he had a wonderful, paranoid eye for details and a genius for asking awkward questions. I've learned a great deal from him, though – or perhaps, because – he usually infuriates me.

I'm so glad you thought the paper worth discussing, and so sorry I can't get to Jerusalem to talk with you. *Inshalla*, next year.

Best wishes,

Morton

---

[356] Xenophanes of Colophon (b. *circ.* 570 B.C.E.) was the first Greek philosopher to condemn the anthropomorphism of the Greek gods, as it is found in Homer and Hesiod.

[357] II Isaiah, or Deutero-Isaiah is the name attributed by scholars to the author of the chapter 40–55 of the biblical book of Isaiah. Scholars believed that it was not written by the prophet Isaiah of Jerusalem but by an anonymous prophet of the Babylonian exile, in the six century B.C.E. The repetitively condemning of idolatry appears clearly in the text.

91

Jerusalem
June 5, 1972

Dear Morton,

I have read with greatest interest the review of the Cambridge History of the Bible,[358] which you kindly sent to me. I enjoyed the frank and very relevant criticism you wrote on the first volume. It made me regret that I have seen so little of your publications in the last few years. I heard from Bill Braude that your magnum opus on Carpocrates is going to appear very shortly. This will be a great occasion for rejoicing. I imagine that the Greek linguists and specialists in patrology will have to take up the cudgels if they want to disagree with the results you brought before us in your first short communication. This one I preserved carefully waiting for the full discussion in your book.

I was much less impressed by Amos Funkenstein,[359] whose pages give evidence of second-hand scholarship which makes me distrust the man. What kind of Jewish scholar is this who can confuse the Ramban[360] with the Rambam[361] and speak about Nachmanides' influence on Christian exegesis and his impact on Meister Eckhart![362]

I asked the Braudes to convey our cordial regards to you. They said they were going to meet you in London. In any case, I hope these lines will reach you in New York.

---

[358] M. Smith [rev.], 'The Cambridge History of the Bible, I: From the Beginnings to Jerome', *American Historical Review* 77 (1972), 94–100.

[359] Amos Funkenstein (1937–1995). Israeli istorian, who taught mainly at the University of California, Berkeley. He reviewed the second volume of *The Cambridge History of the Bible* in the *American Historical Review* 77 (1972), 100–106. Funkenstein subsequently published on Scholem's work: 'Gershom Scholem: Kairos und Charisma', *History and Memory* 4 (1992), 39–52.

[360] Moses, son of Nachman (Ramban, or Nachmanides) (Gerona, 1194–Palestine, 1270). Influential halachist, kabbalist, philosopher and Biblical commentator.

[361] Moses, son of Maimon (Rambam, or Maimonides) (Cordova, 1135–Fostat, Egypt, 1204). Leading halachist, philosopher and physician.

[362] Meister Eckhart von Hochheim (1260–1328). German mystic, theologian and philosopher, influenced by Maimonides.

Please tell me whether you have received from Schocken my book *The Messianic Idea in Judaism.*[363] If not, I will send you a copy. I would like it to be in your hands.

Kindest regards from Fania and myself,

As ever yours,

92

Columbia University in the City of New York
Department of History
Fayerweather Hall
New York, N.Y. 10027
July 4, 1972

Dear Gershom,

Thank you very much for your letter; I am delighted that you liked my review of the Cambridge History of the Bible, and I should be very happy to have a copy of your *Messianic Idea in Judaism*, which Schocken has not sent me.

Bill Braude and I did not make connections in London. My hotel was a cheap one and they economized by using for staff a lot of foreigners who could scarcely speak English. So when Bill tried to reach me he was told they had no one by my name! I never realized *Smith* was so difficult to recognize.

During my stay in London I wrote detailed descriptions (with transcriptions of inscriptions, and a good many drawings of details) of some 330 magical gems of the British Museum collection; I also photographed some 400.[364] During the coming winter I shall try to

[363] G. G. Scholem, *The Messianic Idea in Judaism and Other Essays on Jewish Spirituality* (New York, 1972).

[364] As he explained in his Research Project (See: Appendix A) Smith intended to describe the archeological material available for a history of Greco-Roman magic. This plan to write a catalogue of the magical gems of the British Museum never came to

condense my descriptions, attach the photographs, and so make a first draft of the first half of the catalogue (there are about 550 gems in all) which I can circulate to you, Barb,[365] Seyrig,[366] and a few other people to comments and corrections.

The book on the Carpocratians, Clement of Alexandria and the Secret Gospel, is now in page proof, and the first boxes of index cards are piled on my desk. So is too much other work, to which I now must turn.

Regards to Fanya, and best wishes to you both.

Morton Smith[367]

93

Columbia University in the City of New York
Department of History
Fayerweather Hall
New York, N.Y. 10027
August 24, 1972

Dear Gershom,

Thank you very much indeed for having me sent a copy of your *Messianic Idea in Judaism*. I've been reading it a chapter at a time for the past month and have enjoyed it immensely – it brings back my days in Jerusalem and has made me quite nostalgic. With a number of the

---

an end, but several articles on the subject were written such as 'Old Testament Motifs in the Iconography of the British Museum's Magical Gems' in L. Casson and M. Price (eds.), *Coins, Culture and History in the Ancient World* (Detroit, 1981), 187–194; 'Relation between Magical papyri and Magical Gems', *Actes du XVè congrès international de Papyrologie, IIIè partie* (Papyrologica Bruxellensia 18; Brussels, 1979), 129–136.

365 Alfons A. Barb (born 1901). German philologist, who specialized in the field of ancient magic. Author of: 'Abraxas Studien', *Latomus* 28 (1957), 67–86.

366 Henri Seyrig (1895–1973). French Archaeologist, Historian of Antiquity and numismatist. Directeur des antiquités de Syrie et du Liban and Director of the Archeological Institute in Beyrouth. Author of *Antiquités syriennes*, 6 vols. (Paris, 1934–66).

367 In Hebrew characters.

essays, of course, I was already familiar, but it was good to read them again and see them in the context of the others and of the theme. The most interesting thing, in this respect, was the disappearance of the theme with the disappearance of Sabbatianism – neither Martin Buber nor the Golem of Rehovot[368] will pass muster as a messianic figure. I should be interested to see a chapter on "Messianic Thought in Contemporary Judaism," but I fear it would have the interest of a chapter on the snakes of Ireland.

About the first chapters – the only ones I can criticize – I have some questions. I think you were misled by modern Christian propaganda, especially German Lutheran, into making Christianity a great deal more spiritual than it really was (with p. 1. cp. p. 39 – so the early Kabbalists were Christian? Reuchlin would have been happy).[369] The Messianic kingdom of Christianity was just as solid and carnal as Judaism's.

pp. 10 14 8c[370] (38)] – There are a few texts in which redemption comes about as a result of historical progress: the Maccabean's success is treated in that way in Enoch 90.13 ff. and 91.12 f. and I think there is something of the same idea at the beginning of the Damascus Document[371] and perhaps in the notion that the end would come if all Israel would repent – or become wholly evil. On p. 18 is there a contradiction between the statements that history ends with the destruction of ben Joseph and that ben David defeats the antichrist?[372]

---

368 One of the chapters in Scholem's *Messianic Ideas* is the transcription of a speech given by Scholem in the Weizmann Institute of Science of Rehovot (Israel) in June 1965, at the occasion of the Institute's new computer, named 'Golem 1', as suggested by Scholem to its builder, Haim Pekeris. Scholem connects the conception of the Golem as understood by the Middle-Ages kabbalists to that of the modern mathematicians and engineers.

369 Johann Reuchlin (1455–1522). German humanist who played a substantial role in Christian Kabbalah. In his *De Arte Cabalista* (1517), Reuchlin holds the view that Kabbalah enables to find in the Old Testament, the advent of Christ. He was a fervent defender of Hebrew language and literature.

370 Handwriting unclear.

371 The Damascus Document is a Jewish eschatological text closely related to those found at Qumran, setting forth a collection of detailed rules and instructions for the members of the community. The first part of the text (chapters 1–8) is a comment on God's salvation plan in history. The Damascus document's presentation of history gave birth to numerous interpretations among scholars.

372 In the Jewish tradition, the eschatological coming of Messiah son of Joseph, in the struggle against the evil, precedes that of Messiah son of David. Scholem, in his *Messianic Idea*, 18, claims that Messiah son of Joseph represents the features of 'the catastrophic' (because of his death in the Messianic catastrophe), while ben David represents the features of 'the utopian' (because of his victory on the Antichrist).

What a wonderful world – the intellectual equivalent of Tibetan art. If only I had twenty lives! There was something to be said for *Gilgul*.[373]

Regards to Fanya and best wishes to you both.

As ever,

Morton

94

Jerusalem,
July 3, 1973

Dear Morton,

I owe you many thanks for the several dispatches of articles, critical book reviews and above all the first volume of your Secret Gospel discovery.[374] I have read everything and have enjoyed your caustic and sometimes devastating criticism of some of our contemporaries. The discussion on Pseudepigraphy has done much to enlighten me about some distinctions that could be made in this field. Still I wonder whether there are many secret texts which would not come under the title of pseudepigraphy, of one kind or another. Of all people, Mohammad seems the only authentic author of a secret text who can claim full credit. And in spite of all this, we will go on speaking of *Moshe Rabbenu*.[375]

Your book is indeed very exciting and I am full of expectations regarding the proof forthcoming in your next volume announced by Harvard. Not so much because I have any doubts about your point

---

[373] In Hebrew characters: reincarnation.

[374] Scholem probably refers here to Smith, *The Secret Gospel* (New York, 1973). The "second volume" is probably Smith's *Clement of Alexandria and A Secret Gopsel of Mark*, the upcoming book from Harvard which was to contain the "proof." (A.P.).

[375] Hebrew for 'Moses, Our Master', the traditional appended to the Biblical figure.

regarding the authenticity of the letter, but because of the consequences you draw. The Jesus of the Sermon on the Mountain and Jesus the Magician, suppressed by the church tradition – what perspectives! Was this the secret reason behind your projected study of Jewish magic in Hellenistic times I once supported vis-à-vis Bollingen?

I hope to see you and to talk with you when I come to New York, as I sincerely hope, for about 10 days in September (17–27). I shall be on my way between Santa Barbara and Toronto, two unexpected poles of my activity this fall. I will be again at the address of Mrs. Feuerring, where we met last time (55 Central Park West). This period may also coincide with the long deferred appearance of the English *Sabbatai Sevi* in Princeton. You are on the list of recipients of a copy, no doubt about that! Nobody took the trouble to explain to me why the book was not ready in April or May. Some say that it is all the better for the book to be used by the Jews as [a] Christmas gift.

I shall leave next week, first to Switzerland and then, unless I return another time to Israel, to California. I shall stop over for one night in New York, presumably on Saturday, September 8 and have asked for a reservation at one of the airport hotels. If you feel like it, we might [...].[376]

Your old telephone number which I have, is still the same. Of course, you may be out of town and far away. Between July 16 and August 5 I can be reached at Hotel Margna, Sils Maria-Baseglia, Switzerland. Fania will not accompany me on this trip and stays in Israel. Therefore, if you should show up in this holy place, you might find her in Jerusalem or one of the beaches.

Kindest regards from both of us,

Yours,

[376] One page is missing.

95

Columbia University in the City of New York
Department of History
Fayerweather Hall
New York, N.Y. 10027
July 13, 1973

Dear Gershom,

I was delighted to get your letter with its kind remarks about my book and, even better, the news that you will be again in New York from the 17th to 27th of September. Unfortunately I expect to be out of town on the weekend of September 8th, so I can't see you then, but I do hope you will plan to have dinner and spend an evening with me during your longer stay. Please let me know which will suit you best, and I'll make sure it's free. (I have to teach until almost 8 on Tuesday and Thursday evenings, so the others are better).

Do you like Bickerman's company? He is a great admirer of yours and I'm sure would be happy to join us if you'd like.

I suppose Harvard has sent the book to you by surface mail, book post, so it will reach Jerusalem about the time of your return – if then. With their usual intelligence and open-handed generosity they sent copies by air mail to people in New York (and, I suppose, Boston!), by surface to those more remote. Thank God I'm done with them. News coverage has been good, reviews are yet to come.

Remember me to Fania, I'm sorry she's not coming.

Best wishes,

Morton

96

June 9, 1974

Dear Morton,

It is a long time since we met last and you gave me the copy of your book on the Secret Gospel of Mark. Since then so many things have happened and conspired to prevent me from an early reading of the book. I left Toronto when the war broke out[377] and was taken up with a lot of other duties and occupations and started to read your book attentively only in the spring months. This is the reason that only now I can really thank you.

Of the three main theses of your work regarding the authenticity of the letter by Clement of Alexandria, the problem of Mark and finally the double problem of the magical and libertinist background of Jesus' career and teaching, I have tried to follow your argument and to separate the evidence from the hypothetical elements. I feel convinced by the first two theses and I cannot imagine that you will be contradicted very much although I have not seen to this date any reviews on your work which certainly must have appeared. As to the magical part, I consider your evidence very good and convincing as far as it pertains to the tradition of the original church, whereas I am not sure whether the story can be truly taken as historical evidence about Jesus himself. That the magical element in these traditions of primitive Christianity was in conformity to generally accepted magical views and practices, I take as proven convincingly by you. As to the last part, the libertine character of Jesus' teachings for initiates, I think it is a hypothesis which remains rather vague and I admit that I have not been convinced. That there were groups who drew libertinist consequences from the teachings about the Kingdom of God, I take as firmly established by you and some of your predecessors. The further step to relate it to Jesus himself remains to me a hypothesis for which no hard evidence can be produced.

[377] The Yom Kippur, (or October) War was fought from October 6 to 26, 1973 between Israel and an Arab coalition led by Egypt and Syria. The war began with a surprise attack on Israel by Egypt and Syria on the Jewish Day of Atonement.

The doubts about your interpretation of the story on the new Gospel of Mark which I expressed in our talk in New York, have remained with me. I am not sure whether you proposed as a possible hypothesis or an unavoidable consequence of the context of this story within the background which you have described. My admiration for the scholarship and insight demonstrated in your book is enormous and I cannot imagine that it will not have its repercussions on future discussions. I have read with special attention what you have said about Carpocrates and I will quote you in my next Eranos lecture on religious nihilism which I plan to give this August.[378] But there seems to me a great difference between the stringency of your other deductions and the hypothetical character of your assumption of Jesus as a mystical libertinist.

Have you assembled a dossier of the discussions which must have followed your publication? You can imagine how interested I will be to follow them.

Fania and I shall leave in four weeks for Switzerland where I expect to spend nearly three months. Are you by any chance passing there or will you be staying in New York? We will have three fixed dates and addresses during this time, and if you cannot write before our departure, it will be fine to hear of you at any of these. They are: August 1st–August 19th – Sils Maria, Hotel Margna. August 20th–31st, Ascona, Hotel Tamaro; all through September – Zürich, Schönberggasse 15, Bodmerhaus der Universität, Gastzimmer 1.

With cordial greetings from Fania and me and my special apologies for being so late in writing,

as ever

yours

[378] G. G. Scholem 'Der Nihilismus als religiöses Phänomen', *Eranos Jahrbuch* 43 (1974), 1–50.

97

Columbia University in the City of New York
Department of History
Fayerweather Hall
New York, N.Y. 10027
July 12, 1974

Dear Gershom,

I was in England till the end of June, working on my catalogue of the magical gems of the British Museum, so your letter of a month ago has reached me only now. From it I gather that you will already have left or will soon leave Jerusalem, so I shall send this to the first of your Swiss addresses and hope it will greet you there when you arrive. Your letter pleased me very much and I thank you most sincerely for writing me at such length about my book. That you are convinced of the Clementine authorship of the letter and find probable my account of the relation of the gospel fragment to canonical Mark, and above all that you agree with me as to the importance of magic and related libertinism in the Christian communities from which the Gospel and the Pauline epistles emerges – *day li*![379] As to Jesus, I should perhaps have emphasized more strongly that *all* accounts of his teaching and practice are conjectural, and I claim to my conjectures only that they fit the reports as well as any and better than most. Of course nothing can be *proved* about this subject. For practical purposes the Gospels are our sole substantial evidence. And they are two generations later than the events and contradict both themselves and each other. Therefore every school of criticism concerned about consistency begins by forming arbitrarily its own concept of what Jesus "must" have been – a pious *'am ha'aretz*,[380] a Hillelite rabbi,[381] an eschatological preacher, a prophet like Elijah, etc. etc. – and then declares authentic the material that supports

[379] In Hebrew characters: It is enough for me.
[380] Hebrew expressions meaning literally: people of the Land. *'Am HaAretz* is a rabbinical term meaning an illiterate person.
[381] A rabbi belonging to the School of Hillel (*circ.* 70 B.C.E.–*circ.* 10 B.C.E.), the most important sage of the Second Templeperiod. The school of Hillel is often opposed in the Talmudic sources to that of Shammai. Jesus' teaching was often in line with that of the Hillel School.

are beginning – there will be a fine one by Helmut Koester (Professor of New Testament at Harvard) in the *American Historical Review*.[386] (You'll be glad to know that his conclusions almost exactly agree with yours). My expectation is, however, that with rare exceptions the reviews will be only preliminary skirmishes, the real battle will be fought out in articles and books over the next ten or fifteen years. It will have to be, because the text is there and has to be explained, and the problems are there, and have to be answered. Already, however, I have a dossier of newspaper clipping and reviews two or three inches thick, and an even thicker pile of private letters, some of them screamingly funny. When you next come to New York (soon, I hope) you may have them, if you want, for an evening's amusement. Meanwhile, I hope you and Fania are well and will enjoy yourselves in Switzerland. My stay in England was almost entirely work, but very pleasant: there are some amazing things in the British Museum magical gems. I'll probably be writing you about them in the fall, when my photographs come in and I can send some for your opinions.

En attendant, best wishes, and again thanks.

As ever,

Morton

---

[386] Helmut Köster's review on both of Smith's books on Secret Mark: *Clement of Alexandria and a Secret Gospel of Mark* (Harvard, 1973) and *The Secret Gospel* (New York, 1973) appeared in the *American Historical Review* 80/3 (1975), 620–622. Koester accepts the veracity and the anteriority of the text to the canonical Gospel of Mark and agreed with Smith's assumption that the Secret Mark, as well as the Gospel of John, derives from a primitive source "from which all the miracles stories of both Gospels derive" (p. 620). However, he disagrees with Smith's interpretation of the baptism and with his use of the category of magic, and points out his lack of sociological analysis.

98

Columbia University in the City of New York
Department of History
Fayerweather Hall
New York, N.Y. 10027
February 3, 1975

Dear Gershom,

I've just finished *Jaldabaoth Reconsidered*[387] and send my thanks and congratulations. It's brilliant and completely conclusive. Scholem's done it again. One more problem settled. If only we had a form *Ial(e/ê) dabaôth*[388] to show that the second vowel of the participle was sometimes kept,[389] or *Ieladabaôth*, if it came from the third person singular. But the lack doesn't bother me, and perhaps one will turn up if we start looking for it. The real insight was that *abaôth* = *sabaôth*[390] and that the first element was verbal, not nominative. I'd never noticed *abaôth* because I always mentally corrected it and took it as *lapsus calami*.[391]

All goes as usual here, which is to say that I have more work than I can possibly do, and that keeps me busy and out of trouble. I hoped to get to Israel next year, but evidently won't be able to – to accept the Academy's offer would have cost me about $5000, since my earnings in Israel couldn't be brought back, and I just couldn't afford it. With retirement looming on the horizon, inflation is a serious threat, especially since the rent of my apartment goes up at 5% *per annum* compounded

[387] G. G. Scholem, 'Jaldabaoth Reconsidered' in *Mélanges d'histoire des religions offerts à Henri-Charles Puech* (Paris, 1974), 405–21. Yaldabaoth is the name of the demiurge in various Gnostic texts.

[388] Italicized words in this paragraph appear in Greek characters.

[389] Scholem (*op. cit.* 419) linked *yald* (of Yald-abaoth) with the Hebrew and Aramic verb *yalad*, and as such, understands the element *yald* as 'begetter'. A form as *yaled* – as suggested by Smith – would have yielded the Aramic participle of the verb.

[390] Scholem pointed out (*op. cit.* 420) that Abaoth became a magical term on its own, so that Yaldabaoth must be understood has 'begetter of Sabaoth'.

[391] Latin for 'a slip of the pen'.

triennially. So I must count on seeing you when you come to the States, which I trust will be soon.

Greetings to Fanya, and best wishes to you both,

As ever,

Morton

99

Columbia University in the City of New York
Department of History
Fayerweather Hall
New York, N.Y. 10027
September 27, 1975

Dear Gershom,

I've just received an invitation for your lecture on the sixteenth and wrote to thank you for having me invited, to tell you how glad I am that you will be here again, and to express my hope that while you are here you will be able to spare some time for a visit with me. Your time, I'm sure, will be limited, and the demands on it infinite, so let me say that I have classes on Tuesdays and Thursdays from 4 to 8 (with short breaks) and I must be away all day on Friday, October 17 (I'm lecturing at Williams).

Otherwise I have no fixed obligations between October 10 and October 21, so please set time and occasion at your convenience. I'd be delighted, of course, if you could have lunch or dinner with me, either *tête à tête* or with Fanya, if she comes and would like to join us, or with other company, too – Bickerman? The Brodskys? Anyone you'd like me to invite.

I hope this will catch you before you leave. In any event, when it does reach you, do remember me to Fanya.

With best wishes for both of you.

As ever,

Morton

100

October 22, 1975

Dear Morton,

I am very sad that your letter dated September 27, took so long to reach me and I found it only on our return from New York. We left here on the 14th and it seems unbelievable that your letter should have taken more than two weeks to get here. It is all the more distressing as I heard only on Friday evening from Lieberman that you were in my lecture but didn't approach me after that when I, of course, would have taken you with me even if you were in the letter "S" – class and assigned to another room for lunch. You really should have come forth. Neither Fania, nor I saw you in the audience which was too large for me to identify people from the rostrum. We left on October 18 and I could not call you up. Before I had a long meeting with my publisher at the only time you would have been available. This is doubly regrettable as I see no chance to spend another time in New York. Is there perhaps any chance that "in case you go up to Providence" you could come over at least for a short visit with us? Over the weekend of November 15 and 16 we expect to be here and there might be some chance of seeing you, which both of us would very much welcome. If you think this is possible, please let us know and perhaps you want to phone us at our home address 65 Bay State Road, Boston 02215, Tel. (617) 266-4278.

I hope this letter will take less time in reaching you.

With kind regards, as ever,

Yours,

P.S. This moment, just having read my letter before signing it, your second letter of October 17th arrived, clearing up some of the things I said above. I am very sorry that you had some other errands to do and can only implore you to consider the possibility to use your probable trip to Providence for a visit with us. Our apartment is 2 minutes from Kenmore Square subway station and you should have no difficulties to find it.

The man who made a long speech against me defending all the things I reject [to] in my books was Professor Samuel Atlas[392] of the Hebrew Union College, who is in a way the last left-over of classical rationalism. It is a pity, indeed, that you were not there to hear my answer. I consider it a highlight of my 6 hours at the place.

Again,

Yours,

101

Columbia University in the City of New York
Department of History
Fayerweather Hall
New York, N.Y. 10027
October 17, 1975

Dear Gershom,

I was very sorry to miss you during your visit to the city. I trust Lieberman told you that I had a speaking engagement in upstate New York that made it impossible for me to come to his dinner on Friday. On Thursday I got to your lectures, but had two errands that had to be done about noon. So I hurried out during the question period after the first lecture to do my first errand, expecting to see you at lunch. But when I got back from lunch you had vanished. So I ate lunch and did my second errand, it took too long, and by the time I got back you were already speaking. I had to get to the University by 4, to teach my seminar. After that I had a lecture from 6:30 to 8, and then the University Classical Seminar which kept me till after 9, so I left a note with a graduate lunatic asking you to call me after 10 if

[392] Samuel Atlas (Kamai, Lithuania, 1899–1977). Talmudist and philosopher. Author of *From Critical to Speculative Idealism: the Philosophy of Solomon Maimon* (The Hague, 1964).

you were free. Either she didn't deliver it or you were not free or too tired – you sounded a little hoarse in your lectures. I trust that by the time this reaches you you'll be well again. The lectures were brilliant, of course; your's always are. I particularly liked your honesty in saying you hadn't learned anything of importance from your critics. Thank God somebody has the courage to kick over aged conventions. Your demolition of the fat little fool at the end must have been fine, too, but I had to hurry away while he was still speaking, and could not wait for the fire from heavens to fall. Who was he?

Since you are in Boston – for how long? – I hope you will presently be in New York again. Do let me know when you're coming and plan to have lunch or dinner with me. I teach on Tuesday and Thursday evenings, but am usually free. Otherwise, Phone 212 799-2787, best in the evenings after 10.

Best wishes, as ever.

Morton

102

Columbia University in the City of New York
Dcpartmcnt of History
Fayerweather Hall
New York, N.Y. 10027
October 25, 1975

Dear Gershom,

Thank you for your kind letter of the twenty second. I'm delighted that you'll be home on the evening of the sixteenth. As you expected, Neusner[393] arranged for me to come to Providence with Lieberman, so after

[393] Jacob Neusner (b. 1932). Leading scholar of Talmudic Judaism. His translation into English of many Rabbinic texts has made this literature available to a wider public. At the time of this letter, Neusner was Professor of Religious Studies at Brown University. At first, he had been a fervent admirer of Smith's works, as shown, for

a halakhic[394] afternoon I shall come on to Boston and spend the evening in the mysteries of the Kabbalah. I don't know just what the transportation available will be on a Sunday evening, nor how long the proceedings at Brown will last, but I shall hope – and do my best – to get to you by 7:30 if possible. By 8:00 for sure. If this is satisfactory, you needn't bother to reply: if I don't hear from you I shall arrive, at 7:30 or shortly after, on the evening of November 16th, at 65 Bay State Road.

It will be a great pleasure to see both you and Fanya again, I look forward to it eagerly.

As ever,

Morton

P.S. I hope your reply to Atlas was taped. But I suppose it can't be published without publishing his nonsense. Do you have a recording? I should love to hear it!

With best wishes MS.

(But how appropriate that the sky should have fallen on *Atlas*?)

P.P.S. in case of problems: (212) 799-2787; evenings are the times I'm most likely to be in. Thanks for sending me your phone number, I trust I'll have no need to use it.

---

example, by his editorship of *Christianity, Judaism and Other Greco-Roman Cults: Studies for Morton Smith* (Leiden, 1975). After a public spat between the two (Smith having accused him of incompetence), Neusner became critical of Smith. In 1993, he wrote a book entirely devoted to the refutation of Smith's Ph.D. dissertation: *Are There Really Tannaitic Parallels to the Gospels?* (Atlanta, 1993) in which he declared that the Secret Gospel of Mark "must now be declared the forgery of the century" (p. 28).

[394] Halakhic: related to the *Halakha*, the Jewish Law.

103

Columbia University in the City of New York
Department of History
Fayerweather Hall
New York, N.Y. 10027
November 17, 1975

Dear Gershom and Fanya,

Thank you for a delightful evening. It was a great pleasure to be with you again. I do hope that next time you come you'll be able to spend more time in New York, and some of it *chez moi*. Meanwhile, *bon voyage* and *bon retour*. I'm sending off to Jerusalem to-day Xeroxes of Merkel's attack on my book in *Zeitschrift für Theologie und Kirche* and my reply in the same;[395] I trust they'll be waiting for you at the academy when you arrive, or will come soon afterwards (I'm taking advantage of the necessary delay to send them by surface mail). The attack was really a piece of good fortune for me, since it was so obviously prejudiced as to discredit itself to perceptive readers even before they knew the facts, and it gave me an excuse to write the reply (which I think you'll enjoy, and I certainly did) and so in effect to review my own book in *Zeitschrift fur Theologie und Kirche* and say many of the things I wanted said about it. I hope the outcome will justify my optimism. Speaking of replies, I forgot to ask if yours to Atlas will be published in the "discussion" supplement (if any) to your speech. It must have been crushing! I've heard several enthusiastic, but, alas, inaccurate accounts.

It was a pleasure to meet Mrs. Früde, we had a long conversation – all the way home – in which she failed to convince me that magic works outside the realms of suggestion and autosuggestion. But it was a good try. And fun.

Again thanks and best wishes,

As ever.

Morton

---

[395] H. Merkel, 'Auf den Spuren des Urmarkus: Ein neuer Fund und seine Beurteilung', *Zeitschrift für Theologie und Kirche* 71/2 (1974), 123–144. Smith's response was published in the same journal: 'Rejoinder to Helmut Merkel' *ZThK* 77 (1975), 133–150.

104

Columbia University in the City of New York
Department of History
Fayerweather Hall
New York, N.Y. 10027
September 27, 1976

Dear Gershom,

I've been slow in writing to thank you for *Pirkei Yesod Behavanat HaKabbalah*[396] because I hoped to find time to read some of it before I wrote – especially the chapters on ritual,[397] *Shiur Qoma*,[398] and *Sitra Ahra*[399] and also that on the golem, all of which should be directly relevant to my work. But the fall semester is just beginning, and I still have my summer's work hanging over my head, so my reading always gets pushed off to tomorrow. Consequently I must thank you by anticipation, but I assure you my thanks are no less sincere. Your work is always invaluable, even to those like me who are working in fields quite other than the kabbalah, because of its illumination of the profundities of the religious mind (or whatever it is that the religious use instead of a mind). Nobody else I know has equalled you in grasping *both* the psychological depths and the historical surface. The surface, of course, is special, but the depths are universal, so *Out of the depths I cry to thee*,[400] "I have read you with an eye to the deeper problems", and I think I've learned more about Jesus from you and Shabbatai Zvi (I'm sometimes not sure which is which) than I have from any other source except the gospels and the magical papyri.

---

[396] In Hebrew Characters. German original: G. G. Scholem, *Zur Kabbala und ihrer Symbolik* (Zurich, 1960). The Hebrew version mentioned here, translated from the German by J. Ben Shlomo, was published in Jerusalem in 1976. English: *On the Kabbalah and its Symbolism* (trans. R. Manheim, New York, 1965).

[397] The chapters of the Hebrew version of the book don't correspond to the German and English versions.

[398] In Hebrew Characters. *Shiur Qomah* is a concept from Jewish Gnostic tradition from the second century referring to the 'Body of the Godhead' or the 'Measure of the [Divine] Body'. See: G. G. Scholem, *On the Kabbalah and its Symbolism*, 128.

[399] In Hebrew Characters. Aramaic for 'the other side'. A Kabbalistic term to describe the powers of the Satan and Evil. See: *op. cit.* 129 ff.

[400] In Hebrew: *mima'amakim keratykha* (Ps. 130:1).

Gospels and papyri have kept me busy all summer. I promised Harper's a book on "Jesus the Magician" which was going to be a mere collection of parallels to the Gospels from the magical papyri, so I expected to finish it in January or February.[401] But once I got into it I found so much more interesting material and so many more lines of argument than I had expected that it kept me busy all summer and I finished it only at the end of last month. The results are worth it, though – wait and see. Now I'm busy writing the articles and reviews I promised to write during the summer, and once those are out of the way I shall get back to the British Museum amulets.

Meanwhile, best wishes for you and Fanya. Will you be back in New York soon? I hope so.

Again thanks,

As ever,

Morton

105

Columbia University in the City of New York
Department of History
Fayerweather Hall
New York, N.Y. 10027
November 19, 1976

Dear Gershom,

Your essays *On Jews and Judaism*[402] have just arrived and I write to thank you for them with real gratitude, but also with a touch of sorrow and envy – sorrow because they are a particularly alluring reminder of

[401] The book was eventually published by Harper and Row: M. Smith, *Jesus the Magician* (San Francisco, 1978).

[402] G. G. Scholem, *On Jews and Judaism in Crisis: Selected Essays* (W. Dannhauser (ed.), New York, 1976).

the great world I have never had time to explore, and envy because you have been able to explore it so widely while at the same time achieving and maintaining the sort of scholarly mastery of your enormous field, that I must also envy.

Well, there is also good envy, as Hesiod said,[403] and I hope this belongs to that class. I also hope I may soon be able to acquaint myself more closely with the worlds you have written about and to. Perhaps my nose has been at the grindstone too long. Whatever the cause, I am getting fed up with research in my field and think more and more of retiring early, taking a trip around the world – which I've always wanted to do – and then reading all the things I've so long wanted to read and pushed aside. So your seed is falling on friendly soil – who knows what will sprout. Perhaps the two trees of knowledge and life.

Meanwhile, thanks and best wishes, both for you and for Fanya.

As ever,

Morton

P.S. By chance I noticed a misprint, p. 304 li. 16 f.b. for on read in. Best, M.S.[404]

P.P.S. I hear you will speak at Ancona,[405] late in the coming summer, on Kabbalah and alchemy. I shall be in London from mid July to the end of August, trying to finish my work on the British Museum amulets. If it would not involve an intrusion, I should be very glad if I might come over to Ancona, see you and hear your lecture. But if this would involve any embarrassment for you, please *don't* let it do so. I ask because I don't know at all what rules govern admission to those lectures, and I should be sorry to miss yours if there would be no difficulty about my coming.

Sincerely,

Morton

---

[403] For the Greek poet Hesiod, envy is a good thing when it stimulates someone to work (*Works and Days*, 26).

[404] Smith is confusing again Ancona (Italy) with Ascona (Switzerland).

[405] G. G. Scholem, 'Alchemie und Kabbala', *Eranos Jahrbuch* 46 (1977), 1–96.

106

Jerusalem,
December 19, 1976

Dear Morton,

I am very pleased to hear that both of my books, the Hebrew and the English volume, have reached you and I am even more pleased that you like them and can make use of them, especially of the Hebrew volume.

I hear with great interest of your plan of possibly retiring early and devoting yourself to the research on Magic, from which I expect a lot. Even better is the news that you will not have to wait for your taking a trip around the world in order to meet again, but that you plan to come over to Ascona in Switzerland (not Ancona in Italy, as you must have written by mistake). As a matter of fact, we hope to be there and I have promised to give a lecture on "Kabbalah and Alchemy", or rather "Alchemy and Kabbalah".[406] If you want to participate in the whole meeting which would last from August 17th to August 25th, you would have to write to them and pay the admission fee which is somewhere around SFr. 200. The Address would be Casa Eranos, Ascona, CH-6612, Switzerland. And you would do well to give my name as reference. But I doubt that you would plan such a thing instead of coming over for my lecture only. In this case, I think I could always get you in as my guest and, if at all, you might have to pay for what they call a 'Tageskarte'.[407] I assume that I would probably be the first speaker, which would mean Wednesday, August 17th, 1977, in the morning. You would, therefore, have to be in Ascona the preceding day and make a reservation at some hotel well in time, because this is the Season and hotels will be booked.

If they put my lecture (2 full hours, with an interval of 45 minutes) at a later date, I would inform you accordingly. At any rate, you should think of being with us on Wednesday evening, having dinner with us at the Hotel Tamaro where we always stay. Maybe you can get

[406] G. G. Scholem, 'Alchemie und Kabbalah', *Eranos Jahrbuch* 46 (1977), 1–96.
[407] German for 'day pass'.

a reservation right there, at least for two nights, if you don't want to stay longer, and in writing to them say that you do so on my recommendation.

I hope very much that this meeting of ours will materialize. My lecture will be a final version of a paper which I wrote in "meiner Jugend Maienblüte",[408] fifty two years ago. You can imagine that in the meantime I have learned something.

Please, send me your forthcoming articles and reviews and especially everything on your special magical studies, amulets, etc. Don't forget that in me you have an attentive reader.

With our cordial greetings,

ever yours,

107

Columbia University in the City of New York
Department of History
Fayerweather Hall
New York, N.Y. 10027
January 15, 1977

Dear Gershom,

Thank you very much for your kind letter of December 19 and your permission to use your name in applying to the Eranos conference and the Hotel Tamaro. I have written them accordingly and hope to be in Ascona in the 16th, hear your lecture on the 17th, and accept with pleasure your kind invitation to have dinner with you and Fanya that evening. As the papyrological congress in Brussels,[409] my next fixed

---

[408] German for 'in my first bloom of youth'. Scholem is referring to his 1925 article: 'Alchemie und Kabbala: Ein Kapitel aus der Geschichte der Mystik', *Monatsschrift für Geschichte und Wissenschaft des Judentums* 69, 13–30; 95–110; 371–374.

[409] The Fifteenth Congress of Papyrology took place in Brussels, from August 29 to September 3 of this same year.

engagement, won't begin until the 30th, I have two weeks of interim and shall therefore stay on the Ascona for the whole congress – alchemy, psychiatry and magic are so closely related that I should find a great deal of it useful – and then go to Brussels by way of a trip down the Rhine. I've always wanted to make that journey and some friends, who went last year, tell me it is still beautiful, in spite of the shipping and industrialization. Fortunately I don't know what it used to be, so that will cause me no regrets. As usual, ignorance is bliss.

Articles and reviews are coming by sea mail; I'm very happy that you want them. It will be wonderful to see you again this summer.

Meanwhile, my regards to Fanya and best wishes for both of you.

As ever,

Morton

108

Columbia University in the City of New York
Department of History
Fayerweather Hall
New York, N.Y. 10027
Thanks giving day[410]

Dear Gershom,

Rumor has it that your eightieth birthday is in the offing, and I take this as an appropriate occasion for thanksgiving, not only for you, but even more for the rest of us. *Blessed is His Name, who has kept you alive, and has preserved you and has brought you to us.*[411] For my self, at least, I count it as one of the great good fortunes of my life that I have met you and have had the privilege of learning from you.

---

[410] November 24, 1977.

[411] In Hebrew: *Baruch Shmo, sh'hechiyacha vekiyamcha vehegiacha lanu.* This is a play on words on the 'shehechiyanu', a blessing said on joyous occasions.

I hope very much that this anniversary will be an occasion of deep joy and satisfaction to you, as you survey an entire field of scholarship which you alone have practically called into light out of darkness. I won't accuse you of creation *ex nihilo*, so this line of comparison has got to lead to identification with the demiurge, and I'd better drop it. But – may you rejoice in your works!

Jesus the Magician is now in proof and I hope you'll like it – I shall, as soon as I get through verifying the references, just at the moment I hate the sight of it. Otherwise all is well. I hope very much that Fanya's operation was successful and has relieved her pain and restored her ability to walk. May you both have many more and even happier birthdays together!

As ever,

Morton Smith[412]

109

Morton Smith
N.Y.
July 26, 1978

Dear Gershom,

Mr. Schwartz[413] brought me your greeting, so I send you mine through him. He wants a copy of my translation of *Hekhaloth Rabbathi* for his private use (*not*, of course, for publication) and you have the only copy of it, so I'd be glad to have you send him a Xerox if you wish.

Greeting to Fanya and best wishes,

Morton

---

412 In Hebrew characters.

413 Howard Schwartz (b. 1945). Professor of English, formerly at the University of Michigan. He is known for his fictional works, in which he retells Jewish folk tales or fairy tales from Talmudic or Medieval Sources. See his *Tree of Souls: The Mythology of Judaism* (New York, 2004).

110

Columbia University in the City of New York
Department of History
Fayerweather Hall
New York, N.Y. 10027
July 29, 1978

Dear Gershom,

A young man named Howard Schwartz recently telephoned me and told me you had told him to get in touch with me. I asked him to lunch, we had a pleasant talk, he gave me a volume of his *Midrashim*[414] and asked if I would let him have my translation of the *Hekhaloth Rabbati* which he said you said I had. As it happens I have only the Hebrew text; the only copy of the translation was the one I left with you. I told him this and suggested that he write you for a Xerox. He was doubtful whether you would feel authorized to give him a copy of my text (even though, he assured me, he would of course not publish anything of it, but merely read it for inspiration and ideas). Wishing to facilitate matters I gave him a card addressed to you, with my authorization of the transfer.

Afterwards it occurred to me that he might have been partially a fakc. Hc may havc mct you, but he showed no special knowledge of you; your memory is much better than mine, so it's a bit odd that you should have forgotten that I had no copy of the translation; he might have learned about it not from you, but from the reference to it in your *Jewish Gnosticism*;[415] and so on. Consequently I thought it best to send this note, explaining what had happened. Not that it makes much difference. He teaches in St. Louis, I believe, so he'd scarcely dare plagiarize the translation extensively and directly; it would lose him his job, even though he couldn't be sued for it (and perhaps he could; I think there's some sort of coverage for manuscript material). Thus I have no objection to his getting a copy, but if you do know his work and *don't* like it, or do know him and don't like him, you should

[414] H. Schwartz, *Midrashim: Collected Jewish Parables* (London, 1976).
[415] Scholem mentions Smith's translation of it in his *Jewish Gnosticism, Merkabah Mysticism, and Talmudic Tradition* (New York, 1960), 11, n. 4.

of course feel free to refuse. He seemed to me pleasant and harmless, and so do his *midrashim*, but one never knows.

Let me take this occasion to ask a favor. Ruth Brodsky (Anshan) talked me into writing a book for her "World Perspectives" and I chose the topic "Hope and History".[416] The text is now finished and has gone off to Harper's to be prepared for publication. Would you be so kind as to look through it and (a) if you like it, write a few kind words that Harper's could put on the cover, (b) in any event, warn me of anything you see that seems false or foolish, so I can cut it out before the book goes to press? As you know, such cosmic lucubrations are for me an entirely new genre, so I'm very uneasy about this. Like Moses de Leon,[417] I did it to make money. Egeria[418] appeared in the form of a fashionably dressed old lady waving a checkbook. But even works produced for mercenary motives can have some merits – if the Zohar seems a dubious case, consider the plays of Shakespeare – and now that this one is done there are some things in it I rather like, and I'd like to know what you think of it.

Lehavdil,[419] I hear your biography[420] is (or is about to come) out. Where? When? I'm dying to see it. The narrative may be uneventful, but the remarks will be immortal.

Best wishes to both you and Fanya

As ever,

Morton

[416] Smith wrote for the 'World Perspectives' series, a book entitled *Hope and History, an Exploration* (ed. Ruth Anshen, = World Perspectives 54, New York, 1980).

[417] Moses de Leon (1240–1305). Generally thought to have been the author of the *Zohar*. Early in life, Scholem held the opinion that Moses de Leon had edited the Zohar from earlier sources. Later, he changed his view and saw in Moses de Leon, the sole author of almost the entire corpus of the *Zohar* as it is known today.

[418] In Roman mythology, the nymph Egeria inspired the religious reforms of King Numa.

[419] In Hebrew characters: though different, as opposed to.

[420] Scholem's biography was first edited in German: *Von Berlin nach Jerusalem: Jugenderinnerungen* (Frankfurt, 1977). English translation: *From Berlin to Jerusalem: Memories of my Youth* (trans. H. Zohn, New York, 1980).

111

Columbia University in the City of New York
Department of History
Fayerweather Hall
New York, N.Y. 10027
September 13, 1978

Dear Gershom,

Thank you very much for the Xerox of my translation of the *Hekhalot.* I'm glad to have it and also glad to have your greetings and know you are functioning – I trust as usual. Here classes are beginning and the sea of papers rises daily nearer to my neck.

Regards to Fanya and best wishes to you both,

As ever

Morton Smith[421]

P.S. I still hope to hear what you think of *Jesus*, and especially any corrections, MS.

[421] In Hebrew characters.

112

Columbia University in the City of New York
Department of History
Fayerweather Hall
New York, N.Y. 10027
July 21, 1980

Dear Gershom,

Von Berlin nach Jerusalem, *The Sleuth from Slobodka*,[422] and your photograph, have just arrived and I write at once to thank you for all of them. The photograph is a brilliant study and gets perfectly the look you have when you've been asked a difficult question, which I suppose is your most revealing look – the one that shows you are doing the thing most important in your life. The difficulty of photographing you is that your face is so expressive and changes so greatly from mood to mood. Next time you come I most try to get a shot that shows your look when you have just discovered an answer. Then I can make a diptych with *quest* and *revelation* side by side.

Your critique of Schwartz seemed to me perfectly accurate and I'm glad you were able to do it so gently – he was an amiable ass. The only thing I should object to is the equation of Wolfson with Goodenough. I was close to both. (and a good deal closer to Goodenough than to Wolfson) and I can assure you that while Goodenough was a very clever man, with remarkable psychological penetration, his lukewarm lyrics about Philo are simply not comparable to Wolfson's analytical study.[423] Not that I agree with Wolfson's conclusions, but the structure

---

[422] Scholem referred to Wolfson as 'The Sleuth from Slobodka" in his review of Leo W. Schwartz, *Wolfson of Harvard: Portrait of a Scholar* (Jewish Publication Society of America; Philadelphia, 1978). Slobodka/Slabodka was a famous Lithuanian Yeshiva, where Wolfson, as a child, had received a traditional Jewish education before moving to the USA with his family.

[423] Both Wolfson and Goodenough wrote extensively on Philo of Alexandria. From a philosophical perspective, Wolfson wrote a study about Philo: *Philo, Foundations of Religious Philosophy in Judaism, Christianity and Islam*, 2 vols. (Cambridge, Mass., 1947). Goodenough looked at Philo from the perspective of the history of religions; see his *The Politics of Philo Judaeus* (New-Heaven, 1938).

of evidence and argument by which he reached them is a masterpiece, like Chartres, a monumental mistake, but what a monument!

Your concluding anecdote and quintessential. (My conviction, by the way, is that Wolfson was a complete sceptic. Philosophy had stripped him of Slobodka, so he never forgave philosophy and detested it to the day of his death. However, he could not successfully adopt to American life outside the university, so he stayed in the university and devoted himself to his revenge on philosophy by detailed dissection and demonstration of its arbitrariness and absurdity (even Philo's assumption turn out to be arbitrary and unreasonable, but he is forgiven because he remained a Jew). The sleuth was investigating a crime and by exposing it became the executioner.

From Berlin to Jerusalem I have just begun and am delighted to find the German not so difficult as I feared from your remarks about Berlinese. No doubt I don't know enough to perceive the difficulties, but at my level it reads easily and I shall read it with great pleasure, not only for what it will tell me of you, but also because the early 1900's have long attracted me and I shall be glad to see something of them from the German side.

Best wishes to Fanya; it was a great pleasure to see you both.

As ever,

Morton

113

Jerusalem
November 27, 1980

Dear Morton,

Your letter of August 1st, 1980 arrived here when Fania and I had just left Israel for Europe. When we came back in October, I had some little trouble with another hernia and did not feel quite well. But now, having been restored to good health, (I hope so) I can at least thank you for your interesting letter and the Xerox of the article by Festugière.[424] I did not know of the second edition of Preisendanz.[425] Does it include the index volume? If you think there would be no need for me to acquire the two editions, I would welcome a Xerox of those parts which are new and of which you wrote in your letter. But if you recommend to buy the whole thing, I shall do so. I suppose it is still on the market, although with the new interest in magic, the magicians may have bought it up. My little book *From Berlin to Jerusalem* has now appeared in an English translation (very readable in my opinion), and if you are interested, I shall get you a copy. But maybe you have had already enough from the German text you took with you in [the] summer.

Did you know, by the way, that Festugière was a furious antisemite? I don't know whether the old Jewish magicians of the Papyri or the modern Jews aroused his ire. When I once approached him, not yet knowing this well known fact, he was most impolite, and I did not understand why.

Cordial Greetings from both of us,

ever yours,

[424] André Jean Festugière (1898–1982). Dominican historian of Greek religion and of early Christianity. Translator of the *Corpus Hermeticum*, and author of *La révélation d'Hermès Trismégiste* (4 vols.; Paris 1944–1954), and of *Personal Religion among the Greeks* (Berkeley, 1960).

[425] The Corpus of the Greek Magical Papyri (PGM) was published by Karl Preisendanz, with a German translation, in 1928–1931. A second, revised edition was prepared by Albert Henrichs; see K. Preisendanz, *Papyri Graecae Magicae. Die griechischen Zauberpapyri*, 2 vols. (2nd ed., Stuttgart, 1973–1974).

114

Columbia University in the City of New York
Department of History
Fayerweather Hall
New York, N.Y. 10027
August 1, 1980

Dear Gershom,

Your letter came just as I was caught in the double malestrom of a summer seminar and the preparations for the XVIth papyrological congress,[426] which has just met here. Now that both these hovers are over, I again have time to write letters, but you and Fanya are about to take off, so this will have to follow you. May it catch you soon, and in a pleasant place. I suppose that as a Biblical Zionist you can justify your chronic absence from Israel by the obligation to perform *Alia* at least three times a year.[427]

I enclose a Xerox of Festugière's 'Amulettes Magiques'[428] and trust you won't mind the notes (from my filing system). As you'll see from them, *CP* is a review *Classical Philology* – by all odds the most scholarly journal on that field published in the States. The second edition of Preisendanz, *Papyri Graecae Magicae*, prepared by A. Henrichs, Teubner (Stuttgart) 1973–1974. 2 vols. is for the most part a Xerox of the first edition. Henrichs made very few changes, but he did make a few, notably in papyri XV, XX, XXXIV, LIX, and P[apyrus] 18.[429] He also added from the unpublished, but printed, third volume of Preisendanz, Preisendanz's texts and notes for Papyri LXI–LXXXI and P 21–24 and the texts of the hymns from the papyri prepared by E. Heitsch and published in his *griechischen Dichterfragmente der roemischen Kaiserzeit.*[430]

---

[426] The Congress was hold in New York, from July 24 to 31.

[427] In Hebrew characters: immigration to Israel. Smith refers to the biblical duty (Ex. 23:17) for any Jew to go up to the Temple in Jerusalem three times a year.

[428] A. J. Festugière, 'Amulettes magiques à propos d'un ouvrage récent', *Classical Philology* 46 (1951), 81–92.

[429] Smith omits Papyrus LXVII from the list of Henrich's emendations (see Preisendanz, *Papyri Graecae Magicae*, vol. I, p. XIII).

[430] E. Heitsch, *Die griechischen Dichterfragmente der römischen Kaiserzeit* (Göttingen, 1963–64).

Of this added material Henrichs reworked P LXVII, but otherwise simply took over Preisendanz and Heitsch's texts, again with a few changes, but very few. The added material can easily be xeroxed. If you'd like I'll send you a Xerox of my copy, but you'll have to pick your way through the annotations. No doubt the Hebrew University has a copy – it certainly should that will be cleaner.

I'm still exhausted from the seminar and meetings – I wrote a paper on the hymn PGM IV.2241–2358,[431] with, I think, a lot of improvements in the text. So I'm tired but happy. Next week I go off to assorted meetings – *Corpus Hellenisticum*,[432] The International Association for the History of Religions,[433] Studiorum Novi Testamentum Societas[434] – and shall take *Von Berlin nach Jerusalem* along to brighten my way.

Again thanks and best wishes,

Morton Smith[435]

[431] M. Smith, 'The Hymn to the Moon, PGM IV, 2242–2355' in *Proceedings of the XVI International Congress of Papyrology* (Chicago, 1981), 643–54.

[432] The Corpus Hellenisticum Novi Testamenti is a research project by the Institute for Antiquity and Christianity which seeks to illuminate the Hellenistic background of the New Testament.

[433] The International Association for the History of Religions (IAHR) is formed by various associations for the academic study of religion. In 1980, the XIVth Congress of the International Association for the History of Religions was held in Winnipeg.

[434] Studiorum Novi Testamentum Societas (SNTS) is an international society for the research of the New Testament. In 1980, the society held its Congress in Toronto.

[435] In Hebrew characters.

115

Columbia University in the City of New York
Department of History
Fayerweather Hall
New York, N.Y. 10027
January 6, 1981

Dear Gershom,

Happy New Year! Your letter came just as the Christmas crunch was beginning, and it took me some time to get the new material in the second edition of Preisendanz xeroxed, hence the delay. I'm sending it off this coming Friday, along with this letter – its now at the university and I'll get to it when I go there. I trust it will reach you soon and safely.

Thanks for offering me a copy of the English translation of *From Berlin to Jerusalem*, but I've almost finished the German and haven't had much difficulty with it; except for an occasional word or idiom it goes quite easily and is delightful. What I don't get is the reason for the basic belief that ancestry entails some sort of obligation to perpetuate the language, literature, and ethnic peculiarities of one's ancestors. Thanks be to the non-existent, I feel no such obligation to devote myself to Anglo-Saxon, nor want to go back to England or try to revive the British Empire. And I don't suppose a comparison between you and Steinschneider[436] (or Trotzky) would show that he suffered serious psychological deprivation. However, in your case the conviction seems to have resulted in a happy life and the recovery of a great deal of interesting material, so glory be to it.

I've been busy with magical gems, writing descriptions of about a hundred that the British Museum intends to put in a show of late Roman and mediaeval objects. Now I must do some more work on

[436] Moritz Steinschneider (Moravia, 1816–Berlin, 1907). Most important bibliographer in the realm of Hebrew books and manuscripts and one of the founders of modern Jewish scholarship. He undertook the cataloguing of many libraries, such as the Bodleian Library in Oxford, and contributed also to the field of Medieval Arabic manuscripts, as well as to the history of mathematics and astronomy. Much of his work appeared in his periodical *Hebräische Bibliographie* (1859–1882).

the coming Chicago translation of *Papyri Graecae Magicae*,[437] and then write some articles on first century Judaism for the Cambridge history,[438] and then I shall be free to spend the summer, I hope, on the big gems catalogue. *Italian Semper adventure*, but I'll get there.

I do hope you keep well and take life easy.

Give my regards to Fanya, as ever, Best wishes for both of you.

Morton Smith[439]

116

Columbia University in the City of New York
Department of History
Fayerweather Hall
New York, N.Y. 10027
March 3, 1981

Dear Gershom,

Did you ever receive the Xerox of *Papyri Graecae Magicae* vol. III that I sent you about Christmas time? I xeroxed everything *except* the indices (which you already have) and also the pages of the earlier volumes that were substantially altered in the second edition. I hope very much that the package reached you safely. It should have done so long ago – I sent it airmail – but some typically intelligent postal clerk may have put it in the wrong box, so it may be coming by boat.

---

[437] Smith was a contributor to the translation of the Greek Magical Papyri (PGM) published by the University of Chicago Press: H. D. Betz (ed.), *The Greek Magical Papyri in Translation: Including the Demotic Spells* (Chicago, 1986). The second edition (1992) is dedicated to the memory of Morton Smith. In the Preface to the second edition Betz writes: "He was the first to suggest the whole project, and he never ceased to give attention to it."

[438] M. Smith, 'The Gentiles in Judaism 125 B.C.E.–C.E. 66', in W. Horbury, W. D. Davies and J. Sturdy (eds.), *The Cambridge History of Judaism*, vol. 3: *The Early Roman Period* (Cambridge, U.K., 1999), 192–249.

[439] In Hebrew characters.

If it has NOT arrived yet please let me know and I'll try to start an inquiry.

Not that inquiries do much good, but at least they put losses record and so perhaps serve to indicate bad spots.

No news here – all as usual. I hope to see you and Fanya at Ascona this summer[440] – thanks to you, of course, and sincere thanks.

With best wishes,

Morton

117

Columbia University in the City of New York
Department of History
Fayerweather Hall
New York, N.Y. 10027
April 4, 1981

Dear Gershom,

At the same time as this letter I'm sending off a Xerox of the indices of *Papyri Graecae Magicae*. I'll send it by air mail, so you should have it soon. They made one mistake – re-xeroxed a loose page instead of plate I – but otherwise it's complete, and I think you have pls. I and II, of which little can be made at best. As for cost, don't consider it. I owe you for so many favors, and so much besides, that I'm happy to have the opportunity of doing ever so small a thing.

I'll be sorry to miss you at Ascona – I must be back here on September 1 to speak to the incoming freshmen, I'll hope you can get away early or, failing that, will have another occasion to come to New York soon (as you probably will).

Otherwise all in well. I looked forward to a summer of uninterrupted work here, before going off to Ascona, and hope to get all my minor

---

[440] Smith's lecture was published as: 'Ascent to the Heavens and the Beginning of Christianity', *Eranos Jahrbuch* 50 (1981), 403–429.

obligations out of the way, so as to settle down to uninterrupted work on the gung when I come back in the fall.

Regards to Fanya and the Sambursky's (whom I hope to see at Ascona) and best wishes to all.

As ever,

Morton

118

Columbia University in the City of New York
Department of History
Fayerweather Hall
New York, N.Y. 10027
May 2, 1981

Dear Gershom,

Thanks for your kind note. I'm glad the Xerox reached you safely. If anything is missing or imperfect, don't hesitate to write; I didn't have time to check carefully, but details can easily be redone.

Alas, I've been assigned to the program for incoming freshmen for this fall, so I must appear here on September 1 and shall therefore be leaving Ascona just a couple of days before you leave Israel. But I hope you'll soon be here again.

Meanwhile best wishes for you and Fania,

Regards to the Braudes and the Samburskys, and my ecumenical sub-apostolic benediction

As ever,

Morton

119

Columbia University in the City of New York
Department of History
Fayerweather Hall
New York, N.Y. 10027
September 9, 1981

Dear Gershom,

I was delighted to get your note and learn that you and Fanya would be nearly during the Eranos conference. I can't locate Sils-Maria-Baseglia[441] on my maps, but suppose it's nearby and hope I can get to see you. The Eranos schedule which I've just received seems to leave *free* the afternoon of Thursday, August, 20 all day Sunday, August 23 the afternoon of Wednesday, August 26. Please leave word for me at the Casa Eranos on which of these days you'd prefer to see me, and I shall make every effort to appear accordingly.

As yet I haven't had any word from Ritsema[442] about accommodations, so I don't know where I'll be staying. I expect to arrive at Ascona late on the 18th and leave for Zurich on the morning of the 28th.

With best wishes for both you and Fanya,

As ever

S. Morton[443]

---

441 Hotel Margna is located near the twin villages of Sils Maria and Sils Baseliga, in Upper Engadine (Switzerland). Sils Maria was cherished by Nietzsche.

442 In 1972, the Dutch Orientalist Rudolf Ritsema (1918–2006) started to lead the Eranos conferences.

443 In Hebrew characters.

120

Columbia University in the City of New York
Department of History
Fayerweather Hall
New York, N.Y. 10027
January 10, 1982

Dear Gershom,

Happy New Year! This will be a trifle late, but I take the occasion of this new article to send you my old wishes. I think the article will interest you. Now that Gnosticism has gone to pieces, matters is what can we make with the fragments remaining from the ruin?

When I phoned Ruth[444] to check on your Berlin address. She told me you had gone back to Jerusalem. I suppose the New Berlin was a dreadful disappointment – you know my rule: *Never* go back to a place that charmed you in your childhood – and anyhow I congratulate you on escaping a winter at the latitude of Labrador. Here, at the latitude of Madrid, we've been lucky enough to escape snow so far, but in the last few days the temperature has gone down to about – 10 Centigrade, so I fear our luck won't last long. Thank heaven, it's only 50 days to March. The best thing about February is that it's short.

Please give my regards to Gruenwald[445] when you see him, my retranslation of *Hekhalot Rabbati* was sidetracked during the fall by a long series of petty problems, but I hope to get back to it and finish it off during the coming term. First, However, I have to dispose of a lot of petty problems...

Greetings to Fanya and best wishes to you both,

As ever,

Morton

---

[444] Probably Ruth Nanda Anshen (Brodsky).

[445] Ithamar Gruenwald. Professor of Jewish Mysticism at Tel-Aviv University since 1967; specialist in the *Hekhalot* literature. Author of *Apocalyptic and Merkavah Mysticism* (Leiden-Köln, 1980).

121

Columbia University in the City of New York
Department of History
Fayerweather Hall
New York, N.Y. 10027
March 1, 1983

Dear Fanya,

I have a letter from Professor Katz[446] of the Leo Baeck Institute.[447] Saying it has decided to sponsor an edition of Gershom's correspondence. He would like copies of his letters to me, and makes this request with your approval.

I suppose all is as it should be, but just want to be sure before sending the copies.

I'm sorry to bother you with another letter. I suppose honors for Gershom continue to come so fast that you have all you can do to keep up with acknowledging them. But it's good for the rest of us to see a great scholar honored – scholarship is being phased out so rapidly by the drive for academic economies. So I welcome everything that can be done to secure it recognition, not so much for Gershom's sake – he doesn't need it – nor for my own – what has been, has been, and I'm content – but for the sake of the students, who need some recognizedly great figures to inspire them.

I hope that all is well with you – apart from overwork. So it is with me.

As ever,

---

[446] Jacob Katz (Hungary, 1904–Jerusalem, 1998). Important historian of medieval and modern orthodox Judaism. Taught at the Hebrew University from 1950 on. Author, inter alia, of *Exclusiveness and Tolerance: Studies in Jewish-Gentile Relations in Medieval and Modern Times* (New York, 1961).

[447] A research Institute founded in 1955 and devoted to study and the preservation of Jewish German History; from the origin of the Jewish community in Germany until its destruction by the Nazis. The Institute has centers in Jerusalem, New York and London.

Morton Smith[448]

122

The British Museum
July 6, 1983
Mrs. Fanya Scholem
28 Abarbanel St.
Jerusalem
Israel

Dear Fanya,

Thanks and greetings from London. (Athens was a rat race, and the poor little, charming, old city is completely overrun by the enormous, third-rate modern one). Fortunately London isn't much changed. I hope to see you in Zürich if I can twist my schedule.

Meanwhile best wishes

Morton Smith

[448] In Hebrew characters.

APPENDIX A

Professor Morton Smith
Department of History
Columbia University

Project

My project is to describe the archeological material available for a history of Greco-Roman magic. The need for such a history has been brought home to me by a number of recent studies of religions cognate to early Christianity (e.g. Goodenough, *Jewish Symbols in the Greco Roman Period* II.153–295; Scholem, *Jewish Gnosticism, Merkabah Mysticism and Talmudic Tradition*) and particularly by Scholem's demonstration that a technique producing the experience of ascent through the heavens was common to rabbinic Judaism, gnosticism and pagan magic, and was derived from a pre-Christian source. In a lecture in 1960 at the Lown institute for Advanced Judaic Studies at Brandeis University I showed that the same technique is supposed by the "Mithras Liturgy" of the "Great Magical Papyrus of Paris". (This lecture will be published in the first volume of the papers of the Institute).[1] While working on this I discovered connections indicating that the abnormal experiences induced by this technique played an important part in early Christian history, and I have now collected material for a number of studies on this subject. (The first of these will be published in the Festschrift for H. A. Wolfson).[2]

In this research I have often been balked by the uncertainly of the history of ancient magic. The large magical papyri are mostly of the fourth century A.D. and since magic was both traditional and syncretistic they offer no assurance as to the date or provenance of their contents. To check on that we have a scattering of earlier papyri, a great deal

[1] M. Smith 'Observations on *Hekhalot Rabbati*', in A. Altman (ed.) *Biblical and Other Studies* (Philip W. Lown Institute of Advanced Judaic Studies. Studies and Texts, vol. 1.; Cambridge, Mass., 1963) 142–160.

[2] M. Smith, 'The Account of Simon Magus in Acts 8' in S. Lieberman (ed.) *Harry Austryn Wolfson, Jubilee Volume*, vol. 2 (Jerusalem, 1965) 735–49.

of miscellaneous archeological material – amulets, inscriptions, reliefs, statuettes, magical implements etc. This material is scattered through the museums of America, Europe and the Near East, much of it unpublished or misunderstood.

My project, therefore, is *A Survey of the Magical Material from the Hellenistic and Roman Periods in America, European and Near Eastern Museums.*

I have no thought of producing a corpus or even a complete catalogue, but hope to describe the quantity, distribution and provenance of the preserved material, classify it by types, and within each type give special attention to datable pieces and to chronological and regional characteristics. Because of the wide influence of magic in ancient life, the importance of such a survey for ancient cultural history is obvious. Therefore, although my reason for the undertaking is need of control for the Christian literary material, the project seems to me independently justified as a contribution to the history of Greco – Roman civilization and I intend to present the survey as such, leaving for later studies the special question of its relevance to Christian history.

I think the examination and photographing of the European and Near Eastern material can be completed in the 15½ months which will be available to me, thanks to my coming sabbatical year, from June 1, 1963, to September 20, 1964. I plan to start in Holland and shall try to do the Rhine-Danube frontier in June-September, Turkey in October, Syria-Palestine in November-December, Egypt and Libya in January, North Africa in February, Spain and Portugal in March, Sicily and Italy in April, May and June, the Dalmatian coast and Greece in July, France in August and England in September. While this schedule will not make possible complete examination of any area, it should yield, from all areas, large and representative samplings. These I can supplement after my return with the material from American collections which are easily accessible. The result should suffice for a reliable picture.

Prof. Morton Smith
Department of History
Columbia University

Account of Advanced Studies

At the Harvard Divinity School, from 1937–40, I worked with Professor Henry Cadbury in New Testament criticism and Professor

H. A. Wolfson in Rabbinical literature. Granted a Sheldon Fellowship,[3] I spent four years (1940–4) at the Hebrew University and the American School of Oriental Research in Jerusalem. At the Hebrew University I worked under Professors Moses Schwabe and Hans Lewy on Tannaitic and Hellenistic Judaism and under Professor Gershom Scholem on Jewish mysticism and magic. For Scholem I translated *Hekhalot Rabbati* and revised the translation of his book, *Major Trends in Jewish Mysticism* (Jerusalem, 1941). Under Schwabe's direction I wrote my Ph.D. thesis, *Makbilot ben Habbesorot leSifrut Hattannaim*, Jerusalem, 1948, of which an English translation, *Tannaitic Parrallels to the Gospel*, has since been published in the Monograph Series of *The Journal of Biblical Literature* (as Vol. VI, 1951).

After my return to the United States in 1944 and three years in the Episcopal ministry (Vicar, St. Ambrose' Mission, Philadelphia, 1945; Curate, St. Katharine's Chapel, Mt. Calvary Parish, Baltimore, 1946–7) I went back to Harvard (1948–1950). There Professors Werner Jaeger and A. D. Nock interested me in patristics and I began a study of the manuscripts of Isidore of Pelusium. A Fulbright grant for 1951–2 enabled me to go to Greece to locate and photograph the manuscripts of Isidore. While there I made check lists and took photographic samples of a number of uncatalogued manuscripts collections; in all I brought back over 5,000 photographs of manuscript.

These took a year to print and while they were printing my attention was called back to Palestinian Judaism and especially to the problem of hellenistic elements. Nock, who was directing my work, advised me to put aside Isidore in favor of a study of the interplay between Hellenism and Judaism in Palestine. The resultant thesis, dealing with the period down to Antiochus Epiphanes, was completed in 1957 and accepted for the degree of Doctor of Theology. In that same year my appointment as Assistant Professor of Ancient History at Columbia brought me a heavy teaching load in a field with which I was only partially familiar. I also was persuaded to write a survey of Greek history (*The Ancient Greeks*, Ithaca, 1960) for the Cornell Series, *The Development of Western Civilization*. Meanwhile, revisiting Palestine, I took the opportunity to catalogue the manuscripts at the Monastery of Mar Saba, and there discovered a fragment of an unknown letter attributed to Clement of

[3] The Frederick Sheldon Traveling Fellowships are awarded to Harvard students for study outside the United States.

Alexandria. Determining the reliability of this attribution and preparing an edition of the text has since taken a great deal of my time. Also, during 1961–2 I was Annual Lecturer for the committee on the History of Religion of the American Council of Learned Societies, and recast my Th.D. thesis as a serzies of lectures. At the same time, I wrote, in collaboration with Professor Moses Hadas,[4] a book on Greek stories of holy men. This will soon be published by Harpers under the title, *The Divinization of Hero*;[5] the Th.D. thesis will be published by Schocken in 1963/4 as *Judaism and Hellenization in Palestine, to the Reign of Antiochus Epiphanes*;[6] the edition of Clement's letter I expect to complete this winter. Thus by June I should have completed all these projects except for edition of the letters of Isidore (which the German Academy has asked me to prepare for their series, *Die Griechischen Christlichen Schriftsteller*). That, however, is work which I can do here at any time, while my coming sabbatical year gives me an opportunity which may never occur again to make the survey of magical material proposed in the accompanying plan.

[4] Moses Hadas (Atlanta, 1900–New York, 1966) Classicist, taught at Columbia University. Author of *A History of Greek Literature* (New York, 1950) and *Humanism: The Greek Ideal and Its Survival* (New York, 1960).

[5] The book was published by Harper and Row under the name *Heroes and Gods: Spirituals Biographies in Antiquity* (Religious Perspective 13; New York, 1965).

[6] See note: 'Th.D. thesis (Smith's)'.

PUBLICATIONS AND WORK IN PROGRESS

Abbreviations

AJA	–	American Journal of Archaeology
ATR	–	Anglican Theological Review
BJRL	–	Bulletin of the John Rylands Library
CW	–	The Classical World
EHBS	–	Epeteris Hetaireias Byzantion Spoudon
GBS	–	Greek and Byzantine Studies
GOTR	–	Greek Orthodox Theological Review
HOP	–	Ho Orthodoxos Parateretes
HTR	–	Harvard Theological Review
HUCA	–	Hebrew Union College Annual
IDB	–	Interpreter's Dictionary of the Bible
JBL	–	Journal of Biblical Literature
JBR	–	Journal of Bible and Religion
JNES	–	Journal of Near Eastern Studies
JRT	–	Journal of Religious Thought
NS	–	Nea Sion
NTS	–	New Testament Studies
RIL	–	Religion in Life

Books

Maqbilot ben habbesorot lesiprut hattana'im, Jerusalem 1948 (Ph.D. thesis, Hebrew University).

Tannaitic Parallels to the Gospels, Philadelphia, 1951 (JBL Monograph Series, VI).

The Ancient Greeks, Cornell University Press, Ithaca, 1960.

The Divinization of the Hero (in collaboration with Moses Hadas), to be published by Harpers this winter.

Judaism and Hellenization in Palestine, to the reign of Antiochus Epiphanes. to be published by Schocken in 1963/4.

Articles

I. *On Classical Studies and Palaeography*

The Manuscript Tradition of Isodore of Pelusium, HTR 47 (1954) 205–10.

Symmeikta, *Notes on Collections of Manuscripts in Greece*, EHBS 27 (1956) 380–93.

Hebrew – Why not Greek?, HOP 24 (1958) 197–198.

An Unpublished Life of St. Isodore of Pelusium, edited from MSS in Athens and Mt. Athos, in *Eucharisterion, Timetikos Tomos Hamilka S. Alivizatou*, ed. G. Kondiares, Athens, 1958, 429–38.

On the New Inscription from Serra Orlando, AJA 63 (1959) 183–4.

A Byzantine Panegyric Collection, with an Unknown Homily for the Annuciation, GBS 2 (1959) 139–55.

Hellenika Cheirographa en tei Monei tou Hagiou Sabba, NS 52 (1960).

New Fragments of Scholia on Sophocles' "Ajax", GBS 3 (1960) 40–42.

Greek Monasteries and their Manuscripts, *Archeology* 13 (1960) 172–77.

II. *On the History of Religion*

Notes on Goodspeed's 'Problems of New Testament Translation', JBL 64 (1945) 501–14.

The So-Called 'Biography of David' in the Book of Samuel and Kings, HTS 44 (1951) 167–9.

The Common Theology of the Ancient Near East, JBL 71 (1952) 135–147.

Mt. 5.43: 'Hate thine enemy', HTR 45 (1952) 71–73.

Comments on Taylor's Commentary on Mark, HTR 48 (1955) 21–64.

The Religious History of Classical Antiquity, JRT 12 (1955) 90–99.

Palestinian Judaism in the First Century, in *Israel*, ed. M. Davis, N. Y., 1956, pp. 67 81.

The Jewish Elements on the Gospels, JBR 24 (1956) 90 ff.

Pauline Problems, apropos of J. Munck, 'Paulis und die Heilsgeschichte', HTR 50 (1957) 107–31.

The Image of God: Notes on Hellenization of Judaism, BJRL 40 (1958) 473–512.

Aramaic Studies and the New Testament, JBR 26 (1958) 304–313.

Toward Uncovering Original Texts in the Zadokite Documents (on collaboration with the members of my graduate seminar at Drew) NTS 4 (1958) 62–7.

The Description of the Essenes in Josephus and the Philosophumena, HUCA 29, (1958) 273–313.

'God's Begetting the Messiah' in IQS a, NTS 5 (1959) 218–24.

What is Implied by the Variety of Messianic Figures? JBL 78 (1959) 66–72.

Notes on the Gnostic Amulet Published by Goodenough, GBS 2 (1959) 79–81.

The Testaments of the Twelve Patriarchs, IDB (1960) vol. IV, pp. 575–79.

The Report About Peter in I Clement V. 4, NTS 7 (1960–1) 86–88.

The Dead Sea Sect in Relation to Ancient Judaism, NTS 7 (1960–1) 347–60.

The Place of Hebrew Studies in the Study of History, to appear in *Judaica.*

The Account of Simon Magus in Acts 8, to appear in the Festschrift for H. A. Wolfson.

Observations on Hekhalot Rabbati, to appear in *Lectures at the Lown Institute of Advanced Judaic Studies*, vol. I.

Major Reviews

Of W. Davies, *Torah in the Messianic Age*, JBL 72 (1953) 192–4.

Of E. Goodenough, *Jewish Symbols in the Greco-Period*, I–III, ATR 36 (1954) 218–20; IV, ATR 37 (1955) 81–4; V and VI, ATR 39 (1957) 261–4.

Of S. Lieberman, *The Tosefta*, I, and *Tosefta Ki-feshuta*, JBL 75 (1956) 243–5.

Of C. Kraeling, *The Excavations at Dura Europus, Final Report VIII, Part I The Synagogue*, JBL 76 (1957) 324–7.

Of H. Schoeps, *Urgemeinde, Judenchristentum, Gnosis*, ATR 39 (1957) 179–81.

Of W. Farmer, *Maccabees, Zealots and Josephus*, ATR 39 (1957) 259–61.

Of C. Rabin, *Qumran Studies*, JNES 18 (1959) 282–3.

Of *Samothrace (Excavations conducted by the Institute of Fine Arts of N. Y. U).* ed. K. Lehmann, Vol. I, AJA 64 (1960) 387–8.

Of J. Sint, *Pseudoymität im Altertum*, JBL 70 (1961) 188–9.

Of G. Scholem, *Jewish Gnosticism, Merkabah Mysticism, and Talmudic Tradition*, JBL 70 (1961) 190–1.

Of G. Downey, *A History of Antioch in Syria*, JBL 70 (1961) 377–9.

Minor Reviews in CW, GOTR, JBL, JRT, ATR, and RIL

Work in Progress

I am preparing an edition of a letter which I discovered in the summer of 1958, in a monastery in Palestine. The manuscript containing the letter attributes it to Clement of Alexandria. A careful check has led to the conclusion that the attribution is correct. My report on the manuscript, to the meeting of the Society of Biblical Literature in December 1960, was covered by the *N. Y. Times* (Dec. 30, 1960, p. l, cols. 2–4, p. 17, col. 3 and ff.) I expect to finish the edition this winter.

The Berlin Academy has asked me to prepare a critical text of the letters of Isidore of Pelusium, for publication in the series, *Die Griechischen Christlichen Schriftsteller der ersten Jahrhunderte.* I have classified and secured photographs of 75 manuscripts and have made some progress in collation.

APPENDIX B

Report on Morton Smith to the Guggenheim Foundation

21 October 1962

Prof. Morton Smith is well known to me over many years and I have the highest regards for his character and personality. He is a perfectly trustworthy scholar with a great amount of energy and perseverance in his devotion to his work. He is highly intelligent and brings to the studies he has undertaken an original approach. He is one of the very few scholars in the United States with a full command if both classical languages and Hebrew which makes him an eminently suited person for undertaking such a project as he has submitted to you. I have no doubt that Prof. Smith should be given every possible encouragement to execute this study and, equally, that his project of assembling and studying the archaeological material available for a history of Greco-Roman magic promises to be of highest value of the study of inter-relation between Judaism and the world of Greco-Roman antiquity. The studies of magical material of this kind which are available up to now, especially the work of Campbell Bonner,[1] are marred by the only too visible ignorance of their author's in the field of Judaism and Hebrew and Aramaic philology. This will be greatly changed by Prof. Smith's work. Being a specialist in early Christian, especially Patristic, literature he will be fully qualified to coordinate his material with many problems arising from Christian literature. I am expecting from him a very distinguished contribution to the discussion of the problems which he proposes do deal with and to the history of Religion in late antiquity in general. I should particularly stress the fact, rightly mentioned by him, that much of the material which has so far been published, has been misunderstood and misinterpreted and it seems high time to have somebody who is qualified to put the record straight.

---

[1] Campbell Bonner (b. 1876). Professor of Greek Language and Litearture at the University of Michigan. Author of *Studies in Magical Amulets, chiefly Graeco-Egyptian* (Humanistic Series 49; Michigan, 1950).

I can, therefore, give my wholehearted support to Prof. Smith's project. I shall be delighted to hear that he would be enabled to carry it out.

[Gershom Scholem]

APPENDIX C

Prof. Gershom Scholem
Professor Emeritus in the Hebrew University, Jerusalem
28 Abarbanel St.
Jerusalem

January 4, 1966

In my opinion Prof. Morton Smith is ideally equipped to undertake the work on the project he proposed to you. A study of magic in the Greco-Roman world is a wide subject and requires a combination of knowledge in very different subjects which is difficult to come by. He possesses not only the knowledge of Greek and Latin, but also of Hebrew and Aramaic, which for wide sections of his study is of paramount importance. Among the scholars who have taken an interest in the study of magic he is unique in this respect. He also combines wide knowledge of profane and religious literature with a keen sense of history and historical criticism, which I find sorely lacking in many of the archaeological studies in this field that have come to my knowledge. His power of combination and imagination will surely make for a lively discussion of new hypotheses and for the advancement of new ideas. I cannot say which will be Prof. Smith's eventual leading ideas, but I am convinced that they will be of a fruitful nature and, even if controversial (which can hardly be avoided), will contribute substantially to a discussion and better understanding of a very difficult and important subject. The international character of magic makes it imperative that the scholar working in this field has a wide knowledge and insight into the problems discussed in this regard among the historians of religion. Prof. Smith has both. I think he would qualify for a second Guggenheim fellowship even under the most severe criteria. His project cannot be finished in a short time, but provided he can devote a whole year to nothing but concentrating on this subject, this should go far towards completion of this study. I therefore emphatically support his application. Since I have also been impressed by the quality of his writing and his lucidity in propounding his ideas, I expect him to produce a work of lasting interest and value.

INDEX

JERUSALEM STUDIES IN RELIGION AND CULTURE

The JSRC book series aims to publish the best of scholarship on religion, on the highest international level. Jerusalem is a major center for the study of monotheistic religions, or "religions of the book". The creation of a Center for the Study of Christianity has added a significant emphasis on Christianity. Other religions, like Zoroastrianism, Hinduism, Buddhism, and Chinese religion, are studied here, too, as well as anthropological studies of religious phenomena. This book series will publish dissertations, re-written and translated into English, various monographs and books emerging from conferences.

Volume 1 *The Nuṣayrī-ʿAlawī Religion.* An Enquiry into its Theology and Liturgy. Meir M. Bar-Asher & Aryeh Kofsky. 2002. ISBN 9004 12552 3

Volume 2 *Homer, the Bible, and Beyond.* Literary and Religious Canons in the Ancient World. Edited by Margalit Finkelberg & Guy G. Stroumsa. 2003. ISBN 9004 12665 1

Volume 3 *Christian Gaza in Late Antiquity.* Edited by Brouria Bitton-Ashkelony & Aryeh Kofsky. 2004. ISBN 9004 13868 4

Volume 4 *Axial Civilizations and World History.* Edited by Johann P. Arnason, S.N. Eisenstadt & Björn Wittrock. 2004. ISBN 9004 13955 9

Volume 5 *Rational Theology in Interfaith Communication.* Abu l-Ḥusayn al-Baṣrī's Muʿtazilī Theology among the Karaites in the Fāṭimid Age. Edited by Wilferd Madelung and Sabine Schmidtke. 2006. ISBN 978 90 04 15177 2

Volume 6 *The Poetics of Grammar and the Metaphysics of Sound and Sign.* Edited by S. La Porta and D. Shulman. 2007. ISBN 978 90 04 15810 8

Volume 7 *Islamic Piety in Medieval Syria.* Mosques, Cemeteries and Sermons under the Zangids and Ayyūbids (1146-1260). Daniella Talmon-Heller. 2007. ISBN 978 90 04 15809 2

VOLUME 8 *Greek Religion and Culture, the Bible and the Ancient Near East.* Jan N. Bremmer. 2008. ISBN 978 90 04 16473 4

VOLUME 9 *Morton Smith and Gershom Scholem, Correspondence 1945-1982.* Edited with an introduction by Guy Stroumsa. 2008. ISBN 978 90 04 16839 8